Thomas Carlyle, Charles Eliot Norton

Letters of Thomas Carlyle

Vol. 2 (1832 - 1836)

Thomas Carlyle, Charles Eliot Norton

Letters of Thomas Carlyle
Vol. 2 (1832 - 1836)

ISBN/EAN: 9783337137243

Printed in Europe, USA, Canada, Australia, Japan

Cover: Foto ©ninafisch / pixelio.de

More available books at **www.hansebooks.com**

LETTERS

OF

THOMAS CARLYLE

send a message to her: she is a quick-tempered, indeed quick-minded, methodic, truthful little creation; and my talk that destiny with tolerable hope. — And so our Mother will be left solitary; and rapid time will have brought another change. But fear not: our brave Mother will take it well; and with the heart she has never be left desolate. Jemmy's wife and she seemed to do very handsomely, and she has the rest about her. Her Houses too, on which her income depends, were likely to get into a better train: Baker Park, a very "sensible" man, was about bargaining for the large House next year, and perhaps even taking the whole set of them under his own charge. That Village of Ecclefechan, which I passed thro', once or twice, gives me the strangest unearthly feeling; very sad, very ugly, yet not without a grandeur even a sacredness in the middle of such squalor. What is Eternal Rome, Jerusalem, or Nazareth itself, but a temporary set of huts and habitations, where Being begins, and is, and then is not — under God's unchanging Heaven? Alas, I often feel as if Hades itself were shifting change to me, from this peaceful and wonderful mystery of a world; surely no greater Miracle it were, — hard finding out. Let us bow down in the dust; and in silence (since for the present one has no words) feel with the old wise, "tho' He slay me, yet will I trust in him". Hier steh' ich; Kenn nichts anders, Gott helf mir! — On the whole, I often meditate on Christian things; but find as good as no profit in talking of them here. Most so-called Christians (I believe I should except the worthy Mr Dunn) treat me instead with jargon of metaphysic formulas, or perhaps shovel-hatted Coleridgean moonshine. I admire greatly that of old Marquis Mirabeau (tho' he means it not for admiration): Il a humé toutes les formules! A man should "swallow" innumerable "formulas" in these days; and endeavour above all things to look with eyes. — But whither this all? Importantly, almost nowhither.

If I tell you that my poor scribble, after above a week of rest, is again under way, and doing what it can, you must not grow weary of me and it: I have next to nothing else at present that seems to belong to me in this world. Whether the Book be good or be bad, it will to me be blessed in that one point, — in its end. Yet after all, it is only my impatient temper that makes me so speak: for the poor thing, full of faults as it can be crammed, will have a thought or two, a genuine picture or two; and so will be worthless: what more would!! The best news is that I hope to have the second volume fairly off at the time you appoint for returning: could all answer, how joyfully would I take my interregnum of vacation with Doil! We would walk together, to Hampstead, to Dulwich, to all places; and be happy in the spring sunshine. Let us wait, and hope. — Mill's new Review making small way, they have purchased the

From a Letter to Dr Carlyle, Munich
23rd Feby 1836.

but a message that, she is a quick-tempered, irritable, quick-minded, irritable, truthful but creation; and the that setting with tolerable hope. — She is our mother will be left behind, and repeatedly, as my thoughts continue change. But fear not: our dear mother will take it well; and will the best have no need to be left desolate. Jenny's life and the learned to so my happiness, and the he she about her. Her House is to, on which her income depends, we like to get into a letter theein: The red about her. Her House is to, on which her income depends, we like to get into a letter theein: Bolton Park, a very favorable man, was about bargaining for the large House next year, and perhaps even taking the whole lot often under his own charge. That village of Edgbaston, which I have - at this, one or twice, given me that strangeful unearthly feeling; very old, very left, yet not without a grandeur even a sacredness in the middle growth expecter. What is stencil home, Jerusalem, or Nazareth itself, but a temporary set of huts and habitations, when things begin, and is, and them is not — under God's unchanging Heaven? Alas, I often feel as if travel itself were slight change to and ugly. — Shelley new railway making small way, by some non persecutor - mine. Let us wait, and

OF
THOMAS CARLYLE

1826—1836

EDITED BY

CHARLES ELIOT NORTON

VOL. II

1832—1836

London
MACMILLAN AND CO.
AND NEW YORK
1888

LETTERS

OF

THOMAS CARLYLE

LXXXV.—To ALEXANDER CARLYLE,
Craigenputtock.

4 AMPTON STREET, GRAY'S INN ROAD,
LONDON, *Saturday*, 14*th January* 1832.

MY DEAR ALICK— . . . Several weeks ago I sent you a little Note for the Dumfries Post Office: this I think you must have got, though no answer has yet reached me. The present will be the third Letter for which you are now in my debt. I am getting very desirous to hear from you; what you are doing and forbearing; how you get on with the preparatives for Catlinns, what you think of it, and of your outlooks generally; how we are likely to find you when we return in Spring. Often does the picture of that lone mansion in the Dunscore wold come before me here; it has a strange almost unearthly character, as it comes before me standing in the lone Night in the wintry moor, with the tumult of London raging around me, who was once your fellow-hermit, and am soon to be a yet more solitary hermit. I am wae to think that this, like all other earthly arrangements, is now drawing to its close; we shall wander no more along the Glaisters Hill: it is the ugliest of hills, and none of us saw cheerfulness on the face of it, or anything but toil and vexation; nevertheless now when it is all past, how can we be other than sad? Alas, we ourselves are quickly passing; a little while, and *no* place that now knows us shall know us any more at all forever! Let us strive to obtain a "continuing City"; for such, by God's goodness, there yet is; appointed for the just man; who (in some to us wholly mysterious way, yet surely as aught is sure) "shall dwell forever with God." Were it not for some faith in this, I see not how one could endure the tossing and toils of the World: but with this, while it holds steady before us, the very sorrows of our present dream of life, for it is but a dream, are blessings for us. Let us never lament then; let us stand to it like brave men; *expecting* no reward in this world, *wishing* for none; feeling that to serve our heavenly Taskmaster is itself the richest of all rewards. . . .

Our plans here are getting a little more fixed: I can now give you some faint foreshadow of them. I pride myself that I have never gone half a foot out of my road in search of what are called "prospects": it is yet and has always been clear to me that I was one whom Promotion was least of all likely to visit. Thank Heaven I know my trade: it is to *write truth* while I can be kept alive by so doing, and to die writing it when I can no longer be kept alive. So feeling, I look upon all mortals with the friendliest humour; let Kings and Chancellors fight their own battles, and all speed to them: let the Devil go his way, and I will go mine. Therefore after settling my Author-business in London, I will not stay an hour, "waiting at the pool," as some advise me. . . . On the whole the world stands related to me very much as I could wish it. I find myself respected by all whose judgment I respect; feared and wondered at by a much greater number; despised, at least openly, by no one. With incessant long-continued exertion, there is *much* possible for me; I may become a Preacher of the Truth, and so deliver my message in this Earth, the highest that can be entrusted to man.—I write all this, because I know well, you love me, and heartily, as a Brother and Scholar, wish me good speed. . . .

         T. CARLYLE.

LXXXVI.—To his MOTHER, Scotsbrig.

  4 AMPTON STREET, MECKLENBURG SQUARE,
    LONDON, 22d *January* [1] 1832.

MY DEAR MOTHER— It is not very long since I wrote to you; yet I make no doubt you are wearying to hear from me again; as indeed I am to write again, for there are few things that give me greater pleasure. A letter from Jack having arrived, I have now a decided call made on me; and snatch a few minutes as I

[1] The day of his father's death.

can get them to fulfil it. You have no notion how hard it is even to command minutes here, such streams of visitors and other interruptions come upon one: for example, since I wrote the first sentence of this, there have been no fewer than six persons, simultaneously and successively, breaking in on my privacy, and I have had to talk almost as much as would make a volume. First, Glen and some insignificant *etceteras*; then John Mill with Detrosier (the Manchester Lecturer to the Working Classes, whom you may have seen mentioned in the *Examiner*), and, much stranger, an actual Saint-Simonian Frenchman, arrived as a missionary here![1] I have since taken my dinner; and now sit writing before tea, after which we have another engagement: to go and hear the famous Mr. Owen[2] (of whom also the Newspapers are full enough) preach in his "Institution" for the perfection of Society, or for something else equally noble, which I forget. So you see partly how I am situated, and will take the wish for the deed.

[1] Gustave D'Eichthal. [2] Robert Owen of Lanark.

My worthy and kind Correspondent "little Jean" has been rather stingy with me of late; though I must speak in regret rather than in blame; for were she to dry up on me, what should I do? Remind her only how very long it is since I had a Letter, and how gratifying a Letter from her always is. I am not in any great *anxiety*, for I struggle always to hope the best: indeed Alick wrote to me last week, bringing down the good news, at least want of ill news, to a recent date: neither will I now let myself believe that anything bad has befallen; but think always that some soon coming day will bring me direct confirmation. Alick said that you, my dear Mother, were fully as strong as usual; that the rest were all well; only that my Father was again afflicted with his old complaint of cold. I pray you take all charge of him; let himself too avoid all exposure to these winter damps: he should get himself warmer clothing, above all sufficient shoes, or well-lined clogs; and not stir out at all, except he cannot help it, especially when the sun is not shining. This advice applies also to you; only that I know you are yourself much more of a doctor than he is.

We are struggling along here in the old way, and now see better what we are going to do, and when we are to move. Jane has been sickly almost ever since the winter began; but by rigorous adherence to regimen is now fairly recovering, and already much stronger than she was. The weather here has been more uncomfortable, and the place altogether more full of annoyances, than one could almost anywhere else experience: *reek* and *glar* and fogs damp and dry, these are the grand elements man lives in on the streets of London. Were it not that the city is full of people whom it is pleasant and profitable to converse with, *this* is nowise the habitation I would choose for myself. You are ill-lodged, in brick houses, thin as shells, with the floors all twisted, and every article indicating its showiness and its weakness. You are ill-fed, unless you can live upon beef; your milk is of the bluest, your water of the muddiest; your eggs rotten, your potatoes watery, and exactly about *ten* times the price they are in

Annandale, namely one penny per pound! You are ill-bedded and ill-clothed unless you prefer show to substance; all these things are against you. Nevertheless there is a great charm in being here; at the fountain-head and centre of British activity, in the busiest and quickest-moving spot that this whole Earth contains. I find myself greatly enriched with thoughts since I came hither; and by no means disposed to repent of my journey. Nor am I without encouragements, such as I need, for holding on my way: in all open minds, I find ready access; and sometimes even grateful invitation: all people, good and bad, think of me not very much otherwise than I want them to think. Let us fight the good fight, then! In due time we shall prevail if we faint not. I esteem it a great blessing that I was born, that I am a denizen of God's Universe; and surely the greatest of all earthly blessings that I was born of parents who were *religious*, who from the first studied to open my eyes to the Highest, and train me up in the ways wherein I should go. My motto is always: Reverence God, and fear nothing; nothing either of man or devil!— . . .

We have settled that we are to leave this in March; though the precise day and date, the manner of our journey, whether we are coming round by Edinburgh *first*, etc. etc., all remains unfixed. So that we shall (God willing) see you all with the first fine weather of Spring! Let us trust and hope that it will be in peace and cheerfulness; in thankfulness to the Giver of all Good, by whom such blessing is vouchsafed us!

I am not going to trouble you with any public news; you see enough of that in the Newspaper; and as for my own ideas on the matter I reserve them till we can speak face to face when I return. It seems as if it would be months yet before their Reform Bill were passed, and in the meanwhile all business is crippled. . . . The poor people are all quiet, though very miserable many of them : it is almost positively painful to walk these streets, and see so many cold and hungry and naked and ignorant beings, and have so little power to help them.—Poor Hogg the Ettrick Shepherd is walking about here; dining everywhere, everywhere laughed at; being indeed the veriest *gomeril*.[1] He appears in public with a gray Scotch plaid, the like of which was never seen here before: it is supposed to be a trick of his Bookseller (a hungry shark, on the verge of bankruptcy) who wishes to attract notice from the Cockney population, and thereby raise the wind a little. He drank whisky punch at that dinner I was at; and clattered the arrantest good-natured *janners*.[2]— Jeffrey often comes here, running over in great haste ; and is brisk and busy as a bee.— ... The Bullers are here, both parents and sons, all in the friendliest relation to me. I dined there lately, and am very soon going back: the two boys are promising fellows, and may one day be heard of in the world. Charles is almost the most intelligent young man I converse with here.

I must now go, my dear Mother, and let you go. It will give you great comfort to find that Jack is so well: his Letter is unluckily

---

[1] Good-natured fool. [2] Idle and incoherent talk.

quite too full of Roman antiquities, about which no one of us cares a penny piece; however it brings nothing but good news so far. . . . You must give my brotherly affection to all the young ones; tell them that I vote with you as to this truth : that the *only* blessing in the world is that of good behaviour, which lies in the power of every one. They must love one another: " Little children love one another," this was the departing farewell precept of the Friend of Men. Tell my Father that I love and honour him. Take care of him, dear Mother, and of yourself, that I may find you both well. God ever bless you all!—I remain, my dear Mother, your affectionate Son,

T. CARLYLE.

The Newspaper comes quite prettily every Saturday about Noon. Punctuality is a great virtue.

LXXXVII.—To his MOTHER, Scotsbrig.[1]

LONDON, 24*th January* 1832.

MY DEAREST MOTHER—I was downstairs this

[1] This letter is printed in Froude's *Life*, ii. 248. It is

morning when I heard the Postman's knock, and thought it might be a Letter from Scotsbrig: hastening up I found Jane with the Letter open, and in tears. The next moment gave me the stern tidings. I had written to you yesterday, a light hopeful Letter, which I could now wish you might not read, in these days of darkness: probably you will receive it just along with this; the first red seal so soon to be again exchanged for a black one. I had a certain misgiving, not seeing Jane's customary "all well";[1] and I thought, but did not write (for I strive usually to banish vague fears) "the pitcher goes often to the well, but it is broken at last." I did not know that this very evil had already overtaken us.

As yet I am in no condition to write much: the stroke, all unexpected though not undreaded, as yet painfully crushes my heart together; I have yet hardly had a little relief from tears. And yet it will be a solace to me to speak out

reprinted here (with the correct date) in order that the record of so important an event in Carlyle's life as the death of his father should not be omitted from this epistolary autobiography.

[1] The two strokes on the newspaper.

with you, to repeat along with you that great saying, which, could we lay it rightly to heart, includes all that man can say : " It is God that has done it; God support us all!"[1] Yes, my dear Mother, it is God that has done it; and our part is reverent submission to His Will, and trustful prayer to Him for strength to bear us through every trial.

I could have wished, as I had too confidently hoped, that God had ordered it otherwise : but what are our wishes and wills ? I trusted that I might have had other glad meetings and pleasant communings with my honoured and honour-worthy Father in this world : but it was not so appointed; we shall meet no more, till we meet in that *other* Sphere, where God's Presence more immediately is; the nature of which we know not, only we know that it is of God's appointing, and therefore altogether *good*. Nay already, had we but faith, our Father is not parted from *us*, but only withdrawn from our bodily eyes : the Dead and the Living, as

[1] Words which his mother had written in a postscript to the letter from his sister.

I often repeat to myself, are alike with God: He, fearful and wonderful, yet good and infinitely gracious, encircles alike both them that we see, and them that we cannot see. Whoso trusteth in Him has obtained the victory over Death: the King of Terrors is no longer terrible.

Yes, my dear Mother and Brothers and Sisters, let us see also how mercy has been mingled with our calamity. Death was for a long time ever present to our Father's thought; daily and hourly he seemed meditating on his latter end: the end too appears to have been mild as it was speedy; he parted, as gently as the most do, from this vale of tears; and Oh! in his final agony, he was enabled to call, with his strong voice and strong heart, on the God that had made him to have mercy on him. Which prayer, doubt not one of you, the All-merciful *heard*, and in such wise as infinite mercy might, gave answer to. And what is the Death of one dear to us, as I have often thought, but the setting out on a journey an hour before us, which journey we have all to travel : what is the longest earthly Life to the Eternity, the Endless, the Beginningless, which encircles it? The oldest man and the newborn babe are but divided from each other by a single hair's-breadth. For myself I have long continually meditated on Death, till, by God's grace, it has grown transparent for me, and holy and great rather than terrific ; till I see that " Death, what mortals call Death, is properly the beginning of Life."—One other comfort we have, to take the bitterness out of our tears : this greatest of all comforts, and properly the only one : that our Father was not called away till he had done his work, and done it faithfully. Yes, my beloved friends, we can with a holy pride look at our Father, there where he lies low, and say that his Task was well and manfully performed ; the strength that God had given him he put forth in the ways of honesty and welldoing ; no eye will ever see a hollow deceitful work that *he* did : the world wants one true man, since he was taken away. When we consider his Life, through what hardships and obstructions he struggled, and what he became and what he did, there is room for gratitude that God so bore him on. Oh, what were it now to us that he had been a king; now when the question is not: What *wages* hadst thou for thy work? But: *How* was thy work done? My dear Brothers and Sisters, sorrow not, I entreat you; sorrow is profitless and sinful; but meditate deeply every one of you on this. None of us but started in Life with *far* greater advantages than our dear Father had: we will not weep for him; but we will go and do as he has done. Could I write my Books, as he built his Houses, and walk my way so manfully through this shadow-world, and leave it with so little blame, it were more than all my hopes. Neither are you, my beloved Mother, to let your heart be heavy. Faithfully you toiled by his side, bearing and forbearing as you both could: all that was sinful and of the Earth has passed away; all that was true and holy remains forever, and the Parted shall meet together again with God. *Amen! So be it!* We your children, whom you have faithfully cared for, soul and body, and brought up in the nurture and admonition of the Lord, we gather round you in this solemn hour, and say, be of comfort! Well done, hitherto; persevere and it shall be well! We promise here before God, and the awful yet merciful work of God's Hand, that we will continue to love and honour you, as sinful children can; and now do you pray for us all, and let us all pray in such language as we have for one another; so shall this sore division and parting be the means of a closer union. O let us all and every one know that though this world is full of briars and we are wounded at every step as we go, and one by one must take farewell, and weep bitterly, yet "there remaineth a *rest* for the people of God." Yes, for the people of God there remaineth a Rest, that Rest which in this world they could nowhere find.

And now again I say do not grieve any one of you beyond what nature forces and you cannot help. Pray to God, if any of you have a voice and utterance; all of you pray always in secret and silence, if faithful, ye shall be heard *openly*. I cannot be with you to speak; but read in the

Scripture, as I would have done. Read, I especially ask, in Matthew's Gospel that Passion and Death and Farewell blessing and command of "Jesus of Nazareth"; and see if you can understand and feel what is the "divine depth of Sorrow"; and how even by suffering and sin man is lifted up to God, and in great darkness there shines a light. If you cannot read it aloud in common, then do each of you take his Bible in private and read it for himself. Our business is not to lament, but to *improve* the lamentable, and make it also peaceably work together for greater good.

I could have wished much to lay my honoured Father's head in the grave: yet it could have done no one good save myself only, and I shall not ask for it. Indeed, when I remember, that right would have belonged to John of Cockermouth,[1]—to whom offer in all heartiness my brotherly love. I will be with you in spirit, if not in person: I have given orders that *no one* is to be admitted here till after the funeral on Friday:

[1] His father's eldest son, Carlyle's half-brother.

I mean to spend these hours in solemn meditation and self-examination, and thoughts of the Eternal; such seasons of grief are sent us even for that end: God knocks at our heart, the question [is] Will we open or not?—I shall think every night of the Candle burning in that sheeted room, where our dear Sister also lately lay. O God be gracious to us; and bring us all one day together in Himself! After Friday, I return, as you too must, to my worldly work; for that also is work appointed us by the heavenly Taskmaster.—I will write to John to-night or to-morrow. Let me hear from you again so soon as you have composure. I shall hasten all the more homewards for this. For the present I bid God ever bless you all! Pray for me, my dear Mother; and let us all seek consolation *there*.—I am ever your affectionate,

T. CARLYLE.

Most probably you are not in want of money: if you are, I have some ten pounds or more which I can spare here, and you have only to send for.

LXXXVIII.—To his MOTHER, Scotsbrig.

4 AMPTON STREET [LONDON],
18*th February* 1832.

MY DEAR MOTHER— . . . Jane's kind, calm Letter gave us great satisfaction: it was wholly in the spirit, and represented you all as wholly in the spirit which I wished and expected. Our sufferings here are not unmixed with mercy: nay, as faith teaches us, they are all mercies in disguise. My mind also is peaceable; and if sad, not, I trust, sad after an unholy fashion. Let us not mourn as creatures that had no Hope. We are creatures that had an All-Good Creator; and this Earth we live in is named the "Place of Hope." For myself Death has long been the hourly companion of my thoughts: I can look upon this earthly world as, in very deed, smoke and shadow; and Eternity the only substance, the only truth. Thus is " Death, what mortals call Death, properly the beginning of Life." How any reasonable being can exist here below otherwise than thus, might justly seem a mystery.—I am also much gratified to learn that Jamie makes worship among you: nothing *can* be more becoming and needful than in all our ways and days-works to address ourselves, as the beginning of every other effort, to Him who has given us our whole Force; by whom our whole efforts are overruled, in whom we live, move, and have our being. Tell Jamie that I take this as a *good* token of him; and will hope all that is good and just and wise from his future conduct. Thank him for his kind and honest little Postscript; which I will answer, by the first opportunity; would fain answer *now.* He must write me again, at any rate. Finally, my dear Mother, *take care of yourself;* that we may find you well, when it shall please God to bring us together again.

. . . What *day* we are to look forward to for setting out cannot yet be anywise fixed. I am in the middle of *Johnson,* which I wish to finish before setting out; it will take me at least twelve days yet, pretty hard work. Then I have to settle about many other little things: Napier indeed wrote to me (to-day) about *another* little Article for the *Edinburgh Review* to be ready "about the middle of March"; but this I rather think I shall try to write in Dumfriesshire,—say to finish it at Scotsbrig! On the whole, nothing can be fixed: only you may take this fact: Jane is about writing to her Mother to engage a servant she (Mrs. Welsh) was speaking of, to be ready *by the first of April;* we mean also to stay some while with *you*, before looking at Dunscore. This fact also is certain: we are neither of us disposed *to lose any time;* so the harder I work, the sooner I shall get into free air, and to the sight of dear Friends!—We were both of us very thankful that you had despatched Betty Smeal to keep the house of Puttock: it makes us quite easy on that score; and Betty can be figured there as bolting and barring, and burning fires, and keeping everything as it should be.—We cannot yet make out what Alick is specially doing; for he has never written: probably he is too busy with beginning his new enterprise; at all events I should like to know *where* he is, were it only for sending the Paper to him. By the way, it did not come this morning; but I reckon, that means *nothing*.

We have Cholera at last in this city, as you will see : such has been my expectation ever since I first heard of the disease. The people affected hitherto are few in number (perhaps not above the *usual* number of deaths) and far off this quarter of the city. I myself feel no alarm, nor does Jane : when they told me that day, "Cholera is here! Cholera is here!"—I answered : "When was Death *not* here?"—Far would it be from me to expose myself without strict necessity; I would even fly were the danger considered in any measure pressing, and did one know *whither* to fly (but which place is safe, or even much safer than another?). At the same time, equally far should I wish to be from pusillanimous terror—as if in the midst of the pestilence, as in the midst of health, I were not *in God's hand*.—The truth is, this "Cholera" is little else, if one look at it, than an opening of men's eyes to behold what their usual blindness prevents them from observing : that their Life hangs by a single hair; that

Death is *great*, and forever *close* at their hand. By a singular arrangement, too, this Disease seems to attack almost exclusively, not so much the poor, as the improvident, drunken and worthless : punishment follows hard on sin. They are passing Acts of Parliament about it, for having the Poor clothed and fed, by assessment, where it is not done voluntarily. This is very right. If the Disease spread and become threatening, you shall instantly hear; and, in this case, may see us sooner than you expect, for we have nothing to detain us here, at any *risk*. But for the present, there seems none that we can calculate : so be not uneasy, dear Mother; commit us to God's good keeping, as we, I hope, endeavour to do ourselves ; and fear nothing.

Jane has a headache to-day ; but considers herself, on the whole, and indeed evidently is, in an improving way, "decidedly better than she was." She has had but a sickly time of it here, yet has not been unhappy, " there is such excellent company." She has seen no "sights" hardly; and cares little or nothing about such. Good talk is what she delights in, and I too ;

and here, amid the mass of Stupidity and Falsehood, there *is* actually some reasonable conversation to be come at. She has met with some valuable people; and I believe has improved herself in more ways than one. Mrs. Austin and she are very fond of each other; Jane is going up to her, on Thursday, "to have a whole day of it:" I also think Mrs. Austin a very worthy solid-minded woman.—

. . . Of work, as I told you, I have plenty and to spare. This *Johnson* is meant for [James] Fraser (an honest, ignorant, simpleton of a creature, knowing little but that one and one make two): but if it do not suit his Magazine, I have other use for it. I must also tell you another thing: Fraser came to me the other morning, and, by Jane's help, got me to "stand for my Picture,"[1] to be published in his Magazine! I suppose it will not be out for several months: however, you need not be impatient; for I do not think it at all *like* me, except in the coat and boots, and hair of the

---

[1] The well-known drawing by Maclise, now in the Forster Collection, South Kensington Museum.

head. Goethe's Picture is to appear in the next Number (of that *dud* Magazine); and I have been requested (just as I was beginning this Letter) to write a little Notice to accompany it; which perhaps I should consent to do.[1]— The "Characteristics" has been well received; approved seemingly by every one whose approval was wanted: I am on all hands encouraged to proceed. Forward! Forward!

Meeting Irving the other day on the street, he appointed me to come and take tea with him. The "inspired-tongue" work, I think, is getting a little dulled; at least I heard or saw nothing of it going on, that night; only Irving still full of its importance, and his Wife (a melancholic half-hollow sort of person, not wholly to my mind) still fuller. Irving had read the "Characteristics," with quite *high* estimation of the *talent*, etc. etc.: nevertheless he seemed to think I was going a very wrong road to work, and should consider myself, and

[1] This brief paper, "Goethe's Portrait," appeared in *Fraser's Magazine*, No. 26. It is reprinted in the *Miscellanies*, iii. 379; the portrait "proved a total failure, and involuntary caricature."

take into the "Tongues." He was nobly tolerant in heart; but in head quite bewildered, almost imbecile. He put into my hands, as "the deepest view he had ever seen," a Paper (in his Prophetic Magazine *The Morning Watch*) written by a namesake of mine in Edinburgh; or rather *not* by him, "for it was given him"—by the Spirit! This deepest view I glanced into, and found to be simply the insanest Babble, without top bottom or centre, that ever was emitted even from Bedlam itself.—Poor Irving! It is still said they are taking steps to cast him out of his Church: what next he is to bring out upon the world I cannot prophesy. A good true-hearted man he will continue; the truer, the more he suffers from the world: but he has once for all surrounded himself with Delirium and with the Delirious; and so stands quite exiled from all general usefulness. Nevertheless if he be spared *alive*, he is nowise *done* yet; but has other outbreakings in store.

. . . And now, dear Mother, take our united filial love; and let us all be joined together more and more in true affection, and in *well-doing* above all, which is the only bond and basis of affection between reasonable beings. Let us live in thankfulness towards the good Disposer of events, faithfully striving to serve Him, as He gives us strength : then what is there that can make us afraid ?—Be very careful of your health, for the sake of us all. God bless and keep every one of you !—Your affectionate Son, T. CARLYLE.

LXXXIX.—To ALEXANDER CARLYLE, at Scotsbrig.

TEMPLAND, *Saturday night*
[14*th April* 1832].

MY DEAR ALICK—Your little Mare carried us up very handsomely, and with wonderful spirit (especially the last half of the journey) considering how she has been worked of late. We gave ourselves and her rather a long rest at Dumfries; and got here all safe and sound, about eight o'clock.

I have nothing but a miserable squirt of a crow-pen to write with; so must make the fewest words possible serve.

. . . At Dumfries, besides Jack's, there was another Letter (from Fraser, the Magazine man) bringing the mournful tidings that Goethe was no more. Alas! alas! I feel as if I had a second time lost a Father: he was to me a kind of spiritual Father. The world holds not his like within it. But it is appointed for *all* " once to die."

. . . Where I am to lodge or how to move for the next week, I cannot yet with any certainty predict; probably I shall be here most part of it; possibly we may have taken up quarters by the end of it at our own fireside: at all events, it is not unlikely that I may contrive to see *you* there when you come up for the pigs: if the Sunday is good weather, it might perhaps be permitted me to ride over on such an errand. But it is all, as you see, unfixed, fluctuating: one thing only you can look upon as certain; that after Monday morning I am to be figured *sitting at my work*. Either here or elsewhere I will have a private apartment, and set to: so have I decided it. In some two weeks, I shall be done with this little job: then I am my own master again, and mean to make a sally into Annandale, and see you all with more deliberation. Perhaps in some three weeks; if Harry get any sort of mettle into him. There is much to be said and considered about the new state our whole Brotherhood is thrown into, now that our Head is gone. Meanwhile, let us all strive, by God's grace, to *do* our parts, each for himself, bearing and forbearing, they that are strong helping them that are weak. O let us all be gentle, obedient, loving to our Mother; now that she is left wholly to our charge! "Honour thy Father and thy Mother:" doubly honour thy Mother when she alone remains.

. . . Bid our dear Mother take care of herself: if you have any time, write me a single line to say whether she is better again; for we left her complaining. Tell her that she is to hold fast her trust in the Great Father, and no evil will befal her or hers.

. . . And so, dear Brother, and dear Friends all, take my affectionate good-night. With special love to my Mother (who *must* finish *Johnson*), I remain always, yours heartily, T. CARLYLE.

XC.—To Dr. CARLYLE, Naples.[1]

CRAIGENPUTTOCK, DUMFRIES,
22d May 1832.

MY DEAR BROTHER—I was very thankful to hear of your continued welfare at Naples, by the Letter of the 30th April, which our Neighbours here brought us up from Dunscore on Sunday evening. I take Tuesday, the very next opportunity of answering it.—There is, as usual, a huge mass of Postage concerns to rectify in the first place; for our correspondence, unhappily, flies out not with one thread meeting another thread, but with a whole ravelled fringe of threads meeting (or missing) another ravelled fringe. Let us be thankful, as you say, that there is *any* post. As to your Letters they seem all to have come. . . . So far well : but

[1] Part of this letter is given in Froude's *Life*, ii. 270, with many errors, *e.g.* " Nature's cornucopia " for " Fortune's cornucopia," " make us all happy and honourable " for " make us all helpful and honourable," " houses with some £28 " for " houses worth some £28," " our pastoral establishment " for " our Puttock establishment."

with my Letters to you again, it is quite *un*well; and I must again write you a long empty way-bill, with the sad doubt whether one item of it may yet have come to hand.[1] . . . Also the cream of all the news I sent was simply "nothing singular; much about our usual way, thank you." Happily this is still the essence of what I write: could I but *shoot* it through space, and reassure your heart from its anxieties!

We are well pleased with your sketches of Naples, with its noisy, empty inmates; its Lazzaroni by profession, or only by practice without profession: there is much to be seen, thought of, and remembered in such a scene. Something it is to stand with your own actual feet on a spot distinguished in some particular beyond all others on our Planet. We are also contented with the appearance of your domestic position; and would fain see further into it,

---

[1] Here follows an account of letters and packages sent. At least one letter mentioned, written "some three weeks ago," is absent from this series of letters, and partly explains the hiatus here in the correspondence between Carlyle and his brother John.

and form a more coherent picture of it. Your noble Patient seems to suffer more than we anticipated. . . . Therein, as in so many other cases, must the Patient minister unto herself. He whom Experience has not taught innumerable *hard* lessons will be wretched at the bottom of Fortune's Cornucopia; and some are so dull at taking up! On the whole, the higher classes of modern Europe, especially of actual England, are true objects of compassion. Be thou compassionate, patiently faithful: leave no means untried, work for thy wages and it will be well with thee.—Those *Herzensergiessungen eines Einsamen* which the late Letters abound in, are not singular to me; the spirit that dwells in them is such as I can heartily approve of. It is an earnest mind seeking some place of rest for itself, struggling to get its foot off the quicksand and fixed on the rock. The only thing I regret or fear is that there should *be* so much occupation of the mind upon itself. Turn *outward;* attempt not (the impossibility) to "know thyself," but solely to know "what thou canst work at." This last is a possible knowledge for every creature, and the only profitable one : neither is there any way of attaining it, except *trial*, the attempt *to work*. Attempt honestly, the result even if unsuccessful will be infinitely instructive. I can see too, my dear Brother, that you have a great want in your present otherwise so prosperous condition : you have not anything like enough *to do*. I daresay many a poor riding Apothecary with five times your labour and the fifth part of your income is happier. Nevertheless stand to it tightly ; *every* time brings its duty. If your Lady require your services another year, you will have as much money as will set you up handsomely wherever you like to try, and then all things lie before you : meanwhile are you not enjoying the inexpressible deliverance of paying off your debts, and inwardly resolving that no earthly influence will ever again lead you into such bondage ? It is in this way, if in no other, that "your present state connects itself with your future"; a most favourable and essential connection. For the rest, as I have said some hundreds of times, it seems to me the most insignificant consideration of all, whether you set yourself down to exercise that noble faculty of Healing, in London or elsewhere, among the higher ranks, or among the lower: among God's immortal creatures, groaning under the fardels of a weary life, it will not fail to be; and if *honest*, your Doctorship must in any and all situations be a *martyrdom*; not a working for wages, which latter exist only for the bond Drudge, not for the free Doer. Think of all this, as you are wont; but think of it rather with a *practical* intent: all speculation is beginningless and endless. Do not let yourself into *Grübeln*, even in your present state of partial inaction. I well, infinitely too well, know what *Grübeln* is: a wretched sink of Darkness, Pain, a paralytic Fascination; cover it up; that is to say, *neglect* it for some outward piece of Action: go resolutely forward, you will not heed the precipices that gape on the right hand of you, and on the left. In Naples, for example, is there not much that you can *do?* I speak not of sight-seeing: doubtless you have been or will be at Virgil's Tomb, their Dog-Grotto,

Vesuvius, Herculaneum, and what not; and have your eyes open, and your *pen* going: but there is much more than all this to be seen. There are *men* at Naples, and their way of Life, their *practice* in all things, *medical*, moral, legislative, artistic, economic. Is there no "Count Manso" now, living in your Parthenope? Alas, I fear, none! Nevertheless you actually should not be so *solitary:* scrape a talking acquaintance with *any* one, rather than with none. Some foolish *Abbate*, or *Signor*, or even *Cicerone* might tell you about many things. See to form some practical notion and theorem of the matter; and do not come home (as Alick's mad serving-man said) "with my finger in my mouth, and two men both alike gleg (*klug*) waiting for me." Salvator Rosa's haunts are close by you: also you must not fail to bring me some authentic intelligence of the wondrous Masaniello; gather whatsoever you can of him; the village where he dwelt and fished is not far from you. Finally, dear Brother, "be alive" (as my Shrewsbury Coachman told a Methodist Parson): be *alive;* all is included in that. We will hope to meet you at your return, a man filled with new knowledge, useful and ornamental; and ready then to begin his Mastership with manly effect, his Apprenticeship being honourably concluded.—I remark only further that your anxiety to send that money is an excellent omen in my eyes: I will take good care of the cash when it comes to hand, and dispose of it punctually; and think, it is the first fruits of a Brother's Endeavour, which is henceforth to go on prospering; of which the securing his own Freedom and civic Independence is to be but a small though a fundamental and preliminary result. And so God keep you, and me; and make us all helpful and honourable to one another, and "not ashamed to live" (as a Voice we have often heard[1] was wont to pray), " nor afraid to die." Amen.

I sent you all the Scotsbrig news in my last Letter. I have been there since; only last week, and found them all struggling along, much as of old. Our dear Mother holds out well; is in fair health; not more dispirited than

[1] His father's.—M. C.

almost any one would be under her bereavement; and peaceful, with a high trust in the great Guide of all. We expect her here in about a week, with Alick, who is bringing me up *the* Cart, with some sort of Horse he was to buy for me. I was over at his Farm too (which is named Catlinns); a mile from the junction of Corrie and Milk towards Lockerbie: it is a large mass of a *rough* farm, with some considerable space of good land in it; somewhat *bare*, and the houses, etc., in bad order: but is thought to be *cheap*, by judges. He is toiling at it very hard, looks lean, but otherwise hearty; diligent and prudent. Jenny has given him a queer lively little girl, which he is very fond of.—We settled everything at Scotsbrig; the Departed had left it all ready for settlement. Your name or mine (as I had myself requested) is not mentioned in the Will: it was all between my Mother and the other Five. Each had to claim some perhaps £120 (each of the *five;* our Mother has the Houses worth some £28 yearly, during life) . . . Your Letter had given them all great pleasure; their affection is as true as steel.

Of ourselves here there is not much new to be said. Jane seemed to grow *very greatly* better whenever she set foot on her native heath; is now not so well again, yet better than in London. I have written two things: a short *Funeral Oration* on Goethe; it is for Bulwer's Magazine of June (the *New Monthly*), and pleases the Lady much better than me: then a paper on certain *Corn Law Rhymes* for Napier, of some twenty-five pages; still lying here, but to go off forthwith. I am now beginning a far more extensive Essay on *Goethe* for the *Foreign Quarterly Review*. I am apt to be rather *stupid;* but do the best I can. Venerable, dear Goethe! But we will not speak a word here.— Our Puttock Establishment is much like what it was: duller a little since Alick went; but also quieter. Our new Neighbours have nothing to do with us; except little kind offices of business; articulate speech I hear little; no wiser man than William Corson[1] visits me. My sole comfort and remedy is Work! Work! Rather an unnatural state; but not to be altered for the

[1] Of Nether Craigenputtock.

present. With many blessings too : a kind, true-hearted Wife, with whom a true man may share *any* fortune; fresh air, food and raiment fit for one. The place is even a beautiful place, in its kind; and may serve for a *workshop*, as well as another. Let us work, then; and be thankful. . . . Now excuse my dulness, dear John; love me always; and may God bless you!

T. CARLYLE.

XCI.—To ALEXANDER CARLYLE, Catlinns.

CRAIGENPUTTOCK, *Friday*, 29*th June* 1832.

MY DEAR ALICK— . . . Your note with the Scotsbrig enclosure got hither that same night : greatly to our satisfaction, to learn that all was well with you. With us too, as Peter[1] will explain, Craigenputtock "stands where it did;" with little change—except that there is a considerable *Peat-stack* now happily added to its other edifices. The fuel is good stuff, and was well got in.

Jane is complaining still; yet undoubtedly in the way of mending. I myself, as you

[1] Peter Austin, of the neighbouring farm, Carstammon.

understand, have been the busiest man since we parted, *writing* what I could: am now in the very heart of it; and think other *ten days* will show me daylight on the farther side; at all events two weeks: so that, say in three weeks, you are most likely to see me in Annandale again. If Jane come with me, we will make for Catlinns *first.*—I have the old still existence, which you know so well here; am quite quiet with it, and happy enough while I am busy. If little good, neither does much evil come to ruffle our solitude: let us be thankful. This is my *workshop*, where there is *room* for my tool-bench to stand, and let me work a little: the Earth can yield no man any more than this same thing, better or worse in some small degree.—. . .

The gray mare gives complete satisfaction: a most gentle Beast; *comes* to be caught when you go for it; refuses no kind of work, will soon be a quite superior rider, agrees with its grass, and troubles no one. So that your journey for me to Longtown was not labour in vain, but will often come gratefully to re-

membrance. . . . Send me up a "scrape of a pen" by Peter: how you are (little Jean included), how you are doing. I could have you a few larch-sticks ready *directly*, if you could come for them. God bless you, dear Brother!
—Ever your affectionate, T. CARLYLE.

XCII.—To his MOTHER, Scotsbrig.

CRAIGENPUTTOCK, *Tuesday night*,
31*st July* 1832.

MY DEAR MOTHER—I meant at anyrate to write you a line to-night, and here comes, on Sabbath from Church, a brave Letter from John, which will make the package better worth carriage. Our good Doctor is well, and has now heard of our welfare: it is altogether a very comfortable Letter. I have written him a long Answer to-day; wherein I failed not to mention how many kind things you *wished* to say to him, and that he must *imagine* them all. . . .

I got up handsomely enough that day; came upon Ben Nelson on Dodbeck Brae, and *scraiched*[1] two or three miles with him (for he

[1] Screeched, shouted.

was on a pony that would not lead), then said good-bye, with appointment to meet again in Town; as accordingly we did, and had a long talk together. He told me of Waugh: how old Peg, his aunt, had died, and left him £50; wherewith what does the possessed person do but go off to Benson's and the King's Arms with it, and sit there till he has eaten and drunk the last sixpence of it: then back to unpeeled potatoes and repose! Bray a fool in a mortar, he will *not* depart from his folly. . . .

Jane was sitting waiting for me, or rather running out half-distracted to meet me: she bids me say she rued right sore not coming on with me, and will surely do so next time. She is still in the way of improvement; proceeding, slowly. We ride, and drive, and drink *trefoil* (*threefold*) and other bitters, and do the best we can. The weather is very sultry and thirsty; rain would do us good, as well as the grass. Jane goes to Dumfries in the Gig to-morrow with the Boy; a-shopping, and will take this along with her. . . .

The peats are all home; a most effectual-looking stack : ninety cart-loads to front the winter with. We have got hay too; Rowantree came and offered me what I wanted at 6d. a stone; I sent Peter Austin down to inspect the weighing for me, and now the loft is quite choke-full : 180 stones of Rowantree's, and perhaps 50 that were left of Alick's. The horses seem very willing to eat it. . . .

As to *my* work, it wears but a sluggish look yet : I have been translating and revising some German things for the Magazine, and am now done ; a larger task must forthwith be entered on. I must not come back to you, till this be finished : *when* I cannot positively say ; you shall hear from me how I get on. Would it be quite impossible that some of you should come up hither and see us before shearing-time : say Jane, my valued Correspondent ; would nobody take her work for a week ; she engaging to do the like for that body some other time ? *You* said once, you would come when the rasps[1] were ready : now here they are, and the blackbirds eating them all.

[1] Raspberries.

In any case, tell Jane to order me a Leghorn (coarse) broad-brimmed Hat from the Grahames, to be got ready with all despatch : the measure of my Hat, *outside*, is just two feet and one half-inch, no more and no less : my *shape* (of a flattish brim, slightly turned up behind) the people already know. Tell her also to write to me with all minuteness very soon. I am taking it for granted that my dear Mother, and the rest of them, are in the usual way: but need from time to time to be assured of it. M'Diarmid, who clatters everlastingly,[1] about *cholera*, declared last week that it was near you; as indeed it may soon be near us all. It will go its course, and keep [the path] appointed it, and do the work marked out for it : why flutter and fluster ourselves? Did our great Creator and sure Redeemer send us the cholera; or did some other send it? I think it is a folly even to *speak* of the subject, unless there is some new light to be thrown on it; such as "the able Editor" has *not* to throw. I enclose you, on a [little card] a small stave

[1] In the *Dumfries Courier*, of which he was editor.

by Goethe, which occurred in the thing I was translating.

Alas, dear Mother, the Paper is done, and I hardly begun. But indeed I know not *when* I should *end*. I must now out for my gloaming-shot[1] on the Glaisters Hill side.—May God keep you all! I forget no day to think of you, to *pray* for you in my way. Be good and faithful, "loving one another," as it is commanded. Good-night!   T. CARLYLE.

XCIII.—To ALEXANDER CARLYLE, Catlinns.

CRAIGENPUTTOCK, 12*th August* 1832.

MY DEAR BROTHER—I am just in the bustle of setting out to avoid the dirty "Gunner-bodies;"[2] and having many things to prepare and adjust, cannot write you more than a line. We had determined on a drive to Kirkchrist;[3] Jane to go with me, if she could: I wrote the people to that effect; and now Jane *not* being

---

[1] Twilight-interval, an idle time before the candles are lit.
[2] Come for the grouse-shooting, and "felt to be a nuisance" by the Carlyles.—See *Reminiscences*, i. 84.
[3] To see his old friends the Churches, late of Hitchill.

able to go with me, I must go myself,—most *reluctantly*, now when it has come to the point! Indeed, I think I would willingly give a couple of guineas, had I liberty to stay quietly at home, and follow my affairs. These wretched Devil's-servants of Gunners! However, I shall try to get round them another year. Meanwhile, this journey, as in spite of all my reluctance I inwardly feel, will do me good. . . .

I have not been idle, at least not at *ease*, since we parted; yet the quantity of *work done* is very small. I have packed off two little (mostly translated) pieces for Magazine Fraser; this is all I have yet *got quit of*. Another thing or two are on the anvil; but in a very rough state. I must not look Annandale in the face till I have done at least one of them. You will hear before then. I have now and then enough ado to keep myself stiffly at work : as you know well, however, there is *no* other course for one in this lone Desert; where if a man did not work, he might so easily run mad. When vapours of solitude, and longings after the cheerful face of my fellow-man are gathering round me, I dash them off, and the first lusty swing of Industry scatters them away, as cock-crowing does spectres of the Night. Let not a living man complain! His little Life is given him for the sake of an Eternity: let him *stand to it* honestly; all else is quite unimportant to him. This time fifty years, as I have often said to myself, the question will not be, Wert thou joyful or sorrowful? but, Wert thou true or wert thou false? Was thy little task faithfully done, or faithlessly? So we will move along; and fear no man, and no devil —but the one *within* us, which also we will to the last war with.

I believe myself to be getting really by some hardly perceptible degree stronger in *health* both inward and outward: perhaps, one day, I may triumph over long disease, and be myself again! Still I know, healthy or sick, conquering or conquered, the son of Adam has no blessedness to look for but *honest toil* (which will never be *joyous* but *grievous*): let him toil at the thing *beside* him, and bless Heaven that he has hands and a head! . . .

T. CARLYLE.

XCIV.—To his MOTHER, Scotsbrig.

CRAIGENPUTTOCK, *Tuesday*,
21*st August* 1832.

MY DEAR MOTHER—Alick would tell you, and the last Newspaper would tell you to expect a word from me to-night. I will tell you that I am well, that we are both well, and this is nearly my whole message. I have sat these two days, in the solitary moors, reading here (at a French Book, which is my task) from nine in the morning till ten at night, with hardly intermission for my meals and my pipes: so that my head is quite filled with foreign matters, and I could almost forget that beyond these Heaths there is a wide Earth, and I myself *am not out* of the world, but still *in* it. You will be thankful, I know, for any sort of stuff I can write you.

There is the last *Edinburgh Review* with my Paper on the *Corn-Law Rhymes* in it; which you are to read but not *detain;* for the first sight of it properly belongs to Alick, and the Parcel was forgotten by accident when the

Boy went down with the Horse. Let Alick have it, I pray you, by the first opportunity (along with that little Note); if you want to see more of it, he will send it back, and you can take pennyworths.[1] The last Number of *Fraser's Magazine* is come to hand; you can return it along with the *Review*, by Notman, when you are satisfied: other little things I might send in the Book way; but this, as I judge, is no reading time with you, but a time for plying sickles, and weary limbs.

My dear Mother, every time I hear that you are well, I hear it as an *unexpected* blessing; and live in a continual kind of apprehension. Let the good Jean take pen again, and tell me all how the matter stands; what you are doing, how you are, and every one is. These foolish fears one should strive to banish; they are unprofitable, perhaps sinful: but a natural cowardice and faint-heartedness is in one. I daresay, the truth is you are all reaping corn; and busy and moderately well: had one only a *glass* to *see* you all at work by, now and

[1] Take it by bits, at your leisure.

then! But it is needless wishing; one would be for a *trumpet* next to *hear* you by, and speak with you by.

I set off, as Alick may have informed you, on Monday morning gone a week, to be out of the road of Gunners and such like: the Gunners, as I found, actually came, and would have staid had I been there. However, I have now set about *letting* the Game of the place, and so shall be troubled with it no more. For the rest, I had a pleasant sort of tour (among the Churches of Kirkchrist, Jeffray[1] of Girthon, etc.); and returned on Thursday evening no worse for my excursion. People were all very kind; the country was all beautiful to behold; I saw various persons familiar to me *very* long ago (at College and elsewhere), whose whiskers were now getting gray, whom I could not look upon without interest. I will *tell* you about it all when we meet. I passed Lochinbreck Well, too, and drank a tumbler of their arsenic water: finally, I was very glad to see the Wife running out to meet me, in her green veil (for

[1] An old college friend, minister of Girthon.

midges), and welcome me to my own solitude again.

. . . Except two little trifles for Fraser, not printed yet, I have done as good as nothing since I saw you! I have not been idle either; but somehow it has *kithed* ill.[1] I have now begun a long thing (on a Frenchman called *Diderot*), and must not stir, if I can help it, till it be done. Alas! I have still upwards of twenty large volumes (one per day) to *read*, before I can put pen to paper! However, it *must* be done; and so shall be done, if I keep my health. You will hear from me again before that: nay, if it threaten to detain me *too* long, I will run and leave it for three days after all. If I go to Edinburgh in winter, both *this* and another long piece ought to be done first: I must struggle what I can. Jeffrey is not paid yet;[2] but can now be paid any day, and leave me a handsome enough sum over. Napier I believe owes me more. I am in debt

---

[1] There is little to show for it.

[2] Probably the money lent by Jeffrey to Dr. Carlyle.—See *ante*, i. p. 314; ii. p. 37.

to no Being—but to you, and the GREAT Lender and Giver; to the rest I pay as well as borrow : what more would I have ?

The Paper on Goethe, I see, is published in London last week; it will be here before very long; after which I will send Scotsbrig a reading of it. I reckon it but little worth, either at Scotsbrig or elsewhere. . . .

I still read in the Bible. Did you ever hear of *John Welsh's* Sermons ? It is the brave old John Welsh of Collieston, son-in-law to Knox. I saw the Book at Jeffray's of Girthon, who said they were among the *best* sermons he had ever read. I think, for the sake of *relationship* and ancestry,[1] we should seek them out : in Edinburgh I will make a trial ; and perhaps find some far earlier and better copy than Jeffray's.

But, at length, dear Mother, good-night ! Bid Jean write,— write with minuteness and despatch. I asked about her getting hither : but, alas, I suppose it is over now till after Harvest ; we will see to it then. My Brotherly

[1] See *Reminiscences*, i. 133.

love to Jamie and Jenny and all the rest of them. Tell them all to be good and true; there is *no other* benefit a man with all his cunning can extract from Life. Life is short, Eternity is long! Wise and good was he who commanded, saying, "Little children, love one another."—Good-night, my dear Mother; may God ever be with you!—Your affectionate Son,

T. CARLYLE.

XCV.—To ALEXANDER CARLYLE, Catlinns.

CRAIGENPUTTOCK, *9th September* 1832.

MY DEAR BROTHER—I have got into a small perplexity here, in which I need your assistance. It relates to the gray mare.

Last Wednesday afternoon, Jane and I thought of having a little drive in the Gig, and got yoked and seated accordingly, with the Beast all brushed and corned, whose behaviour on the last occasion, as on all previous ones, had given us no reason for distrust; least of all on the score of *temper*. Nevertheless, at the first crack of the whip what does the brute do but whirl round upon the Green, and attempt rearing; to the infinite terror of the Leddy, who forthwith dismounted, declaring she would venture no step farther! I reassured her; led and then drove, still with some uneasiness, to the outer gate; where, having discovered that the *choke-band* was tighter than it should be, and slackened it, Jane was persuaded to get in again, and away we drove without further sign of obstruction. All went well as possible, till we got to M'Knight's,[1] whose wife and children were busy disloading his cart (about five in the afternoon): the Beast made a kind of volunteer halt there, but easily enough went off again; and then about ten steps farther, we met one of the shoemaker's children trailing a child's cart, at which our quadruped took offence, and shied considerably, yet got past without splutter, and *then*—simply set to work and kicked and plunged as if Satan were in her, till her harness is all in tatters, and, as she still cannot get away, *lies down;* whereupon I (who had sat doing or saying very little) step out with my reins, seize the bridle, get Jane out,

[1] John M'Knight, the Glenessland carrier.

get the foolish brute free of her straps,—and our gigging has reached an untimely end! The suddenness and then the quietness and calm deliberation of the business were matter of astonishment: one minute we are driving prosperously along, in three minutes more we are *gigless*. M'Knight's wife kept disloading her cart all the while, as if it had been nothing out of the common run. The poor woman is very stupid, and indeed in the family way at present. John, however, arrived before all was over, and helped us what he could. We borrowed an old saddle from him, and walked off; leaving the gig-wreck in his warehouse: at Sundaywell I set the poor Leddy on this old saddle, and leading the mare myself in all quietness arrived home in quite other equipment than we had departed. The Boy took Harry and a pair of Cart-ropes, and had the *Clatch*[1] home at dusk: it was far less injured than you would have thought; nothing broken but the leather-mass and two leather straps that fasten on the *splinter*-bar (*swing*-tree bar)

[1] Old gig.

which the traces hook upon; and the under wood-work (I mean the *continuation* of the shaft, nearly above the axle-tree on the left side) rather bruised and twisted than broken. This the Vulcan has already mended, quite effectually, without difficulty. As for the harness it is done utterly; flying in dozens of pieces: you never witnessed such a piece of work as I had to get it thrummed together in any way, so that it would drive as far as the smithy; a *saddle*-crupper fixed on it; one trace lengthened and a new *eye* cut, the other shortened to the utmost (to make both equal): spliced bridle, etc. etc. : the most Irish-looking vehicle perhaps ever seen in these parts. The question now remains : What is to be done?

As for the harness, all things considered, I ought not perhaps to be sorry that it is finished: we seldom went out without something in it breaking; and nobody knows how long one might have gone on cobbling and stitching, always throwing new money away. A quite fresh harness can be got (a Saddler at Thornhill anxiously showed me one, nay two) for little more than five pounds; and it will be best that we are obliged to get a new one. I have no skill at all in these matters; and will not deal with the Thornhill man, till you and I have investigated Dumfries together, and found nothing better there. Harry will draw us at any rate through winter; with the present tackle, one may bring the vehicle down to get new tackle, and that is all we can expect of it.

With regard to the Mare, I must now leave you to act for me, and judge for me. Jane has declared that she will drive with her no more; and indeed I think it were very unwise, unless with quite other security than any skill of mine. We must sell her then, I suppose, if anything like the value is to be had for her. The *old money* would please me sufficiently; or indeed any money you think her worth. I may mention, however, my own persuasion is that the Beast, after all, is thoroughly what is called *quiet;* that it was my poor driving that mainly caused the accident; had I given her an effectual yerk with the whip when she first began kicking, or rather offering to kick, it had been all right.

No shadow of *vice* in the creature have I ever seen before or since.—Unfortunately, as you see, she is in poorish condition for sale; one of the hind feet too has got the hair peeled, which perhaps could not grow in time. The Rood Fair[1] is in two weeks. I have no food here to fatten any quadruped; but Jamie, I think, has plenty of *clover*, and you must take him into counsel. Indeed, he was once talking about *keeping* her, or some like her, for her work till grass-time again; so here is another possibility for us. My persuasion is that any handy man could make this mare do anything he liked without difficulty: and perhaps had she got a winter of carting and ploughing and other sobering, she might be easier to deal with next summer. Manage as you see best. I think the horse a good one and very cheap: however, I have no reluctance to part with her. I do not think she will ever *ride* very handsomely with me; she is *flail-legged*, skittish a little, and does not seem to thrive

[1] An annual fair held at Dumfries the end of September.—M. C.

here (she has had oats and grass and *very little work*); she does nothing well but the *jog-trot*, and about *forty yards* of cantering ; her *sy*NEWS are quite loose under you. Larry was quite another at her age. I believe I must renounce the thought of a *riding* horse ; at all events, your little black mare would ride as well as *she* yet does, and for all else would content me infinitely better. Again, I say, decide for me and act for me.

I think there never was such a long-winded deluge of a Narrative poured out by me, as this same, on so small occasion ! I am excessively stupid to-night, and in haste too. So, my dear Brother, you must just interpret what I mean by your own acuteness of wit. Send the Boy off *early* on Tuesday morning ; he has things to get at Dumfries. Of course you can send no *positive* word what is to be done with the mare, till you have seen Jamie and consulted with him, and considered with yourself : but tell me when you can meet me at Dumfries to buy new Harness, and whether the Rood Fair is the only day shortly you could come on, and whether that would do for the purpose. I like such gatherings very ill. Moreover, do not by any means leave your *harvesting* for that errand: we are in no pressing haste.—And so I conclude this confused interminable story of *The Gig Demolished, or Pride gets a Fall.*

I am tolerably well (and so is Jane); my *reading* is done within two days, and then I have five stern weeks of writing. Wish me goodspeed! I must and will be through it. We shall meet before then, I hope.—I often think of you here, in these solitudes; and how the places that once knew you, now know you no more, and I am left alone on the Moor. Courage! Let us stand to our tasks, and give the rest to the winds. We shall meet often yet, in spite of all; and often hear each that the other is behaving *like a brave man*. I know no other *welfare* in this Earth.—Jean writes us that your house is roofed again; we rejoice to fancy you free from rain-drops; and fronting the Winter with better shelter. Catlinns will have a new face when I come,—which will be, I trust, when this "Article" is over.—You would see John's Letter; you would get the Review and the Printed Piece on Goethe. I can lend you other things of the Magazine kind: but suppose you to be far too busy for reading as yet. Tell me how goes your harvest; when you hope to be done; how you are all.—You will soon see our dear Mother; tell her of our welfare, and that she will before long hear of us again. Thank Jean for her two letters; say the Hat does excellently; no news I can get is so valuable to me as that our Mother and all of you are well. Love one another. One day we shall *not* all be well any longer. Our kindest wishes to little Janekin and her Mother. The "new creature" will be a great solace to you; receive her and retain her as "sent from God."— Remember me and my Leddy to our Mother and my good Letter-writing Jean, and every other one of them, and say we shall *both* be down ere long, were my Article but done.— God be with you, dear Brother!—Ever your affectionate,

T. CARLYLE.

XCVI.—To ALEXANDER CARLYLE, Catlinns.

CRAIGENPUTTOCK, *Tuesday*,
18*th September* 1832.

MY DEAR ALICK— . . . The Limbs of the Law summoned me down to Dumfries, on Saturday last to "serve as Juryman;" I went; and answered to my name, about half-past ten o'clock: this was all the duty I had to do. The case was a Sheriff's one; of a wretched *sagtail* chimney-sweep, who had stolen an Ass, value twenty shillings, in the Parish of Ewes: they sentenced him to imprisonment; after which the fifty or sixty men who had been obliged to throw by their work and mount their horses on his account, were dismissed, and went their way. I contrived, however, to get my little bits of business done; and so, being very much pressed by work here, was obliged to resolve on not losing *another* day, even though I had the prospect of meeting you there.

The rather as I now find that we can do a while *without new Harness*. I got an awl and threads up from Dumfries by the Boy, and have made the most surprising job of it; you would not know that anything had happened. Then, as we are to be away in winter, and so forth, it seemed to me the new Harness might spoil: besides, what is true, there is no superfluity of money going just now. I have paid the Advocate (last Saturday), and have still a few pounds over, and more due; but it will all be wanted, and more, too, that I have yet to earn for Edinburgh and its expenses. So we will let the Harness lie: if you have any chance, pray inform yourself at the Saddler's what such a thing can be had for; it will be to purchase by and by, if we keep the *Clatch* running; which, while resident here, I see not how we can help doing.

Jemmy and you, I daresay, will be at the Rood Fair: can you not come up hither at night, and see what we are doing, and rest yourselves till Saturday? I fear, not; and yet it is perhaps possible, if you are through the corn, and the Potatoes not begun yet. We shall see. . . .

We know not yet when we go to Edinburgh;

I have still much work to do ; it cannot be till a month or so after Martinmas. We have hired the old servant, whom you gave a ride to last Whitsunday : she can ride, yoke, etc. ; so that we think of dismissing Robert, for whom there will be no work. Now on this latter point I had a message to you from Jane, and partly from myself : it is to see whether Jamie needs a Boy of that kind through winter, for I think he had one last winter, and that this might suit him. He is expert enough with horses, rather a *good* carter I think ; willing to work, but totally unable to get through with almost any work, unless there be some *commander* near him, when he will stretch himself really handsomely enough. He performs pretty well (not exorbitantly) with the *spoon*, is not ever in the least troublesome : but the thing that interests us above all things in him is the natural *sense* the poor creature manifests ; his love of knowledge in all sorts ; and what is of infinitely greater moment even than this, his innocence and veracity. We have never detected him telling the smallest falsehood, or so much as prevaricating. I could like well to fancy the poor creature in good hands, where he would see and hear honest sensible things said and done; and be stirred up and *sharpened*, even by *roughish* usage to put himself forth into exertion. He is very desirous, it seems, to learn husbandry work; and could easily learn it, had he a tight stirring master. Tell the Scotsbrig people about all this; and see whether they say anything. We shall likely send him down to the Fair at any rate, and he will see some of you at Beck's.[1]

I have taken up all your sheet with this small *charitable* matter, which is of a sort one ought not to neglect.—There are four Numbers of *Fraser* for you, and a *Life of Mary Wollstonecraft* (once a famous woman): I think they will serve you till we come down.—Alas, I have a long *dour* job before me first; but I am toiling at it, and it cannot last me long. Tell my dear Mother that I am as impatient to come as she can be to have me; that I will

---

[1] A coachmaker's, in whose stable the horse was lodged when at Dumfries.—M. C.

set off the very day I am at liberty ; lastly, that I think surely in four weeks from this date we may hope to see you.

It was cleverly done to slate your house with your "own hand" (as Edward Irving used to sign his name), and get it over before Tirltrees[1] season. You will have a very tolerable place of it, heartsome in summer, stormtight in winter ; I hope and believe it will not disappoint your honest calculations in other respects. Courage, my dear Brother! The willing arm will yet find work, and wages for it : "There is aye life for a living body." We are all born to hard labour ; and might easily have been born to worse.—I have filled up all your sheet with "mere nothings ;" and must now desist, and wrap up. God be with you always! Ever your affectionate, T. CARLYLE.

XCVII.—To JAMES CARLYLE at Dumfries.

CRAIGENPUTTOCK, *Tuesday night*,
25th September 1832.

MY DEAR JAMIE — If Alick saw you, he

[1] See *ante*, i. p. 236.

would be speaking something of this Boy. Since then we have altered our figure a little. The poor honest slut of a Boy would very gladly have gone to Scotsbrig, if he went anywhither; but looked so inexpressibly *wae* to go away at all, that we could not but resolve to leave him in peace. If he is worth his victuals to you, when we set out for Edinburgh, or at any time till we return, you shall have him: if not, he "will go home; and get to the school a while." So it is settled.

I hope you are come[1] to get me rid of that Mare, and will prosper some way. I believe her well worth the money you gave for her; but care not if I never see her face again. Catlinns[2] and you will, I know, make the most of the market, and do for me far better than I could for myself.

We are in great "wishfulness" to know what is going on at Scotsbrig and at Catlinns; whether your Harvest is done, and well done, etc. etc. Will you come up, and tell us: either, or both of you? Otherwise send word with

[1] Up to Dumfries.   [2] His brother Alick.

the Boy. At worst, I will *come* by and by, and see.

The Boy has a Basket of wares, and messages to do, then leave to look about him *till four o'clock*. *Forward* him at that hour, if he come in your way.—My best Blessing with you both!—Your affectionate Brother (very busy),

T. CARLYLE.

XCVIII.—To Mr. JOHN AITKEN, Dumfries.[1]

CRAIGENPUTTOCK, 16*th October* 1832.

MY DEAR UNCLE—Judge if I am anxious to hear from you! Except the silence of the Newspapers, I have no evidence that you are still spared. The Disease,[2] I see, has been in your street; in Shaw's; in Jamie Aitken's; it

[1] This letter is reprinted from the *Dumfries Standard*, 9th February 1881.

[2] Cholera, which was exceptionally severe at Dumfries, owing, it is supposed, to its unwholesome "Closes" (a survival from old Border warfare times, when houses had been crowded near the castle for safety); but chiefly to its water supply, taken in carts from the river which served also as the only conduit for the drainage of the town. The population was then 10,000; between the 15th September and 27th November over 500 persons died,—340 lie buried in one grave.—*Macdowall's History of Dumfries*.

has killed your friend Thomson: who knows what further was its appointed work! You I strive to figure in the meanwhile, as looking at it, in the universal terror, with some calmness, as knowing and practically believing that your days, and the days of those dear to you, were now, as before and always, in the hand of God only; *from* whom it is vain to fly; *towards* whom lies the only refuge of man. Death's thousand doors have ever stood open; this indeed is a wide one, yet it leads no farther than they all lead.

Our Boy was in the town a fortnight ago (for I believe, by experience, the infectious influence to be trifling, and quite inscrutable to man; therefore go and send whithersoever I have *business*, in spite of cholera); but I had forgot that he would not naturally see Shaw or some of you, and gave him no letter; so got no tidings. He will call on you to-morrow; and in any case bring a verbal message. If you are too hurried to *write* in time for him, send a letter next day "to the care of Mrs. Welsh, Templand, Thornhill": tell me only that you are all spared alive!

We are for Annandale, after Thornhill, and may possibly enough return by Dumfries. I do not participate in the panic. We were close beside cholera for many weeks in London: " every ball has its billet."

I hear the Disease is fast abating. It is likely enough to come and go among us; to take up its dwelling with us among our other maladies. The sooner we grow to compose ourselves beside it, the wiser for us. A man who has reconciled himself *to die* need not go distracted at the *manner* of his death.

God make us all ready ; and be His time ours ! —No more to-night.—Ever your affectionate,

T. CARLYLE.

XCIX.—To Dr. CARLYLE, Rome.

18 CARLTON STREET, STOCKBRIDGE,
EDINBURGH, 8*th January* 1833.

MY DEAR BROTHER— . . . It was but last night that we got our household transported hither, by the Thornhill coach ; and as neither Jane nor I slept much, Jane not at all (thanks to the Watchman's care about the *hour*), I am not in very bright spirits at present: however, I have a vacant forty minutes, and will *begin* to do a duty, which is always one's best resource. I have yet seen but little of Edinburgh beyond a few of the cloth-making, shop-keeping sort: I am to go and dine with old uncle Bradfute[1] (at a *precise* moment); will therefore reserve all Edinburgh things till the end of my Letter, which will not be accomplished till to-morrow. —I have been *once* at Scotsbrig since I wrote you (if not twice, for I am dim about my last date); I set off exactly this day gone a week, through a world of frost-mist and snow-*slush*, being almost superstitiously determined to see my Mother once more before we went. She was sitting at tea (in the low end-room), and stood silent with amazement to see me there all swimming with *slobber*[2] (for she had despaired of me two days before); but soon got me stript of travelling gear, and otherwise lovingly attended to; and then we sat talking

---

[1] A relation of Mrs. Carlyle, a partner in the firm of Bell and Bradfute, booksellers, in Edinburgh.

[2] Slush, liquid mud.

the whole night; for the rest of them were all gone to Brand's of Craighouse to a New-year's Party.¹ She looks older, our dear Mother, within these two years; yet her health is still wonderfully tolerable: her spirits, as we can all understand, have been much weighed down, so that her *old* cheerfulness is gone, perhaps for long; nevertheless the faith she has sustains her from despondency, and the love we all endeavour to show her is most lovingly responded to. She depends much on me, as the eldest; and I feel it as a sacred duty to divide my last fraction of earthly substance or faculty in her cause. One of her very first questions is always: "Hast thou heard onything fra the Doctor?" She speculates greatly about your home-coming; and says if it be the Almighty's good pleasure she shall yet live to meet you. A Letter from you to herself, not so much filled with expressions of feeling, as with minute details about your way of life, purposes, *Befinden und Hoffen*, would gratify her much. She often

¹ The Brands were relations of the Carlyles.—See *Reminiscences*, i. 40.

speaks of you with more joy perhaps, not with more love than formerly; and now and then makes us laugh by some such phrase as " when the Doctor was *sucking!*" The rest were all in their usual heart. . . .

This is not properly a noisy place but the reverse; in a little while we shall learn the train of things, to endure or to avoid, and so do well enough. It is an excellent Floor of its sort; two really dashing Rooms, with three Bedrooms, Kitchen and all *etceteras*, for £4 a month. We have engaged it for three months, that is till the beginning of April. You remember Stockbridge, and a smart street, with large trees growing through the pavement, looking into the river (Water of Leith), called *Dean Street?* You just cross the Bridge, from Edinburgh, and Dean Street stretches to the *left.* Now Carlton Street is the first street at right angles to that; our house is the corner one (the corner *farthest* from the River), and fronts two ways; both beautiful, one of them into a sort of circus or double-crescent, where are such trees that a rookery has established itself in them. So much for our whereabout, which I know you will take pleasure in figuring. The question: what we expect or intend here? is also not very ill to answer. I expect little; to see some Books, some People; to *live* for twelve weeks, with eyes and ears open; and wait *das Weitere*. In some days too I shall have my writing-desk in order, and compose somewhat; were it only to pay expenses. I have long been very remiss in the matter of writing; indeed have not had so long an interval of reading and idling for above twelve months. But my head is not vacant; neither has that past time been wholly barren,—though nearly enough so. I know not what I shall write first; perhaps something for Fraser (who pays best, and is the sweetest to deal with); but you shall hear. Naso I saw yesterday walking along the streets, but kept clear of him—for a day or two. He has but one fault but that one is a thumper: he seems very scarce of money! He only paid that Paper *Characteristics*, after twice being dunned, some three weeks ago, and then rather sparingly I thought. Another Paper he still owes me; but will and must pay it. Cochrane[1] is keeping the *Diderot* I conjecture for his *next* Number; that will be some four months hence. That is all of my Scriptory Economics I had to tell you.[2] By Heaven's grace, I nowise want merchants (of a sort) for my ware; and can still, even in these days, live. So long as that is granted, what more is there to ask? All Gigmanity is of the Devil, devilish: let us rather be thankful if we are shut out even from the temptation thereto. It is not want of money or money's worth that I could ever complain of; nay often too it seems to me as if I did *best* when no *praise* was given me; and I stood alone between the two Eternities, with my feet on the rock: but what I mourn over is the too frequent obscuration of Faith within me; the kind of exile I must live in from all classes of articulate-speaking men; the dimness that reigns over all my *practical* sphere, the etc. etc., for

---

[1] Editor of the *Foreign Quarterly Review*.
[2] Part of the remainder of this letter is in Froude's *Life*, ii. 327.

there is no end to man's complaining. One thing I have as good as ascertained, that Craigenputtock cannot forever be my place of abode; that it is, at present, and actually, one of the worst abodes for me in the whole wide world. One day I will quit it; either quietly, or like a *muirbreak*¹—for I feel well there are things in me to be told which may cause the ears that hear them to tingle! *Alles mit Mass und Regel!* As yet I decide on nothing; will nowise desert the whinstone stronghold till I better see some road from it. I could live again in Edinburgh; perhaps still more willingly in London, had I means; my good Wife is ready for all things: so we wait what the days bring forth.² Perhaps *your* place and mode of settlement might do something to determine us; we shall see how it turns. Meanwhile clear enough it is that *I*, in these very present days, ought to—write something true for the Periodicals!

---

¹ Burst of waters from a lake.

² Froude leaves out, without omission marks, what follows here, as far as to " against the evil " on p. 80.

I said I had no Edinburgh news: I have yet seen only the houses and pavements. The whole place impresses me as something village-like; after the roaring Life-floods of London, it looks all little, secluded, almost quiescent. But again it is very *clean*, and orderly in comparison; on the whole, a desirable place. One thing village-like is the number of known faces I have met on the streets; all old friends, grown a little grayer in the whiskers. I encountered Brewster yesterday; in a canvassing for the Natural Philosophy Professorship, vacant by the death of Leslie. There seems great doubt whether he will get it. The Tory Town-Council driven desperate and distracted by the figure of the time are bent, as their last act, to make a signal job of this; and put in a certain Forbes, age about twenty-three, never till this moment heard of by any man.[1] This seems to be the main article of Bookshop gossip for the time. The elections are over: Jeffrey and one Abercromby (a Liberal Whig) defeated the Tory

---

[1] James David Forbes; afterwards much and well "heard of." He held the Professorship till 1860.

wholly, and were chaired with great glory and renown. Jeffrey does not know yet that we are here; otherwise he would be through, for it is but a stone-cast. They had an election contest at Dumfries too; a monstrous-looking joiner's shed which they called a hustings stood erected at the west end of the mid-steeple, and there the people were perorating, one day when I happened to be down. Sharpe prevailed over Hannay; pot over kettle: a shallower mortal never travelled so far in such a trade. But so it must be: they that took *such as they had* never wanted. Buller is returned for Liskeard. The Whigs prevail everywhere: only some five or six *perfect* Radicals, among whom Cobbett for Oldham. The Tories may drink hemlock when they please, for they are extinguished not to be re-illumed. As for me, I take no hand in it, speak no word in it, whatsoever; for the whole struggle is poor and small; in *thought*, I am the deepest Radical alive in this Island, but allow it to rest there, having other to do. There will be infinite floods of contentious jargon emitted were the poor men got together; and so they will "*carry* on till Loansdeal coom,"[1] and then—. I suppose you see *The Times* still, and know all these things as well as I. . . .

We see by the Newspapers that Lady Clare and Mr. Burrel are still at Rome, at least were lately: you must tell me all your movements and intentions. Your difficulties and disquietudes hide from me no less; such I know you have, for you are on this Earth: *ubi homines sunt injuriæ sunt.* Let us be thankful each of us that he is rich enough to have a Brother; one whose fidelity and love will *never* fail, let the contentious flesh introduce what superficial Discords it may. I say we should be thankful for such a possession; and try to draw from it what good it will yield, taking deliberately precaution against the evil. Perhaps the Future will be kinder to us both: but is not the Present kind, full of work to do? Write me *all* things, my dear Brother, and fear not that you

---

[1] Till (Lord) Lonsdale come: "Old Cumberland woman, listening as the Newspaper was read, full of battling, warring and tumult all over the world, exclaimed at last: 'Aye, they'll carry on till Lonsdale coom, and he'll soon settle them aw!'"—Note of Carlyle's in *Letters and Memorials*, i. 91.

shall ever want my sympathy. Keep diligent in business, fervent in spirit, serving God: that is the sum of all wisdom.—My Paper is near done; I feel sure I have forgotten much. No news from Irving or of him: the Tongue concern is quite out in this quarter: my poor lost Friend! Lost to me, to the world and to himself. . . .

And now, alas, dear Jack, I am done also, and must close. Jane (whom I have gone to ask) sends you "no word but her *kind* love," which is better than nothing. Write soon. God bless you, dear John.—Ever your true Brother, T. CARLYLE.

. . . . . .

C.—To his MOTHER, Scotsbrig.

18 CARLTON STREET [EDINBURGH],
27th January 1833.

MY DEAR MOTHER— . . . In my particular craft there seems to be nothing or very little astir; all people are either selling Penny Magazines, or lying on their oars. I get no good of any Editor or Publisher I have yet seen; come into no closer terms with them; I suppose they rather think me a dangerous sort of fellow: happily too I need not disturb myself a jot about one of them; having work enough elsewhere if I had three hands to work with. The truth is they are all at a kind of stand, poor fellows; and know not clearly on what side to turn them. We see abundance of people; most of them, unhappily, are but unprofitable sights, yet at worst harmless, and good compared to *none*. Jeffrey is here very often; talking like a pen-gun[1] (of very *light* calibre), always brisk and in good humour: he looks a great deal stronger than he did in London, is a little delighted with his Election; and ready again to go and have himself half-killed—for nothing! Such is men's lot. . . . The best man I see here, indeed the only man I care much about, is Sir William Hamilton; in whom alone of all these people I find an earnest soul, an openness for truth: I really think him a genuine kind of man. His learning is great, his talent considerable; we have

[1] Pop-gun.

long talks and walks together. He is the descendant of that " Robert Hamilton of Preston" (rather "a foolish man," as Sir William calls him) who commanded the Cameronians at Bothwell Brig. So much for my society here.

I wish I could say that I had fairly begun work, and was once in the middle of some hearty piece of writing, all on fire about it : but, alas, such is not yet my case; I am still only preparing and threatening to write. I go almost daily to the Advocates' Library, rummaging among Books, and searching out a variety of things : by and by, I shall get buckled to the gear, and certainly do something notable,—one would think! In the meantime you can fancy us sufficiently : breakfasting about nine; reading, or innocently though still more idly employed receiving visitors till one or two; about which hour I generally go out to walk ; then home to dine at four; after which the night is very generally our own, and we spend it in some sort of study till eleven, and then, if all have gone right, are sound asleep by twelve. This is the history of our day. . . .

But now here is the end. Give our kind love to all, let all be assured of our continual love. And so God bless you and guard you, my dear Mother!—I am ever, your affectionate Son, T. CARLYLE.

CI.—To ALEXANDER CARLYLE, Catlinns.

18 CARLTON STREET, STOCKBRIDGE,
EDINBURGH, 27*th January* 1833.

MY DEAR BROTHER—I sympathise truly with the painful incident that has befallen you. Your little Son has been lent you but a short while; has but, as it were, opened his eyes on this strange Chaos of TIME, and then as if affrighted, shrunk back into ETERNITY, hiding himself from the sin and woe in which we that are left on Earth must still struggle. There is something infinitely touching in a history so brief and yet so tragic; something infinitely mysterious too; but indeed the longest life is scarcely longer than the shortest if we think of the Eternity that encircles both; and so it is all mysterious, all awful and likewise holy; and our sole wisdom is to bow down before our inscrutable Author, and say heartily in *all* things, God's will be done. The Lord giveth and the Lord taketh away; blessed be the name of the Lord!—I have many times pictured to myself that stern awakening you got: "I dinna hear the bairn breathing!" Yet surely, as you observe, it was a blessed mercy that you found the event to have happened, as it were by the will of Providence alone; and without mischance on your part, which would have rendered the affliction doubly severe. In all our griefs, it is truly said, there is something of mercy mingled. And so we will bid the little Wayfarer, whose journey was so short, Farewell: he is but gone whither we too are hastening to follow.—This winter I can figure you out in your country home, a little less lonely than the last: your household is more stirring, and you are in a neighbourhood where one likes better to fancy you. I trust piously still that the change was for your good. Continue to be diligent and prudent, and you have nothing evil to apprehend. The times and the country we live in press heavy on us all: but a certain hope of improvement is still reasonable; nay, far better than any hope, a perfect assurance that if our Task be well done (which is always in our own power) all else will be well with us. So let the evil of the day be sufficient for the day: what the future may offer we will try to be ready for. Time and chance, as Solomon long since declared, happen unto all.

It is pleasant for me to consider you as now once more in a Neighbourhood: I need not counsel you to study "as much as in you lies" to live in peace, in goodwill and sympathy with all men, more especially with those nearest you, whom you have most to do with. It is this mainly of having persons one takes interest in around one's house that makes a House into the far more precious thing, a Home. In all mortals one finds flaws; nay *in one's self* more than in any other; therefore let us pity and pardon; even the poor creature that *wrongs* us was sore driven to his shifts, or he would not have wronged us; he too is pitiable and pardonable. . . . Next time you write I hope you will farther have to tell me that your financial reckonings have not disappointed you; but that the Rent is actually all ready, if not paid; and so the Catlinns speculation looking as we all wish it. We will pray always, May the worst of our days be past! In fine I will ask only one thing: that you would mend that Bridge (down at the old Mill): assuredly some one will get a mischief by it, if you do not; at present I cannot think of it without a kind of horror. Mind this, now, and take warning in time.

I have been living here in a curious unsatisfactory half-awake state: the transition is so singular from bare solitary moors, with only myself for company, to crowded streets and the converse of men. . . . I am carrying on a sort of occupation; but not with so much energy as I could desire; still only with the assurance that I shall grow energetic. The people (of whom we see abundance) are all kind and courteous as heart could reasonably wish : nevertheless I feel myself singularly a stranger among them ; their notions are not mine ; the things they are running the race for are no prizes to me. In Politics, especially as here manifested, I take no pleasure at all : the Tories, now happily driven into holes and corners, are quite out of date ; all the rest is Whiggery and Reform-Bill-for-ever, a most sandblind, feeble sort of concern ; a few Radicals of the Henry Hunt[1] sort are a still more pitiable set. The men stare at me when I give voice ; I listen when they have the word, "with a sigh or a smile." One great benefit I have, and can enjoy without drawback : abundance of Books. I am almost daily in the Advocates' Library, ransacking many things ; my appetite sharpened by long abstinence. On the whole we do well . . . ; and one way or other, generally to profit, the mind is kept full. Edinburgh affects me quite peculiarly after London : it looks all so orderly, so quiet, so little. I incline often to wish we had never

---

[1] A noted political agitator and charlatan, who died soon after this time.

left it: yet properly I cherish no regret for what is gone; that too had its worth, its influence on me for good, and lay among the things I had to do. I feel however, more and more plainly that Craigenputtock will absolutely never prove a wholesome abode for me; that I must try to get away from it, the sooner the better; however, there is evidently no immediate prospect of such a thing, and in any case, we will do *nothing rashly*. I privately think sometimes we should not settle upon anything till Jack come home; of which I am very glad that there is now a prospect. Dr. Irving, Keeper of the Advocates' Library, of whom you have heard me speak, has been talking lately very often about a Professorship at Glasgow, which will soon be vacant, the present incumbent being very old: this, as a thing that will be in the Lord Advocate's gift, our worthy Doctor thinks were the very thing for me. I bite at it with no eagerness; yet have hinted it to Jeffrey, and will not neglect it if it come in my way. We shall see. My own private impression is that I shall never get any Promotion in this world; and happy shall I be if Providence enable me only to stand *my own* friend. That is (or would be) all the prayer I offer to Heaven.—In Literature all is as dull here as it could possibly be; my old Manuscript is lying by me quiet; there is no likelihood of its being printed this winter, for I have not the cash just ready, and it is a thing that can wait. I do not think of vexing my soul with *Booksellers* about it or any other thing again,—so long as I can help it.—But alas, dear Alick, my sheet is done. Our Mother has a Letter too, which she will read you, where will be found a little more news. By the way, may I trust that Jamie and you have come to some final measures about those Ecclefechan Houses[1] and their management; and so relieving our good Mother from anxiety on that score. I know you will do what in you lies, it is well the part of us all. Jane sends her best wishes to her Namesake and every one of you. Let us find you all well and thriving in the month of April! Write to me soon and

[1] The property of his mother.

explain all your hopes and cares to me. Bless God that in a too unfriendly world we are not without Friends.—Ever, my dear Brother, your affectionate,   T. CARLYLE.

.   .   .   .   .   .

CII.—To ALEXANDER CARLYLE, Catlinns.

EDINBURGH, 4 GREAT KING STREET,
26th March 1833.

MY DEAR ALICK—I am making up a Parcel to go this day, by the Dumfries Bookseller, to Scotsbrig; and will not neglect, as the very first thing I set about, to answer your kind and acceptable Letter, which we have now had in hand since Saturday morning gone a week. You will not expect much sense of me; for I have many Letters to write, little time, and many interruptions. Mrs. Welsh, and her Niece from Liverpool (a very pleasant young damsel) have been here for about a week; our servant Nancy has *plotted*[1] the skin off her foot, and goes *hirpling*[2] along in most lame style, so that for the time, it is but a confused kind of

---

[1] Scalded.   [2] Limping.

house. We removed into it out of the old one at Stockbridge. . . .

It gave us great satisfaction to hear from you so good an account of everything at Scotsbrig and Catlinns; and to see that for the present at least your labour does not prove in vain. It is saying much as things now go in this distracted country. Millions (a frightful word but a true one!) millions of mortals are toiling this day, in our British Isles, without prospect of rest, save in speedy death, to whom for their utmost toiling, food and shelter are too high a blessing. When one reads of the Lancashire Factories and little children labouring for sixteen hours a day, inhaling at every breath a quantity of cotton *fuzz*, falling asleep over their wheels, and roused again by the lash of thongs over their backs, or the slap of "billy-rollers" over their little crowns; and then again of Irish Whitefeet, driven out of their potato-patches and mud-hovels, and obliged to take the hillside as broken men,—one pauses with a kind of amazed horror, to ask if this be Earth, the place of Hope, or Tophet, where hope never comes!

A good practical inference too, every one of us may draw from it : to be thankful that with him it is *not* yet so, to be content under many griefs, and patiently struggle on towards a better day : which, even in this world, cannot fail to dawn for the afflicted children of men. One grand remedy against the worst still lies partly open : America and its forests, where you have only the wild *beasts* to strive against !¹ I understand there never was such emigration from these parts, at least from Edinburgh, as this year. People of all sorts are going: labourers, shopkeepers, even Writers to the Signet, and country Lairds. They are very right ; *they* will be all the better, and the country all the better for the want of them.—But, in the meanwhile, do you, my dear Brother, go on tilling the Dryfesdale clod, while it will yield you anything : surely it is probable, the Government, before matters come to the utmost press, will apply itself in earnest to Emigration, as the sole remedy for all that most

---

¹ Alexander Carlyle did, in 1843, emigrate to America, settling on a farm of his own, near Brantford, Canada West, where he died in 1876.

immediately presses on us. Let us "possess our souls in patience, and await what can betide." . . .

Edinburgh continues one of the dullest and poorest and on the whole paltriest of places for me. I cannot remember that I have heard one sentence with true meaning in it uttered since I came hither! The very power of Thought seems to have forsaken this Athenian City; at least, a more entirely shallow, barren, unfruitful and trivial set of persons than those I meet with never that I remember came across my "bodily vision." One has no right to be angry with them: poor fellows, far from it! Yet does it remain evident that "Carlyle is wasting his considerable talent on impossibilities, and can never do any good." Time will show : for the present, poor man, he is quite fixed to *try*. At any rate there are some good Books here, that one can borrow and read; kindly-disposed human creatures too, who, though they cannot without a shudder see one spit in the Devil's face so, yet wish one well, almost love one. The best is that I have been rather busy writing, and have finished a long sort of thing for *Fraser's Maga-*

zine, to be called *Cagliostro :* it is very wild, but not untrue, so may do its part. Write away my man! that is thy only chance : these poor persons, demean them as they may, "*can do th' neither ill na' good.*"[1] We have liberty to stay here till near Whitsunday ; but shall not likely continue far beyond the end of April : in May we can hope to see you at Catlinns. Except house-rent it seems hardly more expensive here than at Puttock, so much have things fallen in price ; or perhaps, mainly, so much has house-wife cunning risen ! We have not so comfortable a roomy life as there ; but all else is far superior.—What we are to make of ourselves next winter, if we be spared so long, is not clear yet; but will become so. . . . Jane does not seem to improve of late : however, she has far more entertainment here. She is out at this moment, or would send her little namesake and you her love. And so God bless you all !—Your affectionate Brother, T. CARLYLE.

[1] "Can do thee neither ill nor good." For the origin of this phrase, "become proverbial" with him, see Carlyle's note in *Letters and Memorials*, i. 278.

CIII.—To Dr. CARLYLE, Paris.

TEMPLAND, THORNHILL, 17*th May* 1833.

MY DEAR BROTHER—If you arrive as you anticipated, at Paris on the 20th, this Letter again will be too late. A consummation which I have striven honestly to prevent; but, as you see, and shall hear, without effect. Excuse this limited size of paper too; for at present I am in the transition-state, and divided from my tools. On Tuesday morning gone a week, our places were all secured in the Thornhill Coach, the baggage happily despatched the week before: but by the foolishest misunderstanding we found on reaching the North Bridge at half-past six, that the Coach was *gone*—three minutes ago! There was nothing for it but wearisomely waiting two days longer; to which painful side of the alternative we reconciled ourselves the best way possible; lying literally hidden, unknown to all our friends except two; scarcely stirring out except at nightfall, and then very much with the feeling of *revenants*. I bathed twice in the Forth; read a *Life of*

Paul Jones, pieces of Sir George M'Kenzie, and meditated about enough of things. One incident that most of all reconciled me to the disappointment was the arrival (some two hours after our return) of your Florence Letter, which otherwise we must have waited for, and run the risk of losing, for it had already been at Dumfries, and might not, without hesitation, have been sent back. I determined to write forthwith; yet not till I had seen the Scotsbrig people, and could tell you a positive tale. Well, on Thursday we did all happily get off, and, after a stifling stew of nine dusty hours, were set down at Glendinning's,[1] all alive, but Jane utterly sick, hardly able to move hither in any fashion, and seized, as it soon appeared, with this universal *Influenza*, which has held her in confinement, generally in bed, ever since. We sent the maid over to Craigenputtock, but no one else has yet been over there. It was Monday morning (for Mrs. Welsh too had taken the *Influenza*) before I could get off for Scotsbrig; writing there I found impossible

[1] Inn at Thornhill.

(for want of time, and even of paper) : and it was only yesternight that I returned. Happily, however, after this tedious preamble, I am enabled to inform you that all is quite well in Annandale, that all in Nithsdale is improving and hopeful; and so in the end your heart is set at rest.

The Monday when I set off with Harry and the Gig was a quite beautiful day, and everything that occurred was of a kind to render thanks for. After the meekest of drives, down Æ water and the rest of them, Catlinns House, whitewashed and hospitable, rose on me over *White-ween Hass*[1] about three o'clock; and in few minutes more Alick, hastening home from his potato ground, had his tea-table covered for me, and question and answer was in full progress. . . . At Scotsbrig they had heard my wheels in time; my Mother was running out to meet me as of old; I could thank God that here too I found everything well. Our Mother seems better rather than worse in bodily health;

---

[1] Probably the local pronunciation of Whitewoolen-hass, a hill close by Catlinns.—M. C.

seems patient, contented, even cheerful. The rest of them seem to go on quite tolerably; all in good agreement, in good heart, and proper behaviour. . . .

And now here once more are we, stranded again on the wold (where we hope to be next Monday) with intent to pass another summer there. We are not out of funds; we are free from debt, have liberty to live and let live. A Paper on *Diderot* was printed about a month ago; character not known. Fraser has just sent me Proofs of a *Cagliostro*, one of the most distorted bad things (not to be *false*) I ever wrote; probably the *last* in that style. These two, worth near £100, the payment of which I reckon sure, form my present disposable capital. My chief project for the summer is to cut Teufelsdreck into slips, and have it printed in *Fraser's Magazine:* I have not proposed it to him yet, and must go warily to work in that, for I have spoiled such things already by want of diplomacy. It will be worth almost £200 to me that way, and I shall get rid of it, which otherwise there is little hope of, to *any* purpose or without great loss; the Book-trade being still dead,—and as I reckon forever. I have much reading too, much thinking; prospects of more *society* than last year: so we shall wait in a kind of *rest*. "*Halte still und seh' Dich um:*" that is every way my posture at present. Outwardly and inwardly a kind of closing of the First Act goes on with me; the Second as yet quite *un*-opened. The world is fast changing, the ways and wants and duties of the world; I myself am also, or ought to be, changing: there must be a readjustment. . . .

Jane thankfully and not without hope accepts your offer of Physicianship; I myself am of opinion that you will do her good. She is much weakened with this Influenza, and may not have her strength again for weeks. A cough too still lingers, loth to leave.—I fancy this will be in Paris by Whitsunday. May it find you safe, waiting to receive it. We shall soon hear from you in reply, and then the next news, if all prosper, is that you are in England! — . . . And for the present, God bless you, dear Brother!—Ever yours,   T. CARLYLE.

CIV.—To his MOTHER, Scotsbrig.

CRAIGENPUTTOCK, *Tuesday night*,
22*d May* 1833.

. . . We got here on Monday, as I had calculated; Jane still weak enough, but glad like me to get to any " bit hadding of her ain fr' a' that." She was rather sick during the drive; but got fresher afterwards. We found everything about the house in complete order; Nancy had been diligent; and Peggy Austin had kept out the damp with great success; indeed Jane says we never were *drier*, and not the smallest thing has gone wrong. Peter too has the Garden all trimmed up as neatly as ever it was: so far as they go nothing could be more perfect than their performance. We have seen none of them yet; but are certainly bound to thank them heartily, "besides payment."

The only thing of any consequence that has gone out of joint is one of the Plantations which M'Adam's people have burnt, in burning their heather. The careless lumber! That men should plant and fence and laboriously rear shelter in this wilderness; and then a hash of hashes come and in one hour consume the fruit of twenty years' industry! However, it is needless to *speak* anything about it. One comforting circumstance is that it was rather a bad Planting; though here again unluckily, it lies close to us, in daily view: it is the one at the north end of the " heathery park ;" between the Glaisters Hillside and the road; on your *left* hand, as you set out from Stumpy to come hither. Joseph [M'Adam] was in a great *fuff* about it, we learn; he also writes to Mrs. Welsh that he will "come good for it." *Good* for it! Can he make these black scrags into green trees again? I have not seen him yet; but will.—On the whole, I disturb myself comparatively little: what good shall I ever get of these woods at any rate? Be not careful over much. . . . We should like you very well, just now; and have even need of you. Jane is still very feeble (she had a wretched ill-turn of headache, etc., this very evening, not an hour ago); and there is no nurse but myself. I feel confident that she is getting strong again; but it may be weeks before she is as well even as she was. . . . Continue to watch over your children, my dear Mother; and let us all continue to love and honour you.—Ever your affectionate,

T. CARLYLE.

Jane had several little things to send: but, poor lassie, she is in bed; and I will not let her rise to seek them. Tell the other Jane to write—directly unless you are coming.

CV.—To Mr. FRASER, Publisher, London.

CRAIGENPUTTOCK, 27*th May* 1833.

MY DEAR SIR—On the Proofsheet of *Cagliostro* I marked an announcement that you would hear from me soon. I write to-day in more confusion than is desirable; but rather so than lose another half-week.

Most probably you recollect the Manuscript *Book* I had with me in London; and how during that Reform hurly-burly, which unluckily still continues and is like to continue, I failed to make any bargain about it. The Manuscript still lies in my drawer; and now after long deliberation I have determined to slit it up into strips, and send it forth in the Periodical way; for which in any case it was perhaps better adapted. The pains I took with the composition of it, truly, were greater than even I might have thought necessary, had this been foreseen: but what then? Care of that sort is never altogether thrown away; far better too much than too little. I reckon that it will be easy for the Magazine Printer to save me some thirty or forty complete copies, as he prints it; these can then be bound up and distributed among my Friends likely to profit thereby; and in the end of all we can *re*print it into a Book proper, if that seem good. Your Magazine is the first I think of for this object; and I must have got a distinct negative from you before I go any farther. Listen to me, then, and judge.

The Book is at present named "Thoughts on Clothes; or Life and Opinions of Herr D. Teufelsdröckh, D. U. J.";[1] but perhaps we

[1] "Now called *Sartor Resartus*," says Carlyle in his Notebook, September 1833. The hero of it, instead of, as hitherto, Teufelsdreck, "I mean to call Teufelsdröckh," he had told his brother John, in a letter of 10th February 1833.

might see right to alter the title a little; for the rest, some brief Introduction could fit it handsomely enough into its new destination: it is already divided into three "Books," and farther into very short "Chapters," capable in all ways of subdivision. Nay some tell me, what perhaps is true, that taking a few chapters at a time is really the profitablest way of reading it. There may be in all some Eight sheets of *Fraser*. It is put together in the fashion of a kind of Didactic Novel; but indeed properly *like* nothing yet extant: I used to characterise it briefly as a kind of "Satirical Extravaganza on Things in General"; it contains more of my opinions on Art, Politics, Religion, Heaven, Earth and Air, than all the things I have yet written. The Creed promulgated on all these things, as you may judge, is *mine*, and firmly *believed:* for the rest, the main Actor in the business ("Editor of these Sheets," as he often calls himself) assumes a kind of Conservative (though Anti-quack) character; and would suit *Fraser* perhaps better than any other Magazine. The ultimate result, however, I need hardly premise, is a deep religious speculative-radicalism (so I call it for want of a better name), with which you are already well enough acquainted in me.

There are only five persons that have yet read this Manuscript: of whom two have expressed themselves (I mean convinced me that they *are*) considerably interested and gratified; two quite *struck*, "overwhelmed with astonishment and new hope" (this is the result I aimed at for souls worthy of hope); and one in secret discontented and displeased. William Fraser is a sixth reader, or rather half-reader; for I think he had only got half-way or so; and I never learned his opinion. With him, if you like, at this stage of the business you can consult freely about it. My own conjecture is that *Teufelsdröckh*, whenever published, will astonish most that read it, be wholly understood by very few; but to the astonishment of some will add touches of (almost the deepest) spiritual interest, with others quite the opposite feeling. I think I can practically prophesy that for some six or eight months (for it must be published without interruption), it would be apt at least to *keep the eyes* of the Public on you.

Such is all the description I can give you, in these limits : now what say you to it ? Let me hear as soon as you can ; for the time seems come to set these little bits of Doctrine forth ; and, as I said, till your *finale* arrive, I can do nothing. Would you like to see the Manuscript yourself? It can come, and return, by Coach for a few shillings, if you think of that : it will of course want the Introduction, and various other "O. Y.'s"[1] that will perhaps be useful. I need not remind you that about showing it to any third party (as I have learned by experience) there is a certain delicacy to be observed : I shall like to hear from you first. Write to me, therefore, with the same openness as I have done to you ; we shall then soon see how it lies between us.

. . . My Brother, I keep hoping, will one day ere long walk in upon you : he ought to be at Paris by this time, on his way homeward. . . . The airs are fresh here, the trees of the greenest ;

---

[1] Notes by "Oliver Yorke."

and my cabbages flourish as briskly as Dioclesian's.

If you send any Books, etc., by Waugh, pray charge him strictly; his Clerk (as our Proverb says) "is not *to ride the water on.*"

And now, in great haste, adieu! Believe me always, my dear sir, most faithfully yours,

T. CARLYLE.

CVI.—To his MOTHER, Scotsbrig.

CRAIGENPUTTOCK, *Tuesday,* 25*th June* 1833.

. . . The *Fraser's Magazine* does contain a kind of Likeness;[1] liker than I expected. Jane specially claims the Number as hers; has got her name on it; and insists much that said title be *respected.* I partly expect from Fraser another copy or two of the Picture; and shall not fail directly to send you one of them as *yours.* The opposite *Page* will edify you very little; in fact, it is hardly intelligible (not at all so except to persons of the craft), but complimentary enough, and for so foolish a business may be considered as better than a wiser thing.

[1] Of himself, by Maclise, see *ante*, p. 25.

The writer is one Dr. Maginn, a mad rattling Irishman; of whom perhaps you may have heard me speak. He wishes me well in his way; which indeed is very far from mine. So let us be thankful for all mercies.

. . . Since my return[1] I have mended and new-stuffed the *Clatch*, which really looks very gate-going;[2] I have read a little, dreamed a little; and that is literally all that I have done. Fraser I believe *is* to have my Manuscript Book; which will therefore require a very little sorting: but on the whole I prefer resting for a while; at least as long as an uneasy conscience will let me. Absolute Idleness is a thing which, were it never so *good*, one *cannot* carry on long here. . . .

CVII.—To Dr. CARLYLE, London.

CRAIGENPUTTOCK, 27*th August* 1833.

MY DEAR BROTHER[3]—All the pains I had

[1] From a visit to Scotsbrig.   [2] Respectable, *road-worthy*.
[3] Since the last letter to him, Dr. Carlyle had returned to England, and made a short visit at Scotsbrig and Craigenputtock, before again going to the Continent as physician to Lady Clare.

taken were well rewarded on Sunday evening, when your Letter came. It has solaced me here, and will give no less solacement to those that love you elsewhere: I will send it off, as you conjecture, to Scotsbrig, to-morrow. We can now know that you are safe so far, and send our wishes after you with new clearness. My Mother said: "We'll no be sae ill, if we had the first Letter frae him." On Friday or Saturday (the former, as I calculate) a like comfort must be provided for you in return.

Your steamboat, that agitated day, had scarcely cleared the Pier-head, when I was stripping and bathing; my head and my heart, like your own, all full of painful obstruction and confusion. It was half an hour before we set sail again, and near two o'clock before we reached the Annan shore.[1]

[1] From Bowness, whither Carlyle had accompanied his brother in the boat. After mentioning his brother's departure, Carlyle writes in his Note-book, "John is a good man; with far more talent than even yet he has unfolded fully, though already he begins to show himself as a skilful Physician, likely I imagine to prove useful and also acceptable. He has a boundless affectionateness; this is his great quality, manifesting itself too at times in strange ways, as in humorous

We could see your vessel storming along with you, already far to the west; and not we only, but all your other Friends each from his several hillside had seen it and watched it, and could tell at what hour it had vanished behind St. Bees. . . . If it be God's merciful will, we shall yet all live to see your steamboat come foaming *up* the Solway, and bringing you safe back to us. I saw it once so from the Landheads Brae; and should be thankful for the feeling as long as I live.

Next morning betimes Jamie and I were mounted for Catlinns, and breakfasted with a numerous hay-making party; conjecturing that you might be already in the Mersey; treating this and all things in the tone of Hope. I soon set forth, and plodded wearisomely through

frolicking (even with pigs and horses, if there is no other *living* thing to frolic with), in the trustfullest abandonment to all kinds of innocently foolish talk and sport, throughout, as a genuine inexhaustible fund of *bonhommie*,—the soul of all manner of useful sympathies and activities, of a character *natural*, at once worthy and amiable. How different from me; how much happier and better! We all love him, and have good reason. May the Unseen Powers, that mercifully look on mankind, bring him safe back to us!"

the moors to Templand, where I arrived before dinner, with such a jaded, road-worn, woe-worn sort of feeling as you can conceive. The Sunday proved too wet for Dunscore, I went to Closeburn,[1] and there heard Corson, uttering the wonderfullest jumble of affectations, imitations, wind and froth: not till next evening did we reach home, and find ourselves once more thoroughly *alone*. The sorrowfullest blank had occurred here; for me, I could not but feel so *harried*, so bereaved; the half of my world was gone. . . .

This, dear Brother, is our history since you left us. Nothing has occurred here, except the arrival, on Friday last, of a Pianotuner, who for the small charge of 5s. 6d. has rehabilitated the Piano, and brought me again the luxury of sweet sounds. We carried the poor instrument into the Dining-room, to avoid the coming frosts, and there nightly I can have my tunes: it stands where the half-table did, against the wall right opposite the window; the sofa is moved into its place, and the half-

[1] The Parish Church.

table into the sofa's, in the Drawing-room. Let me add also (for you love all these things) that Napoleon,[1] as too large for his station, has been moved into this Library of mine, under his Kinsman Byron, and your little Italian vase, with Goethe's medals in it and other *etceteras*, now stands in his place. The only other arrival was, on Sunday at dinner-time, that of the American Emerson, Gustave d'Eichthal's man; the most amiable creature in the world, who spent an apparently very happy four-and-twenty hours with us, and then went his way to Wordsworth's Lakes, to Liverpool, and home to Massachusetts on Sunday next. We regretted that you had not seen him, as he that he had not found you in Rome. Of d'Eichthal he could tell me nothing, except that they parted a few weeks ago where you left them, the one for Florence and England, the other for Naples: indeed it appeared they had in reality met only once or twice. If you fall in with d'Eichthal, it will perhaps be friendly if you rather press yourself on him; I figure him to be somewhat

[1] A small copy in bronze of the Place Vendôme statue.—M. C.

shrouded up within his own sorrow and regret, and understand his family are anxious to have his mind by all means diverted and cheerfully aroused. Tell him that he has much affectionate esteem from me; that if he will come and see us here, we will give him the most cordial welcome. I suppose you will see his friends in Paris at any rate; and be able there to tell me something more definite about him. . . .

I cannot but see too that your mood of mind is the right one for you: nay, at bottom, as you often urged, were the right one for me also: your earnest counsels for Tolerance will not fail of their effect on me; such are at all times wholesome mementoes, and forever true on their own side, and I know not why I should so often have taken them up at your hands under the argumentative aspect. Perhaps it was like a patient wincing under a bitter drug, which yet when over had its salutary tendencies. . . . God guide and keep you, dear Brother! Amen!

T. CARLYLE.

One Major Irving of Gribton came here the

other day, and *took* the shooting of Puttock for £5 rent (of his own fixing), and even insisted on paying the notes down on the spot! I gave them to the Dame for pin money civil services: the *first* help this place ever brought us. . . .

CVIII.—To Dr. CARLYLE, Milan.[1]

CRAIGENPUTTOCK, 1*st October* 1833.

MY DEAR BROTHER—All your Letters came punctually to hand; the last one from Calais on the Sunday, as you hoped; greatly to our solacement, and to our Mother's, to whom this like the others was without delay transmitted. . . . I reckoned favourably of your company, from the little glimpses you gave us into it: there is, to all appearance, goodness enough in it to ensure moderate peace, and let the diverse elements there brought together work with moderate harmony. Discords too will come, discords are nowhere wanting and can be nowhere wanting in this Earth; but these, as you know, are properly but "*unregulated* concords," and I think will prove no deeper or greater

[1] Part of this letter is in Froude's *Life*, ii. 369-371.

than are essential for the music. You are all kindly people, trustful and deserving trust; of few travelling or resting Parties can so much be said. As for you, continue to remember always that even in *regulating* those same "unregulated concords" does, in all situations, the wise man's task and happiness lie.

With regard to Craigenputtock and ourselves there has nothing of the smallest moment happened since you heard last: no news either here or at Scotsbrig; which means at least no bad news. We have had visitors enough; too many sometimes. On that Wednesday night before you left London, William Graham[1] made his appearance; the white horse glimmered on me through the trees as I stood pruning among them, and next moment the honest man and I were exchanging our somewhat boisterous salutations. He staid till Friday, amid rather bad weather, and rather wearisome conversation (for he has become altogether *rustic* in his ideas), yet with much honest feeling on all

[1] "Who might in his way be called a friend, . . . so long as his life lasted."—See *Reminiscences*, ii. 78-84.

sides; and then on Friday, he and I rode over together to Templand, and spent the night (tolerably enough) there; and parted next day at Auldgarth. . . . Some days after this Jane went off with her Mother and Helen[1] to Moffat, leaving me here in perhaps the most perfect seclusion any European man was suffering or enjoying. I made a point not to be *idle ;* and spent those ten days better than I have done many: was glad enough nevertheless to seek my little companion home again from Templand; who for her share seemed no less glad to get back to me. Moffat was "detestable" enough: she had found the Anderson's there, however, and could report handsomely of them. . . . The next visitor we got was poor Glen's Brother Archy; one night late, his rap sounded strange through the house; he had come to Dunscore by the Glasgow Coach. A most amiable, sensible creature we found him, one of the best youths I have seen for long. What a blessing, in the mournful state of his household, now all resting on his

---

[1] Her cousin, from Liverpool.

shoulders alone. We talked greatly about his poor Brother; strove to sift out his true position in *all* respects; in conclusion we came upon this project: to have Glen boarded and lodged with Peter Austin . . . ; we shall then have the poor fellow close by, can endeavour to put him on some employment and amusement, and *try* if any influence of ours can assist him. . . . If he come here I will set him to read Homer with me, or something of that kind, and see him as often as I can.[1] Alas, what wreck of young hopes there is in this Earth! Archy Glen was not gone, with his sad errand when, with a whole bevy of biped and quadruped attendants, arrived William Gray and Wife. A couple not very unlike the Badamses. . . .

---

[1] "Glen and I are nearly through the second Book [of Homer]. Nothing I have read for long years so interests and nourishes me : I am quite surprised at the interest I take in it. All the *Antiquity* I have ever known becomes *alive* in my head : there is a whole Gallery of Apelleses and Phidiases that I not only look upon but *make*. Never before had I any so distinct glimpse of antique Art ; those Pompeii Engravings of yours, and all of the sort I have seen, first get their significance."—Letter to Dr. Carlyle, 25th February 1834.

If you ask now, What in suffering and witnessing all these little matters I have performed and accomplished for myself? the answer might look rather meagre. I have not yet put pen to paper. The *new chapter* of my History as yet lies all-too confused; I look round on innumerable fluctuating masses; can begin to build no edifice from them. However, my mind is not *empty*, which is the most intolerable state. I think occasionally with energy; I read a good deal; I wait, not without hope. What other can I do? Looking back over the last seven years, I wonder at myself; looking forward, were there not a fund of tragical Indifference in me, I could lose head. The economical outlook is so complex, the spiritual no less. Alas, the *thing* I want to do is precisely the thing I cannot do. My mind would so fain deliver itself adequately of that " Divine Idea of the World "; and only in quite *in*adequate approximations is such deliverance possible. I want to write what Teufelsdröckh calls the story of the *Time-Hat;* to show forth to the men of these days that they also live in the Age of Miracle! We shall see.

Meanwhile, one of the subjects that engages me most is the French Revolution, which indeed for us is still the subject of subjects. My chief errand to Paris were freer inquiry into this: one day, if this mood continue, I may have something of my own to say on it. But to stick nearer home: I have as good as engaged with myself not to go even to Scotsbrig till I have *written something*. With which view partly, on Saturday last, I determined on two things I could write about (there are twenty others, if one had any vehicle): the first a *History of the Diamond Necklace;* the next an *Essay on the St. Simonians.* I even wrote off to Cochrane, as diplomatically as I could, to ask whether they would suit him. Be his answer what it may, I think I shall fasten upon that *Necklace* business (to prove myself in the Narrative style), and commence it (sending for Books from Edinburgh) in some few days. At this then you can figure me as occupied. For the rest, I have Books enough: your great Parcel came about a fortnight ago; some of the Scotsbrig volumes a little crushed on the back; otherwise uninjured: I sent these latter forward to their place; and have already read what Mill sent for me. Finally, yesterday, no further gone, I drove over to Barjarg[1] (in the middle of thick small rain) to get the *Keys of the Barjarg Library;* which accordingly, after negotiation enough, I found most handsomely left for me by the Hunters; so that I could seize the Catalogue and some half-dozen volumes and hasten off with them, to return at discretion! It is really a very great favour; there are various important works there; reading which I am far better than at any University. For the first time in my life I have free access to some kind of Book-collection; I a Book-man. One way and other, we look forward to a cheerfullish kind of winter here.

. . . Your sister-in-law seems to me and to herself very considerably improved since you first prescribed for her; Moffat did her considerable mischief; nevertheless she is getting

---

[1] About eight miles from Craigenputtock, where was, and still is, a fine library which the owner, Mr. Hunter Arundell, had kindly placed (in September 1833) at Carlyle's service.

into heart again, into good looks, and anticipates the winter with more spirit than usual. She gives me a little tune or two many a night; and so we sit as still as we can. . . .

Mill tells us in person that he is going to Paris and cannot see us this year. . . . I set him on investigating Paris for us; will probably write him again, for books to be bought, before he go. I find Mill one of the purest, worthiest men of this country; but, as you say, much too exclusively *logical*. I think he will mend: but his character is naturally not *large*, rather high and solid.

. . . I will try for Fea's *Winckelmann* this week at Edinburgh; yet with no great hope of getting it: the only representative I found of the work last winter was a poor French one with few plates or perhaps none. For you it is naturally the most appropriate study of all; there where you sit in the very scene of it. Study to profit by your place whatever be the produce of it, all places (even Craigenputtock) produce something. I wish I might get *Fea*, for then I should read it with you: I almost need company to carry me through it. In my own heterodox heart there is yearly growing up the strangest crabbed one-sided persuasion, that all Art is but a reminiscence now, that for us in these days *Prophecy* (well understood) not Poetry is the thing wanted; how can we *sing* and *paint* when we do not yet *believe* and *see?* There is some considerable truth in this; how much I have not yet fixed. Now what under such point of view is all existing Art and study of Art? What was the great Goethe himself? The greatest of contemporary men; who however is not to have any follower, and should not have any.

In the *Conversations Lexikon* I find sundry curious things; but sadly huddled together, in the way carriers *pack*, to take up least room: there is a notice about me, almost every word of which is more or less wrong. . . .

I asked Jane whether she had anything to say: she "would read the Letter and then see." I leave the margins; and will not yet (till bedtime) take final farewell.—Ever yours,

T. C.

When you write tell us the biographic doings of your travelling party; dramatically, especially, lyrically. Little touches in all these kinds will bring us far nearer you than all "general views" could. Explain all with copiousness, frankness. Above all be autobiographic as you see I am. Jane says there is nothing that *can* be added to this so minute Letter; nothing but her sisterly love! . . .

CIX.—To Dr. CARLYLE, Rome.[1]

CRAIGENPUTTOCK, 21*st January* 1834.

MY DEAR BROTHER — It is exactly four weeks since I wrote to you; and three since I received your last Letter: perhaps it had been more in the order of time to wait till next Tuesday;[2] but as I may be busier then, and had rather be too soon than too late, I set about it now while nothing hinders me. As I conjecture, there are few occurrences in your Roman month that bring more pleasure than

---

[1] Part of this letter is in Froude's *Life*, ii. 391, 408.
[2] *i.e.* In time for Wednesday, the market day at Dumfries, when there were opportunities of sending and receiving letters.

news from home: let me be careful then to furnish you as regularly as I can.

On Wednesday gone a fortnight (two weeks since, all but a day) I drove down to Dumfries, by appointment, to fetch up our Mother. . . . Jamie's marriage is still understood to be fixed upon. . . . He presses my Mother to retain the two upper rooms at Scotsbrig, and live if not with him, yet under the same roof with him. An arrangement which none of us approves of, except perhaps as a *bad best*. A month or two must now decide. Our Mother says, she knows *who* will provide her a home while she shall need one; and so remains quite quiet and patient. I spoke of building her a house here; and she was gratified at the offer: but my own uncertainty of continuance, the foreign neighbourhood, and its loneliness and dulness, render this a hazardous speculation. We shall struggle to do the best possible. . . .

Glen is just gone to Peter Austin's since I began this paragraph; Jane accompanying him. We were to have both gone down with him last night, and (with Tea) warmed the house for him : but it was a deluge of rain, and none of us stirred out. Archy Glen has sent down a carpet and bed-mattress, with various *etceteras;* and now it is really quite a respectable little apartment ; where the poor fellow may wait what Providence has decided for him. We can yet form no *fixed* prophecy about him ; our experience of such things is so limited. He has two states : one a most quiet, almost languid state, like a kind of collapse ; with an appearance of consciousness that delusion is in him, an apprehension to commit himself by speaking ; his answers are perfectly sane, even judicious and intelligent ; but he originates nothing, or next to nothing ; sits silent or reads in an inattentive wandering manner. His second state is one of much more energy, when his crotchets get the force of beliefs in him ; and he will utter, and even maintain them, though with a singular tolerance of contradiction, and with *arguments* of such a sort for feebleness as you never heard man utter. Mostly however, with me, even in these states, he draws back again ; says he cannot discuss such things at present till he "get sentience." These varieties I have found depend altogether almost on the *state of the digestive organs*. It is here that you could be of the best service; but I with my utmost care can do too little. . . .

But now, my dear Brother, I have a very mournful piece of news for you; though hardly an unexpected one. On Saturday came a Letter from Tom Holcroft; wherein quite incidently, as if speaking of a thing known, he mentions that poor Badams died in September! How this affected and affects me you may figure. A deep Tragedy, transacted before one's eyes, you might say in one's very household circle; for Badams was among the men I loved most in the world. Poor fellow! With such endowments too, with such worth; but the spirit of the world, its distractions and its persecutions were too hard for him. . . . It is all over now. I have written to Holcroft to tell me at least where he lies buried; whether his Father and Mother still live. Jane speaks of trying if a Letter will find Bessy Barnet[1] (whom we

[1] See *Reminiscences*, ii. 146.

love for his sake and her own), and whether, if she stand desolate and destitute, she could not in some way be attached to us. . . .

Environed as I have been ever since you last heard of me, I could naturally do no work, only wait for a better time. The house within this half hour is clear for the first time these five weeks. . . .

James Fraser writes me that *Teufelsdröckh* meets with the most unqualified disapproval; which is all extremely proper. His payment arrives, which is still more proper. On the whole, dear Jack, it is a contending world, and he that is born into it must fight for his place or lose it. If we are under the *right flag*, let the world do its worst, and heartily welcome! I will now go and walk till Dinner, the weather is not fair, is not absolutely wet.—God bless thee, dear Brother! *Auf ewig.*

T. CARLYLE.

. . . I did drink your health, though not on New Year's Day (for that was the day I went for my Mother, and so *got* no dinner); but next day here, mindful of my duty. Have you begun to any study of Artistics? Or do you find it a pursuit too unproductive for you? My own impression is that the Cant in it is great; but also that there is a Reality in it, though of smaller magnitude.[1] . . .

Jane sends this message, when I ask if she has aught to say: " My kindest affection to him; that I have a headache, and that everything is said."—What trust can you put in woman? She engaged to write, and see!— —I go to Glen's to-night yet and smoke a pipe with him. He was *very wae.*—Adieu! I do end here.

CX.—To Mrs. AITKEN,[2] Dumfries.

CRAIGENPUTTOCK, 18*th February* 1834.

MY DEAR JEAN—I will with great pleasure lend you any Book I have; on one condition, which I doubt not you would prescribe to your-

[1] *Cf.* remarks on the modern gospel of Art, in the *Life of Sterling*, p. 213.
[2] His sister Jean, married, in November 1833, to Mr. James Aitken of Dumfries.

selves, that they be kept free from dirt and damage. Nothing is more gratifying than to afford so useful an accommodation so easily, to any one that will employ it; much more to a Brother and a Sister. On the other hand few things vex a methodical character more than thumb-marks when the volume returns : spot of grease, above all, seems to deserve death without benefit of clergy!

I have sent you to-day : *Holcroft's Memoirs*, 3 vols.; Mackintosh's *England*, 1 vol.; *Marmaduke Maxwell*, 1 vol.; *Young* (for Sundays too), 1 vol.; Two Magazines: of the latter kind there are whole barrowfuls here; but it may be questioned whether they will profit you much. — When you want more, let me know. On the whole I am very glad that you and James take to reading in leisure hours: leisure, of which every mortal has some, cannot in any other way that I know of be so profitably employed. If one *do* not read, wherefore *can* he read?

We are going on here in the common way; nothing new except the favourable change of the weather. I have many Books about me, many Thoughts in me: if not *happy*, may hope to grow *happier*.[1]

If Alick come to-morrow, you can give him that Letterkin; if not, you can commit it to the Lockerbie Carrier (whose name I forget), or to any other conveyance you think better.

Mary tells me our Mother is well; but there seems to be no kind of settlement made yet, or capable of being made, which I regret, but do not yet see means of mending.

I know not exactly when I shall be down; but probably it will not be very long.—Commend me to James.—I am, ever your Brother,

T. CARLYLE.

CXI.—To Mrs. AITKEN, Dumfries.

CRAIGENPUTTOCK, 25*th February* 1834.

... I have a piece of news that will surprise you, and not so agreeably. Nay perhaps you have it already (if M'Diarmid[2] have put in the

---

[1] Jeffrey's occasional form of salutation was, "Are you happy?"—M. C.

[2] See *ante*, i. p. 199 *n*.

Advertisement, that our House is to let), and are already surprised at it. We are speaking quite seriously and practically about setting off for London at Whitsunday! I did not mention it to Alick last Wednesday; because it was not till last Thursday that we started it ourselves. As yet none knows of it but our two selves,—and M'Diarmid, who has if not inserted, got orders to insert the Advertisement. We have long had it in the wind; we are quite buried alive here, and must try to rise of ourselves. Tell nobody of it (at least not Rob[1]) unless the Newspaper have already made it public.—Unless there come something in the Letter way tomorrow I think I must go down about Friday or Saturday and tell our Mother. You shall see me by the road, and hear all about it. God bless you, dear Sister! Commend me to the Goodman.—Ever yours, T. C.

CXII.—To Dr. CARLYLE, Rome.

CRAIGENPUTTOCK, 27th *March* 1834.

MY DEAR BROTHER — There is no bigger

[1] Probably the man who brought the letter.

sheet in the house, except monstrosities of scrolling-sheets, and to procure another, as you know, will detain us some two weeks. My hand shall be cabin'd, crib'd, confin'd to the very uttermost: you shall have my news, and my blessing with them, still. We had a kind of hope of hearing from you yesterday, which was Wednesday; but it yielded nothing; so, as we are for Thornhill to-morrow, I will not wait another week. My last despatch to you was dated some four, or more likely five weeks ago; either of which is far enough back. . . . Time passes here in so noiseless, unproductive a way, one has no natural feeling of its course; each day being the express image of last (and most of them, like Macadam's Dutch crockery-image, "clean *toom*"[1]), you are apt to lump large masses of them together, and wonder how they went.— For me, if you received my last Letter, there will be nothing of great moment to add to it: wherefore, as I have been at Scotsbrig since, I will begin with that. It was yesterday gone three weeks that I yoked my *clatch* again, after wait-

[1] Altogether empty.

ing out all the winter deluges, and looked abroad again into the living world, not without a kind of gladness and almost surprise to find that there still was a living world. At Dumfries whole bags of Letters lay waiting me : about our London Expedition from Mrs. Austin and Mill, about the finer sensibilities of the heart from Mrs. Montagu; an inarticulate shriek from poor Mrs. Badams, as late announcement of her loss, long rambling speculations on the same sad subject from Tom Holcroft, whereby *nothing* I think was learned except that the mortal body of our poor Friend lay in Paddington Churchyard, and that while alive he had been wont to step over from Bartlett's Buildings and drink in Fearon's shop some large measure of brandy every day: alas, the whole of it is a Tragedy all too heart-oppressing ; such as has often been, such as we also were appointed to witness! Hastily glancing over these Documents, and hastily despatching them home, I dined on " three light-boiled eggs with salt " (a favourite travelling dinner of mine) at Jean's, whom I found well and doing well; and again taking the road was at Alick's about sunset. He was mending a stone-dyke near yon old ruinous mill of his, and the "Brig of Danger"; he joyfully answered my hail, led me over, and up the brae, to a clean house, two clean rosy children, and a blazing coal fire.

I learned from him the particulars of an occurrence I had been apprised of quite unexpectedly at Dumfries by a funeral-letter: the death of our poor old Aunt Fanny.[1] She had been buried the day before. The end of her Life was like the course of it; resolute, indomitable: and as soft almost as the falling asleep of a tired labourer, his day's work being done. She was out (among the cows, overseeing something done to them), though weak as weak could be, the very day before: that night (or rather next morning) about two o'clock, she bade Will, who was watching with her, go to bed and leave her, for he was nothing but disturbing her; Will obeyed, but rose again about four, and went to look: his Mother had been up, had lighted her pipe, had smoked it, and

[1] His father's eldest sister.—See *Reminiscences*, i. 32.

laid it, with the candle first carefully extinguished, on the back-bar of the bed; and fallen asleep—to awake no more! She was the last of a race: one generation we have seen pass away; we ourselves are the next, also rapidly passing. . . .

But to collect my scattered threads and go on knitting: you are to fancy that Alick has rolled me down, like Jehu, with lamps burning, to the astonishment of the country, and the joyful surprise of Scotsbrig, part of which was even to bed. Our Mother came rushing out of Mary's: one thinks of all these things with joy yet with sadness. Of *all* things there are only *so many times;* one time is the last.

Various plans were agitated for our Mother's Whitsunday settlement, with much vague speculation, out of which it was not easy to frame any practical result. All things that could be thought of offered objections: it was only a choice of the bad best. Our Mother herself was quiet, yet sad as was natural, and recoiled from the prospect of change, which nevertheless by the adventurousness of the younger ones had become inevitable. . . . It was judged better, since both Jamie and she so objected to a change, that she for this year should continue under the Scotsbrig roof, occupying the two upstairs rooms as her own house, with Jenny, who, however, meant to pass most of the summer in Dumfries, improving herself in sewing and the like. . . . Poor Mother! I was very sad to see all the old scaffolding of her life falling asunder about her; and I doubt not, all of us very heartily vowed that nothing we could do should be wanting to repair what she loses. . . . Our departure for London naturally grieved her much, but she bears up as well as possible; admits willingly that we are doing no good here, and *must* go. I drove her up to Catlinns that morning I returned; and left her there; Alick escorting me with his "black mare" through Lochmaben, when again the "must" interfered, and we went thoughtfully each his way.

This then is the Scotsbrig business, which mainly concerned us at present. With our Craigenputtock doings I must be much briefer. The house has been twice advertised to let; but no tenant offers, or indeed is rightly expected : Mrs. Austin writes in the most cheerful way about undertaking to get us a house. . . . We have further determined now *not* to "burn our ships," in the way of sale by auction which would involve us in much trouble with uncertain issue, but to use them in the way at worst "of firewood," laid up here, or sold as chance opportunities may occur.¹ The disposal of the House and *etceteras* lies still dubious ; but perhaps something *may* be made of it. Let me mention too, that we heard last night, for the second time, from Bessy Barnet : she is with the old Badamses at Warwick ; will go and serve us anywhere under the heavenly sun ; "wages are the last of her thoughts," kindness and to be with those she likes are the whole matter. Poor Bessy! So you see we are provided with a servant, on whose fidelity at least we can rely. As to London generally, my thoughts are of the dimmest, earnest, huge character. To go thither seems inevitable, palpably necessary ; yet, contrasted

---

¹ The kitchen table of the Carlyles still stands in its place at Craigenputtock.—M. C.

with these six years of rockbound seclusion, seems almost like a rising from the grave. Like an issuing from the Bastille at least: and then the question is, Whether we shall not, like that old man, request with tears to be *taken back!* On the whole, I hope; and my little Dame (whom I often call 'Spairkin, Despairkin) declares naively that "she is not a coward for all that she is desperate." Forward then and try! As to "fame" and all that, I can honestly say I regard it *not:* my wish and hope is that I may live not dishonestly, nor in vain; and it is my confidence too. Soon, soon does a high Eternity swallow up *all* the littleness of Time, were it joyful, were it painful. Curiously enough, the Rhetoric Chair at Edinburgh, just about this time, has fallen vacant: but I make no whisper of pretention to it; Jeffrey as good as assured me *he* could do nothing for me, beforehand, and we hear and shall likely hear nothing further from him. They will give it to Thomas Campbell, or let it lie vacant: at bottom, I believe this better for me. And so I go on reading and studying here, and for exercise digging up and trimming the garden flower-borders, though I shall not see them blow. Glen, whom, in spite of all contradictory appearances, I consider as improving, looks at *Homer* nightly with me; we are nearly through the Fourth Book, and my delight is still great. Glen is very perfunctory in his scholarship, vague and inaccurate here as in all things; knows much Greek, but knows it very ill. I have got Heyne's Homer now and Voss's Translation, etc., and really make something of the business, or try to do it. Voss's is the best translation I ever in my life looked into: it is poetical even, yet *closer* than Clarke's school one. I have also a heap of *Annual Registers* (very interesting) from Liverpool, and abundance of Books from Barjarg.—O this dirty little sheet! It has quite lamed my fingers, writing so small; and lamed my *thought* too: besides I have been interrupted by a woodman coming to clear and prune the woods. Next time better! God bless you, dear Brother! Farewell, and love me, and come safe back to me! T. CARLYLE.

CXIII.—To Mr. HENRY INGLIS, Edinburgh.

CRAIGENPUTTOCK, 28*th April* 1834.

MY DEAR SIR—Your Books return to you to-day, which have lain here finished these two weeks, waiting for an opportunity that seemed safe. I hope you will receive them uninjured; you certainly receive them with many just thanks, for they were most kindly sent, as many others have been, and afforded me great entertainment, as well as a fair modicum of profit too. *Heyne* is a huge quarry; in which, however, though under chaotic quarry-like arrangement, all manner of needful materials lie: I have dug hither and thither through him, and found several things. *Blackwell*[1] one may call a *flare* of trumpet-music, in the bravura style too common in his time and since; sweet enough, but meaningless, or nearly so. The best of all, to his bulk, is *Payne Knight*,[2] a

---

[1] Dr. Thomas Blackwell's *Enquiry into the Life and Writings of Homer*, published in 1735, is now seldom read. Bentley said, he forgot it before he finished reading it.

[2] *Prolegomena in Homerum*, 1820.

sound, methodical, compact man, worthy of all acceptation. Let me add only of the brave *Voss*, that if you at any time want a Translation of *Homer*, you will find Voss's not only the best of that old Singer, but perhaps the best ever executed of any Singer, under such circumstances; a really effectual work, which one rejoices to look into, true, genuine to the heart in every line. And so here ends for the present my intercourse with *Homer:* I have read several Books of his Rhapsody as with spectacles, and diligently surveyed all the rest; and leave it with increased knowledge, and love it better than any other Book, I think, except the Bible alone. It is not the richest intrinsically perhaps, but the richest-oldest, and stands in such an environment as no other.

Here, too, I believe, my kind Friend, ends your Book-dealings with Craigenputtock, for all things have an end! Never more, it is like, will you send me Books hither; this scene of your activity terminates now, and truly, in retiring, you have a right to say *Plaudite*, or rather *Plaude*, for it is I that am interested in it, which, thinking of all your attentiveness, I can well assure you that I heartily do. Probably the Newspaper I sent last might indicate to you that we were bound for London. It is even so: we go there at Whitsunday; to what fates the Upper Powers have provided us, for hitherto it is as dark and vague as you could fancy. One must take the flood, and swim in it with a stout heart and an open eye. The whole aspect of Existence has long ceased to give me any transcendent terror; I know it of old to be hollowness and foam and theatrical sham, yet with an Eternity lying beyond it, looking through it, *which* is *true*. Considering all this, what manner of men ought ye to be, —whether your forks be of silver, or ye have no forks at all? The life of an Author, which is now mine without remedy, is externally, and too often internally, among the most difficult and painfullest given to man; nevertheless, to this also, with all its heights and depths, one must address himself: pray for me only, That I do not become a Scoundrel;—in the highest garret, I have no other prayer.

Our address, I imagine, will be 4 Holland Street, Kensington; but till after to-morrow this is not *quite* certain: however, I will take care to send you some token: some special *written* notice, if we are *not* to anchor there. A Dumfries Newspaper or some such thing may serve to affirm, if that is all that is wanted; for I am like to be very much hurried. We count too that we shall see you from time to time; oftener there than we should do here. I would not have you forget me: when I look up towards Edinburgh now, there is almost nothing else that it gives me much pain to part from. My much-respected Motherland has given me much, much of priceless value, but of men that I love, no great overplus.

And now, my Friend, quitting your end of the Island, my last and continued advice is, Stand by the Truth, though the Arch-Devil hindered you! A man has no other footing in this world, but what is mere pasteboard, which vanishing in reek, *he* sinks to endless depths. Another precept, which perhaps I myself need more than you, is, Not to hate, only to pity and avoid those that follow Lies. Patience! Patience! whosoever is not against us is for us. The noisiest of Gigmen, is not his Gig-spring *already* breaking? Alas! it inevitably breaks; and he—whither goes he? Out of thy way at anyrate. And so,

> Jog on, jog on the footpath way,
> And *merrily* hent the stile-a;
> A merry heart goes all the day,
> Your sad one tires in a mile-a.

You see in what a state my Pen is; otherwise I had much more of this sort to dilate on. Better as it is!

Did I tell you that your friend Teufelsdröckh is publishing his lucubrations in a London Magazine? The Public seems to receive him with fixed ——.[1] Little wonder! I hope to forward you a · complete copy, so soon as the business is done; perhaps some two months hence. . . .

With friendliest wishes and hopes, I bid you farewell. May God bless you always!

T. CARLYLE.

[1] Word illegible.

CXIV.—To his WIFE, Craigenputtock.

4 AMPTON STREET, GRAY'S INN ROAD,
LONDON, 17th *May* 1834.

DEAREST HEART—Here am I once more seated on the sofa, by this old rickety table, where you have so often sat looking over on me: I have had my frank since yesterday, with Sister Jean's address on it, who will not let the sheet loiter in Dumfries; I give you the top of the morning, and will write down my whole confused experiences for you with as little confusion as I yet can. What a time it seems since we were parted, though by the calendar it counts only some nine days! Oh, my Love, if I were to write all the loving things I have thought of thee, whole quires would not hold it. Blessed be the Heavens, I have thee to wife; my own, while existence is granted us; we are not yet parted forever, but only, by God's grace, for some few days longer. As I have quantities of the most perplexed matters to write of, and all things yet stand at sixes and sevens with me, I will take the old-established order of time, and endeavour to sketch you the whole of it that seems sketchable.

You remember the Friday, what a bright day it was. . . . Fancy that I spent the day, as one might in a Solway steamboat of but moderate arrangements (for having declined Dinner at two o'clock, there was *nothing* afterwards to be had but the miserablest Tea, at seven: this I mention for your own guidance); that as the Night sank, the gleam of Liverpool arose far over the waters, and the red Light of "The Rock," and other Lights floating and fixed, amid which steering with address, yet not without bellowings and swearings, we came rushing up to the Clarence Dock about two in the morning, and were informed we could not enter, but might land over planks. . . .

But figure me now mounted at noontide of Monday, on your old *Umpire* Coach (for it has changed its hour), and bowling off towards London at one stretch. Figure us rushing down the steep street of Lichfield, and along my old familiar ways in Warwickshire about midnight; and the dirtiest little chill drizzle beginning, from which on the Coach-box with the breeze on the right cheek I had no means of guarding myself; though your Uncle, good man, had a bran-new umbrella waiting for me at the Liverpool starting-place, having failed to get back my own from Porcus M'Minn, who had staggered off with it the night before. Alas, the drizzle continued, and became a rain, and I sat nodding there, and starting awake again at the threshold of most comfortless sleep, till about eight in the morning three cups of scalding coffee brought some motion back into my fingers. Particulars to be *often* recapitulated when we sit by the fire together! Not till two o'clock did I see the huge monstrosity of a London, through the Arch at Holloway, again amid rain, and enter it with a kind of defiance. In few minutes, from "the Angel of Islington," I was here, and the glad Mrs. Page recognising me, and the whole house welcoming me, safe so far from my perils. Our old rooms had been vacant for about a week. . . . All hands here express the truest joy at hope of seeing you again. . . . I feel comparatively at home;

and so, in respect of lodgings am as fortunate as you could wish.

That same Tuesday evening I strode off to Bayswater, and was welcomed[1] (what think you of that?) with a most graceful little kiss. Alas! in the course of five minutes' speech, I learned that my whole hurry had been useless, that I might have staid with you perfectly as well; that our whole Scotch notion of London houseletting was erroneous from top to bottom. Heard poor man, heard poor wife ever anything so provoking? Whitsunday is no day at all in London:[2] they have four term-days in the year. . . . But now in Kensington Gardens (no delved garden, but the beautifullest immensity of a Park, with water-pieces and grass-pieces, and sky-high clumps of frondent beeches, where you shall often walk), there starts from a side-seat a black figure, and clutches my hand in both his: it is poor Edward Irving![3] O what a feeling! The poor friend looks like

---

[1] By Mrs. Austin.   [2] For the renting of houses.
[3] See *Reminiscences*, ii. 212, for a fuller account of this accidental meeting.

death rather than life; pale and yet flushed, a flaccid, boiled appearance; and one short peal of his old Annandale laugh went through me with the wofullest tone. . . .

[Wednesday was spent in house-hunting without result.] Next morning, or Thursday, . . . I soon got out with Hunt in wide quest of houses. Chelsea lies low close by the side of the river; has an ancient, here and there dilapidated look; the houses apparently a tenth cheaper; some market articles, especially coals, said likewise to be cheaper. I liked it little. . . .

Hunt gave me dinner, a pipe even and glass of ale; was the blithest, helpfullest, most loquacious of men; yet his talk only fatigued me mostly; there was much, much of it; full of airiness indeed, yet with little but scepticising quibbles, crotchets, fancies, and even Cockney wit, which I was all too earnest to relish. He sent his kind regards to Craigenputtock, and left me on my way to Edwardes Square. . . . Next morning, Friday, I set out westward, and took Buller by the way [house-hunting again, again without success]. . . . Mill did not come till nine o'clock, and then with a strange gaunt-looking "disciple," and so all three sat talking till near one o'clock.

You have thus, dear Wife, my whole history since we parted. Was ever anything more confused? . . .

Thus, dear Goodykin, have I filled you two of the longest sheets you ever read. Dinner is just here, and I dare not begin another. O my wee Wifiekin, how art thou, in these tumults? Alick promised me that he would as far as man could take the burden off you, screen from all toils, of which in spite of him enough would reach you. Take care, take every care. Tell Alick that if he send thee well to me, I will never forget him,—as indeed I never will any way. And now do you ever think of me? Not you, you little wretch! But oh me, I am too serious for jesting; yet not sad. I feel very fearless in this business; "though desperate not cowardly." Be of good cheer; it is for my Dearest's good too. And so God bless and keep thee!   T. CARLYLE.

CXV.—To his MOTHER, Scotsbrig.

4 AMPTON STREET, GRAY'S INN ROAD,
LONDON, 17*th May* (*Saturday*) [1834].

MY DEAR MOTHER—I am arrived safely here, and living in my old quarters. I got in on Tuesday, having suffered no damage; had good weather all the way, but the last twelve hours, when it rained, but could not wet me. I have great cause of thankfulness: friends are all kind to me; I seem to meet nothing but friends.

. . . Many times, my dear Mother, has your image come over me; but I let it not be with sadness. Nay, what will you think if I often hummed " Fairest Phillis "[1] on the coach-roof,

---

[1] Carlyle would sometimes, in his late years, repeat this old song, the first and last verses of which are :—

> " Haste, haste, fairest Phillis,
> To the greenwood let's away,
> To pull the pale primrose :
> 'Tis the first of the May.
>
> .   .   .   .
>
> " Then all you pretty, fair maids,
> To the greenwood do not go,
> Till the Priest joins your hands,
> Let your answer be No."—M. C.

and actually, when I first saw the great, smoky, immeasurable London, sung to myself with a kind of real defiance, and the right tune, "There's seven foresters in yon forest, and them I want to *see!*"

You shall have plenty of news from me were we settled, a frank every two or at furthest every three weeks; the newspaper weekly: and remember I am very punctual.

Finally, my dear Mother, commit me in your prayers to God, by whose will I desire to live and to die. With whom are we not all present?

My health is good, rather better even.—You must learn to *write;* you must *try* to write, let me rather say, and you can already do it.— There is no fair chance here for *reading:* but I will write plainer the next time. . . .

Send me a Newspaper directed hither. May God's blessing be with you, my dear Mother, and with you all!—Ever your affectionate,

T. CARLYLE.

You shall very soon hear more of me.

CXVI.—To Dr. CARLYLE, Naples.

4 AMPTON STREET, GRAY'S INN ROAD,
LONDON, 18*th May* 1834.

MY DEAR BROTHER — Doubtless you are thinking long to hear from me, as I have done these two weeks to write to you. I pitied but could not help you. I hope you yourself have *Heiterkeit*, and do not torment your mind with vain fears on our account. Be of good cheer: all is well with us. Here also, at length, is another broad and long sheet of that "foreign Post" of theirs, with pen and ink, and the length of a whole still Sunday before me: to have a table that would *stand* on its feet were another completion of comfort; which, however, for the present, I must dispense with. My brave true-hearted Jack shall hear to all lengths how it goes with us.

Your last Letter but one arrived only a day after my last was despatched. The last was found lying at Dumfries now nearly a fortnight ago; and in the very best time; for our dear Mother was beginning to call exceedingly often at the Post-office, and no reasoning could have

saved her from considerable anxiety, had it
lasted long. She had been at Craigenputtock,
for a fortnight, on her "*last* visit" there. I
took her down on the Friday as far as Alick's,
who would not let us go farther; then next day
forward to Annan to show her Mary, who had
actually removed thither into a temporary house
a week before; from which, the same evening,
up to Scotsbrig. Passing through Ecclefechan
we "called,"¹ as usual; but poor Postie had
nothing for us. However, on the Monday following, as I returned through Dumfries, there
lay, in very deed, the long, most kind, most
brotherly letter; which I could read to Jean on
the spot, and send our Mother hint of by a
Newspaper, with hope of seeing *itself* in the
course of that week. Jean went on with me to
Puttock, and staid there talking and sewing
shirts, till the Thursday when I was to bring her
so far down on my road—to London. For you
must know, our Holland Street, and all other
Austinian house-speculations had, after the most
provoking vicissitudes of hope and even of

¹ *i.e.* At the post-office for letters.

assurance, come suddenly to nought; whereby, as Whitsunday was so near, it became for us self-evident that I must off in person to do the work, lest it altogether miswent for year and day. Poor Jane was to be left with the Furniture herself; Alick undertook to come for a week and take the burden off her, which I believe he is now at Craigenputtock struggling with his best effort to do. And so I, wetted with poor Mrs. Welsh's tears (whom Jane seemed anxious to see *done* with her visit, as she then nearly was), lumbered off in my *Clatch*, in rainy weather, to seek new habitations. Alas, five minutes after arriving here, I found that my whole hurry had been superfluous; that Whitsunday is no day at all in London,[1] or this very *Sunday;* and houses are to be had at any season, and most plentifully of all some two weeks hence! However, intrinsically there is little ill done: I shall have a House *ready*, I hope, for the poor tired Wife, and as our Goods, having a quick path all marked out for them, will not linger, we shall all the sooner have it

[1] See *ante*, p. 149.

over. Let me first, meanwhile, wind up Scottish matters; then tell you, as far as I can, what London has brought forth.

With regard to our dear Mother, I bid you comfort yourself with the assurance, then, that she is really moderately well; better, I can say, than you are likely to fancy her. . . . She adjusts herself with the old heroism to new circumstances; agrees that I *must* come hither, parts from me with the stillest face, more touching than if it had been all beteared. I said to Alick, as we drove up the Purdamstown brae[1] that morning that I thought if I had had all the Mothers I ever saw to choose from I would have chosen my own. She is to have Harry, and can ride very well on him; will go down awhile to sea-bathing at Mary's; up to Dumfries; to Catlinns; and spend the summer tolerably enough. For winter I left her the task of spinning me a plaid dressing-gown, with which if she get too soon done, she may spin another for you. She has Books; above all, her *Book:* she trusts in God, and " shall not

[1] Close to Scotsbrig.

be put to shame." I am to write once in the three weeks; you also are pressingly charged to keep writing; your Letters to me I shall get forwarded in Franks. I told her, there would be railways too (which is a fact) which, in few years, would bring us to Liverpool in ten hours. If I once again saw you safe here, in September come a year, we would come home together, and once again provide her with some happy days.—To show you several things I will mention a fact: while at Craigenputtock, I made her train me to two song-tunes, and we often sang them together, and tried them often again in coming down to Annandale; nay, one of them, I actually found myself humming with a strange cheerfully-pathetic feeling when I first came in sight (through that Arch on the road) of huge smoky Babylon: "For there's *seven foresters in yon forest*, and them *I want to see*, see, and them," etc.! I wrote her a little Note yesterday, and told her this.[1]—As for Jamie, you can fancy him providing for a love-mar-

---

[1] A part of the preceding portion of this paragraph is in Froude's *Life*, ii. 416.

riage, which is to take place shortly. He is no ill-conditioned fellow; very far from it; and with a great natural talent, had he given it any culture. We will heartily wish him joy, and hope well of him.—Jean seems also to be doing very well, to be happy in Dumfries, interested in it, and able to give a good account of what she sees there. I think she loves her husband, and will help him to be an honest man, which, with very good faculty in all ways, he is truly anxious to be. She wept at parting, when I had eaten my last Dumfries meal with them: I bade them ever remember that it was but a short, short time we had to be tumbled about here, and that all Eternity depended on our way of spending that. And so I left poor Jean; *guter Hoffnung* (they say) in the German sense; and I with good hope of her in the universal sense.—My good Alick stood waiting for me at the end of Shillahill Bridge with his black mare, thinking my horse would be weak. It is one of those apparitions I shall never forget. He whirled me, like an arrow, direct down to Highlaw, Breconhill, Ecclefechan, and

Scotsbrig, through old scenes unvisited for years: we were within cry of Mainhill (for the new road now goes by the horse-loch almost); it stood there still, and we had never more aught to do with it. Alick still votes for Annan, and I fancy will probably accomplish it: he has gained hitherto at Catlinns; but has no assurance that in a wet year he will not greatly lose: the proprietors also will not afford him the palpably needfullest encouragement; he will do well to cast it from him.—At Annan, I told you, Mary already was: her husband has had constantly some work from the very first day, and shapes fairly for doing well enough. He is a blithe man, strong, steady. . . . Poor Mary had her two children as clean as new shillings, and the whole little housekin swept and cleared, and the neatest breakfast laid out for us all that morning I went off. It had been appointed so: I went in the "new steamboat from Annan" (which is also to carry our Furniture); Alick and Jamie, with Ben Nelson, etc., were down with me at the shore; and before noon, at the

Waterfoot I had waved my hat to my two Brothers, and gone on my way.—Of Jenny I think I told you all last time; I got her Chambers's two volumes of Songs bound into one, for a most acceptable parting-gift, and so left my little "Prudence." Your Iliad and Odyssey I also got bound then, and have appropriated them for the present.—Alas, how my Paper wanes! I must merely huddle up the rest. . . .

With respect to London, where we are now arrived,[1] I must spare you many details: understand in general that I walk myself daily into lameness and utter lassitude (taking all advantage of *omnibii* too) in search of houses, but still find none, or hardly any: see only that I shall find some. My present view is fixed on two points: one in Edwardes Square, a little quiet green place, far west in Kensington; the second, which as yet I like distinctly better, a detached new-[brick] cottage in Gloucester Terrace, Brompton; built on the very model of Craigenputtock, only

[1] *i.e.* After having described Liverpool, etc.

wider, without adjoined kitchen (servant's-room being kitchen), and lower in the upper story; a solid-looking, clean-yellow house, in the middle of a garden with an Omnibus road in front, and perhaps [half a] mile to Hyde Park: rent, I think, £40. That is my outlook tomorrow. Bayswater I like best of all, especially for the glorious Kensington Gardens; Chelsea is cheapest of all, but I like it not, and also shall be better not too near the Hunts, who overwhelm me with kindness, but will never do good with me. In Kensington or Brompton you are to figure me then; certainly almost, in some western suburb: Bessy Barnet is warned to be here in twelve days, when our Goods arrive; Jane follows instantly, and so with good heart we begin the world. As you must write to me *instantaneously*, it will be better to direct to [James] Fraser, 215 Regent Street: but I expect to hear of you before that also, by Scotsbrig. Our Mother took lessons in writing from me; and really can write quite tolerably, though slowly.

In point of employment here I have yet made

no accurate calculations: Literature seems *done*, or nearly so; all enterprises languish; Tait has given up his Magazine (or joined it with a certain *Johnstone's*); Cochrane,[1] who really proves no bad fellow, and received me very kindly, I suspect to be in lowest water for money, and not to occupy me mainly on *that* ground. *Fraser's Magazine* is here, and a lot of Books for you from Mrs. Badams: but the man[2] himself I have not seen. Nothing seems to thrive but Penny Journals: are we at the *End*, then? Meanwhile be gratified to know that these things and twenty times as many cannot dispirit me. I feel in general that I have wit enough in my head to live; and look upon many things with the cheerfullest "still defiance" I have known for long. A scoundrel, by God Almighty's grace, no man shall ever see me: the rest is leather and prunella. I find friends too, kind friends; will *survey* my element, will understand it, then see whether I can swim there. Here is a professed Teacher, there are innumerable Ignorants: doubtless there *is* a way of bringing

---

[1] See *ante*, p. 76 *n*.   [2] Fraser.

them together. Rejoice also that whether by such walking or by the humour I am in, or by what, my health feels especially good since I arrived. Who knows but I shall one day be *healthy!* So Courage! *Andar con Dios!* ...

T. CARLYLE.

.   .   .   .

CXVII.—To his WIFE, Liverpool.

AMPTON STREET, 30*th May* (*Friday*) 1834.

God be thanked, my own Dearest, here is word from you again! It is long since I have been so happy as when I found your Letter yesterday, as I came in to dinner. The last one, which I had longed and languished four days for, left me in the absurd predicament of neither accurately knowing your motions, nor even understanding how to address a Letter to you. I had prepared a Frank for my Mother at Scotsbrig, as the only thing possible; but now that is superfluous for your part of it: you have done as I hoped and calculated you would do if it lay in your power; like a dear Child you are hastening to me; in few days

I shall hold you in this bosom, and now once more "it is all right." Could I have spoken I would have said, Do not hasten if your health is to suffer, much as, on all accounts, I long to see you. However, you have heeded none of these hindrances: at this hour I fancy you on the Solway Brine, with one sure hope in your heart, all too overclouded otherwise. God bless you for it; and bring you safe to my heart! But O, my little Lassie, take care of yourself; rest, if rest be possible, when you get to land. I see not how I can forgive myself if you suffer mischief by haste to obey me. But we will hope and pray, it may still not be so. . . .

As to Craigenputtock, take my thanks for your cleverness, adroitness and despatch: I find all quite wonderfully well settled; there is hardly one thing I think of which I would have voted otherwise. . . . Is Chico[1] actually with you? Thou little fool! Yet dear even in thy follies. . . .

But the question is, When is my Goody coming? *When!* Warn me, my little Darling. If

[1] The canary-bird.

you go by Birmingham (which except for Bessy, quite easily managed otherwise, there is not the slightest *need* of your doing), your Uncle must choose you a good Coach *thither;* from Birmingham to London I believe they are all good. Would you not like to sleep? or do you feel as if you could not sleep? Decide thy own way, my pretty one. Only tell me pointedly which way you come, and at what hour: I would not miss you for a sovereign. You will jump out round my neck?—For shame! . . . O Dearest, Best, when *wilt* thou come?—Jeffrey is gone two days ago: I saw him *again*, at Mrs. Austin's, where he was taking leave. His manner to me tremulous and shy; mine kinder and graver than ever. Peace be with him!—By the bye it is reported here that his Majesty is gone mad; and the "present excellent Ministry" in this alarming state. *Eheu! Eheu!*— . . .

Dearest, it is close on five! Thousand thanks for your kind sentiment of *staying at home.* That *is* it, my little brave one. We will be true to Heaven and one another, and fear *nothing*.—Now when will it be that I hear?

Monday? Tuesday? God guide thee home to me, my Own! I fear I have forgotten many things; but the interruptions have been numerous; my hurry greater than I looked for.—Ever thy own, heart and soul, T. CARLYLE.

My kindest regards to Uncle and Aunt and all in kind Maryland Street. Ask Helen to come and see us here: I did.— . . .

CXVIII.—To his MOTHER, Scotsbrig.

5 GREAT CHEYNE ROW, CHELSEA, LONDON,
Thursday, 12th June 1834.

MY DEAR MOTHER—I promised you that the first frank I filled from our new House should be for you; and here I am, in the middle of a most miscellaneous collection of operative men and women, accomplishing that promise. It is not only the first Letter I have written, but the first time I have put pen to paper. However, I have for the present (while the Bell-hangers are absent) a room to myself; I have my old *firm* writing-table, firm as a rock; my old inkbottle and penholder; and the quietest outlook, through an open window, into green fields and trees; I have even my old Highland bonnet on: so I will tell you the completest story I can, with moderate composure after all.

Jane gave me, in a Letter from Liverpool, a sad tale of your parting at Annan, and how you stood waving your handkerchief to her, in front of a great crowd of people, to make amends for your tears, and keep up her heart. All *that* is past, and too sad to dwell on. Carlyle of Waterbeck[1] was abundantly civil to the poor Traveller; as indeed all people had been and continued to be helpful and civil: so finally, on, I think, the Wednesday afternoon, as I returned to Frederick Street from Mrs. Austin's (where they had kept me to dinner), I was met by the *chirling* of a little Canary-bird (the same as I hear even now, from the under-story), and in the next room, safe in bed, and already well-rested, lay my little Wife, "actually" engaged in drinking tea! She was well, she assured me, and all was well. Let us be thankful; and trust that the rest, too, will be well!

[1] A relation of the Carlyles.—M. C.

With our renewed house-huntings, and how we dashed up and down for three or four days, in all manner of conveyances, where such were to be had cheap, and on our legs where not,— I need not detain you here. We saw various Houses; but the Chelsea House (though our Dame did not think so at first, but thought and thinks *doubly* so afterwards) seemed nearly *twice* as good as any other we could get at the money: so on Saturday afternoon we finally fixed; and moved hither, according to appointment, on Tuesday forenoon. Bessy Barnet had joined us from Birmingham the night before; and we came all down in a Hackney Coach, loaded with luggage, and *Chico* (the Canary-bird) singing on Bessy's knee. Jane says the little atom put great heart into her frequently through the journey: *he* sang aloud, wherever he might be; praising, in his way, the Maker that gave him Life and Food and fine weather. How much more should we!

. . . The House, which we have now inhabited (in the *Gillha'*[1] style) for two days

[1] *Make-shift.*

and nights, is certainly by many degrees the suitablest I could find far or near. . . . We lie safe down in a little bend of the river, away from all the great roads; have air and quiet hardly inferior to Craigenputtock, an outlook from the back-windows into mere leafy regions, with here and there a red high-peaked old roof looking through; and see nothing of London, except by day the summits of St. Paul's Cathedral and Westminster Abbey, and by night the gleam of the great Babylon affronting the peaceful skies. Yet in *half an hour* (for it is under two miles to Piccadilly) we can be, with a pair of stout legs, in the most crowded part of the whole habitable Earth; and, even without legs, every quarter of an hour, from sun to sun, a Coach will take you for sixpence from your own threshold, and set you down there again for another. We are south-west *from* the smoke; so during great part of the year we shall have no more to do with it than you. Nay even, in East winds, we are near *five* miles from the old, manufacturing part of London, and the smoke is all but gone before it reaches us.—As for the House itself, it is probably the *best* we ever lived in: a right old strong roomy brick house, built near one hundred and [thirty] years ago, and likely to see *three* races of their modern fashionables fall before it come down: it has all been put in perfect repair, and has closets and conveniences without end. Our furniture suits it too; being all of a strong *weighty* sort. . . . In addition to the many properties of our House, I should have mentioned a little Garden behind; where all is as yet barren or weedy, except a cherry-tree with almost *ripe* cherries on it, and two miserable rose-bushes: however, I have got a new set of Garden-tools (for six shillings), and will soon give it at least a clean face. It is of admirable comfort to me, in the *smoking* way: I can wander about in dressing-gown and straw hat in it, as of old, and take my pipe in peace. I think, were the Railways done, you must see it all with your own eyes, my dear Mother; that were the shortest way.

Of Bessy Barnet I dare not yet say much:

we have seen so little of her; and that little seems so *very* favourable. She is by far the orderliest, cleverest worker we ever had in the house (hardly even excepting Grace Macdonald), and has manners and an appearance of character totally beyond the servant class: if she go on as we hope, and as she has begun, it will be our duty and pleasure to treat her not as a servant but as a friend. On this side too, therefore, we have as yet *great* reason to be thankful.

You see all things painted here in the colours of Hope: there is no doubt but by and by we shall have them (House, Place, Servant and all) painted in the dingier colours of Reality: nevertheless I think and calculate there will still be much more than Tolerability to boast of; much which, with grateful hearts, we should thank the Giver for, and above all study to improve by welldoing, which is the acceptablest sort of thanks.—I write all to you; because I know there is not *any*thing (down to our very water-barrel) that you do not feel a motherly interest in for our sake.

The Literary craft is bad, though hardly *so*

bad as I expected. I find I shall get my Book (on the French Revolution) *printed* without cost; but probably nothing more. In the meantime I have some Magazine things in my eye, of a slight kind, to work at, and keep "*mall in shaft*" by; and then if my Book were *well* written, and out, I shall have a better name to start Lecturing, etc., with; and so, on the whole, we *shall* make it out, by God's help, better or worse. If to " His glory and my own eternal good," all else will be as dust on the balance, and an exceeding little thing. " They cannot hinder thee of God's Providence :" that is the beautiful part of it.

For the rest, my Friends here continue all very kind, and do more for me than I had any right to expect, or even to wish; I who profess to depend on no friend, but only on God and myself. Hunt who lives close by, is not only the kindest but the politest of men; has never yet been near us (which we reckon very civil), but will always be delighted when I go and rouse *him* for a walk; and indeed a sprightly sensible talker he is, and very pleasant company for a stroll. Jane greatly preferred his "poetical Tinkerdom" to any of the unpoetical Gigmandoms (even Mrs. Austin's) which I showed her. The Hunts, I think, will not trouble us, and indeed be a pleasure so far as they go.

And now, my dear Mother, here surely is enough about London and me for once. As for you and Scotsbrig, I begin to feel exceedingly disheartened about my prospects of news thence. Not one *scrape of a pen* have I yet realised from any of you; not so much as a Newspaper: the very *Courier* has not come, I think, for three weeks. You really must not treat me so; nay I know it is not *you*, dear Mother: but do you, if none else will, get the *Courier* Newspaper yourself, and in your own hand, as you can, write our address upon it: that, with *two strokes*[1] (if happily you can still send them) will be a great comfort to me. But, indeed, I do wrong to accuse the rest of negli-

---

[1] "By a certain pair of *strokes* [on the Newspapers], unmeaning to the uninitiated, we inform one another that all is well."—From Letter to Dr. Carlyle, 22d July 1834.

gence; for surely there is some mistake in it: they are too much occupied otherwise, or perhaps had not rightly understood how to direct to me. Give my love to them all; and not reproaches but entreaties. . . .

O my dear Mother! how much there was to say, which there is now no time for! May the Almighty Father of us all bless you, and guide all your footsteps! Through Time and through Eternity.—Blessings with you all! Ever your affectionate, T. CARLYLE.

[Postscript by Mrs. Carlyle.]

Is not all this very satisfactory, my dear Mother, and have we not great cause of thankfulness? I declare to you I could not have made myself a better house if I had had money at command; and for my servant, I expect she will be sister to me as well as servant.—No fear but we shall get a living, and my Husband will be healthier and happier than he has been for long years.—I will write you a long letter "with my own hand" when I am a little settled, at present I am so busy *fettling* up things! but Bessy is equal to all, and Eliza Miles is come to help me besides. Everybody is kind to me—and *has been* kind to me. I shall ever remember you all with gratitude as well as love. God be with you every one.—Your affectionate, JANE.

CXIX.—To Dr. CARLYLE, Naples.

CHEYNE ROW, CHELSEA, LONDON,
17*th June* 1834.

MY DEAR BROTHER — . . . You can fancy what weary lonesome wanderings I had, through the dusty suburbs, and along the burning streets, under a fierce May sun with East wind; "seeking through the nation for some habitation"! At length Jane sent me comfortable tidings of innumerable difficulties overcome; and finally (in, I think, the fourth week) arrived herself; with the Furniture all close following her, in one of Pickford's Track-boats. I carried her to certain of the hopefullest-looking Houses I had fallen in with, and a toilsome time we anew had : however, it was not long; for, on the second inspection, this old Chelsea mansion pleased very decidedly far better than any other we could see; and, the people also whom it belongs to proving reasonable, we soon struck a bargain, and in three days more (precisely this day week) a Hackney Coach, loaded to the roof and beyond it with luggage and live-passengers, tumbled us all down here about eleven in the morning. By "all" I mean my Dame and myself; Bessy Barnet, who had come the night before; and —little *Chico*, the Canary-bird, who, *multum jactatus*, did nevertheless arrive living and well from Puttock, and even sang violently all the way by sea or land, nay struck up his *lilt* in the very London streets wherever he could see green leaves and feel the free air.[1] There then we sat on three trunks; I, however, with a match-box, soon lit a cigar, as Bessy did a fire; and thus with a kind of cheerful solemnity we took possession by "raising reek," and even dined in an *extempore* fashion, on a box-lid

[1] See *Reminiscences*, i. 101; the strong grasp of Carlyle's memory on the events of the past is strikingly illustrated by a comparison of the passages.

covered with some accidental towel. At two
o'clock the Pickfords did arrive; and *then*
began the hurly-burly; which even yet has but
grown quieter, will not grow quiet, for a fortnight to come. However, two rooms and two
bedrooms are now in a partially civilised state;
the broken Furniture is mostly mended; I have
my old writing-table again (here) *firm* as Atlas;
a large wainscoted drawing-room (which is to
be my study) with the "red carpet" tightly
spread on it; my Books all safe in Presses;
the Belisarius Picture[1] right in front of me over
the mantel-piece (most suitable to its new wainscot lodging), and my beloved *Segretario Ambulante*[2] right behind, with the two old Italian

---

[1] A French print of Belisarius begging alms. The print was valued only because the face of a young Roman soldier in it reminded Mrs. Carlyle of her father, Dr. Welsh.—M. C.

[2] Brought by Dr. Carlyle from Italy. A little common coloured lithograph of a ragged old man, seated behind a board on trestles (a quill in his hand, another behind his ear and a third in his inkbottle), plying his trade, the writing of letters at dictation for illiterate passers-by. Carlyle says, in a letter of the 18th November 1833, " He is a delightful fellow; shows you Literature in its simplest quite steadfast condition, below which it *cannot* sink." Carlyle always liked the little picture, which to the last hung in his bedroom at Chelsea.—M. C.

Engravings, and others that I value less, dispersed around; and so, opposite the middle of my three windows, with little but huge Scotch elm-trees looking in on me, and in the distance an ivied House, and a sunshiny sky bursting out from genial rain, I sit here already very much at home, and impart to my dear and true Brother a thankfulness which he is sure to share in. We have indeed much reason to be thankful every way.

With the House we are all highly pleased, and, I think, the better, the longer we know it hitherto. I know not if you ever were at Chelsea, especially at Old Chelsea, of which this is portion. It stretches from Battersea Bridge (a queer old wooden structure, where they charge you a halfpenny) along the bank of the River, westward a little way; and eastward (which is our side) some quarter of a mile, forming a "Cheyne Walk" (pronounced *Chainie* walk) of really grand old brick mansions, dating perhaps from Charles II.'s time (" Don Saltero's Coffeehouse" of the *Tatler* is still fresh and brisk among them), with flagged pavement;

carriage-way between two rows of stubborn-looking high old pollarded trees; and then the River with its varied small craft, fast-moving or safe-moored, and the wholesome smell (among the breezes) of sea *tar*. Cheyne Row (or Great Cheyne Row, when we wish to be grand) runs up at right angles from this, has some twenty Houses of the same fashion; Upper Cheyne Row (where Hunt lives) turning *again* at right angles, some stone-cast from this door. Frontwards we have the outlook I have described already (or if we shove out our head, the River is disclosed some hundred paces to the left); backwards, from the ground floor, our own gardenkin (which I with new garden-tools am actually re-trimming every morning), and, from all the other floors, nothing but leafy clumps, and green fields, and red high-peaked roofs glimmering through them: a most clear, pleasant prospect, in these fresh westerly airs! Of London nothing visible but Westminster Abbey and the topmost dome of St. Paul's; other faint ghosts of spires (one other at least) disclose themselves, as the smoke-cloud shifts; but I have not yet made out what they are. At night we are pure and silent, almost as at Puttock; and the gas-light shimmer of the great Babylon hangs stretched from side to side of our horizon. To Buckingham Gate it is thirty-two minutes of my walking (Allan Cunningham's door about half way); nearly the very same to Hyde-Park Corner, to which latter point we have omnibuses every quarter of an hour (they say) that carry you to the Whitehorse Cellar, or even to Coventry Street, for sixpence; calling for you at the very threshold. Nothing was ever so discrepant in my experience as the Craigenputtock-silence of this House and then the world-hubbub of London and its people into which a few minutes bring you: I feel as if a day spent between the two must be the epitome of a month. . . . The rent is £35; which really seems £10 cheaper than such a House could be had for in Dumfries or Annan. The secret is our old friend, "Gigmanity": Chelsea is unfashionable; it is also reputed unhealthy. The former quality we rather like (for our neighbours still are all polite-living people); the latter we do not in the faintest degree believe in, remembering that Chelsea was once considered the " London Montpelier," and knowing that in these matters now as formerly the Cockneys "know nothing," only rush in masses blindly and sheepwise. Our worst fault is the want of a good free *rustic* walk, like Kensington Gardens, which are above a mile off: however, we have the "College" or Hospital Grounds, with their withered old Pensioners; we have open carriage-ways, and lanes, and really a very pretty route to Piccadilly (different from the omnibus route) through the new Grosvenor edifices, Eaton Square, Belgrave Place, etc.: I have also walked to Westminster Hall by Vauxhall Bridge-end, Millbank, etc.; but the road is squalid, confused, dusty and detestable, and happily *need* not be returned to. To conclude, we are here on *literary* classical ground, as Hunt is continually ready to declare and unfold: not a stone-cast from this House Smollett wrote his *Count Fathom* (the house is ruined and we happily do not see it); hardly another stone-cast off, old More entertained Erasmus: to say nothing of Bolingbroke St. John, of Paradise Row and the Count de Grammont, for in truth we care almost nothing for them. On the whole we are exceedingly content so far; and have reason to be so. I add only that our furniture came with wonderfully *little* breakage, and for less than £20, Annan included; that Jane sold all her odd things to Nanny Macqueen on really fair terms; and that we find new furniture of all sorts exceedingly cheap here, and have already got what we need, or nearly so, for less than our own old good, brought us on the spot. . . .

There is now a word to be said on Economics, and the Commissariat Department. Bookselling is still at its lowest ebb; yet on the whole *better* than I expected to find it. Fraser is the only craftsman I have yet seen: he talks still of *loss* by his Magazine; and I think will not willingly employ me much, were I never so ready, at the old rate of writing. He seems a well-intentioned creature; I can really pity him in the place he occupies. I went yesterday with a project of a series of Articles on French Revolution matters; chiefly to be translated from *Mémoires:* but he could not take them, at my rate, or indeed at almost any rate; for he spoke of £10 a sheet as quite a *ransom*. He has got my name (such as it is), and can do better without me. However, he will cheerfully print (for "half-profits," that is, *zero*) a projected Book of mine on the French Revolution; to which accordingly, if no new thing occur, I shall probably very soon with all my heart address myself, in full purpose to do *my best*, and put my name to it. The *Diamond Necklace* Paper his Boy got from me, by appointment, this morning; to be examined whether it *will* make a Book: as an *Article* I shall perhaps hardly think of giving it to him. For, you are to understand, that Radical Review of Mill's, after seeming to be quite abandoned, has now a far fairer chance of getting started: a Sir W. Molesworth, a young man whom I have seen at Buller's and liked, offers to furnish all the money himself (and can do it, being very rich), and to take no further hand in it, once a Manager that will please Mill is found for it. Mill is to be here to-morrow evening : I think, I must appoint some meeting with Molesworth, and give him my whole views of it, and express my readiness to take a most hearty hold of it; having the prospect of right companions; none yet but Mill and Buller, and such as we may further approve of and add. It seems likely something may come of this. In any other case, Periodical Authorship, like all other forms of it, seems *done* in the economical sense : I think of quite abandoning it; of writing my Book; and then, with such name as it may give me, starting some new course, or courses, to make honest wages by. A poor Fanny Wright (whom we are to hear to-night in Freemasons' Hall) goes lecturing over the whole world: before sight, I will engage to lecture twice as well; being, as Glen once said, with great violence, to me, "the *more* gigantic spirit of the two." On the whole, I fear nothing. There are funds here already to keep us going above a year, independently of all incomings: before that we may have seen into much, tried much, and succeeded in somewhat. "God's providence they cannot hinder thee of": that is the thing I always repeat to myself, or know without repeating. . . .

God bless you, dear Brother! *Vale mei memor.*   T. CARLYLE.

.   .   .   .   .

CXX.—To his MOTHER, Scotsbrig.

5 CHEYNE ROW, CHELSEA, LONDON,
6th July 1834.

. . . I have got a heap of Books about me and am actually employing myself daily in preparation of that Book of my own! It is on the French Revolution, which seems far the eligiblest for my first: there is an appetite for it; there are plenty of Documents and materials; Mill himself laid me out the other day a whole barrowful, and insisted on my getting them over all at once. They are not come yet, but are coming—by the "Carrier," for we have Carriers between district and district of this huge city, some with horses, some with asses, some for aught I know with *dogs*—the lightest draught-cattle in use here.—I am determined to do my very best, and shall, like Cowthwaite, "*mak' an a'f-f-f-u' struggle.*"[1] Do you prophesy well of me? I hope you do. Of your *wishes* for me there could be no improvement. . . .

CXXI.—To Mrs. AITKEN, Dumfries.

5 CHEYNE ROW, CHELSEA, LONDON,
6th July 1834.

MY DEAR JEAN—Your Letter, which was the first I had received from any of my Friends in Scotland, proved one of the welcomest I ever got. The Postman's two knocks (for all Postmen give two smart thumps, which are known here and elsewhere as the " Postman's Knock ") brought me it and the Newspaper, and delivered me from a multitude of vague imaginations. Newspapers indeed had come the week before, and persuaded me that nothing material was wrong: however, it was still the best that could happen to have it all confirmed in black-on-white.

---

[1] Cowthwaite, an Annandale neighbour, doubtless a *stutterer*.

Tell James that, in spite of his critical penetration, the Letter "*could* go," and did go, and was welcomed as few are.

Whatever you may think, it is not a "ten minutes" matter with me, the filling of a frank that will carry an ounce of thin writing paper: it is a decided *business* which breaks the head of a Day for me; which breakage, however, I am generally well disposed to execute. Do you also take a large, even a *long*-shaped sheet, a clear-pointed pen, and in the smallest hand you can master, repay it me. By no means must I want Dumfriesshire news, especially news about my Mother. The tax-loaded Post-office is still the most invaluable of Establishments; and the ancient men, that invented *Writing*, and made the voice of man triumphant over Space and Time, were deservedly accounted next to gods. I would have you in particular, do your endeavour by assiduous practice (there is *no* other method) to perfect yourself in that divine art, the uses of which no man can calculate: in time, as I predict, you will acquire very considerable excellence. As for good composition, it is mainly the result of good thinking, and improves with that, if careful observation as you read attends it: the Penmanship is a secondary matter, and has only three points of perfection, or at most four, that I know of; in all of which one may advance indefinitely by exertions of one's own : that it be straight across the paper, that it be distinct, that it be rapid,—to which if you like, add that it be *close*, or *much of it* in a given space. "These are good advices"? They are not mine, but the Apostle Butterworth's![1]

I did not design answering you so soon by a week or ten days; as I said in Alick's Letter: but there has come a sheet from Naples, which I was beginning to be very impatient for, and I would not keep it back an instant from my Mother, whose impatience probably is still greater. She has already got hint of it in the last *Examiner*, and also that it is coming by you on Wednesday : so I take occasion by the forelock, and hope I shall not miss the day again, as I fear was done in the Catlinns case, after

[1] Of spelling book celebrity in those days.

all my exertions : as for you, make up the Parcel again, instantly for Jardine[1] and Scotsbrig, or there will be no forgiveness for you.

As you have doubtless seen or will see the copious despatches I have sent to Annandale about our Household Establishment, wherein nothing from the very watering-pan and marigold flowers upwards is forgotten, I need not dilate farther on that topic. We have at length all but got the last stragglers of the upholsterer squadron handsomely conducted out of doors, with far less damage than might have been apprehended ; and sit quietly in a Dwelling-place really much beyond what could have been anticipated ; where, if Providence but grant us grace not to be wanting *to ourselves*, the rest may pass quite uncriticised. We have not yet ceased to admire the union of quietness, and freshness of air, and the outlook into green trees (Plum trees, Walnuts, even Mulberries, they say), with the close neighbourhood of the noisiest Babylon that ever raged and *fumed* (with coal smoke) on the face of this Planet. I

[1] The carrier.

can alternate between the one and the other in half an hour! The London streets themselves are a quite peculiar object, and I daresay of almost *inexhaustible* significance. There is such a torrent of vehicles and faces : the slow-rolling, all-defying waggon, like a mountain in motion, the dejected Hackney-coach, that "has seen better days," but goes along as with a tough uncomplaining patience, the gay equipage with its light bounding air, and *flunkies* of colour hanging behind it; the *distracted* Cab (a thing like a Cradle set aslant on its foot-end, where you sit open in front but free from rain), which always some *blackguard* drives, with the fury of Jehu; the huge Omnibus (a painted *Corn-kist*, of twenty feet long, set on four wheels : no, it cannot be *twenty* feet!) which runs along all streets from all points of the compass, as a sixpenny or shilling stage-coach towards "The Bank" (of England); Butchers' and Brewers' and Bakers' Drays: all these, with wheelbarrows, trucks (*hurlies*), dogcarts, and a nameless flood of other *sma' trash*, hold on unweariedly their ever-vexed chaotic way. And then of foot-passengers! From the King to the Beggar; all in haste, all with a look of care and endeavour; and as if there *were* really " Deevil a thing but one man oppressing another." To wander along and read all this : it is reading one of the strangest everlasting *Newspaper Columns* the eye ever opened on. A Newspaper Column of *living* Letters (as I often say), that was printed in ETERNITY, and is here published only for a little while in TIME, and will soon be recalled and taken out of circulation again!

For the rest, we live exceedingly quiet here ; as yet visited by few, and happily by almost *none* that is not worth being visited by. At any time, in half an hour, I can have company enough of the sort going; and scarcely above once or twice in the week is my Day taken from me by any intrusion. I am getting rather stiffly to work again ; and once well at work, can defy the whole Powers of Darkness, and say in my heart (as Tom Ker the mason did to Denbie and "the Marquis" or some military minion of his) : "Ye will go your lengths, Gentlemen; my name's Tom Ker." By and by, if all go right, you shall see some book of mine with my name (not of "Tom Ker") on it, and the best I can do. Pray that it be honestly done, let its reception be what it will.

Of "amusements," beyond mere strolling, I take little thought. By acquaintance with Newspaper people (such as Hunt), I fancy we might procure free admission to the Theatres, even to the Opera, almost every night: but, alas, what would it avail? I actually went, one idle night before Jane came, to Covent Garden; found it a very mystery of stupidity and abomination; and so tiresome that I came away long before the end, and declare that the dullest sermon I ever heard was cheery in comparison. The night before last, looking out from our (back) Bedroom window, at midnight, I saw the many-coloured rockets rising from Vauxhall Gardens, and thought with myself: "Very well, gentlemen, if you have 'guinea admission' to spare for it; only, thank Heaven, I am not within a measured mile of you!"—There are a few good, even noble people here too; there must be a few; if there were not, the whole concern would take fire : of these I even know some, and hope to know more.

But now, my dear Sister, you have enough of London : let me turn a little northward. I am much obliged by your description of Mother's settlement ; I can form a very tolerable notion of her arrangement in the two well-known rooms, and find it the most natural that could be made.[1] I hope, however, the *Clock* is now got safely hoisted up : surely, among so many stout hands, any task of that kind could not be difficult. However, where a Honeymoon is in progress one must *thole*,[2] one must *thole*. I also like very well to hear of your Jamie's boarding with our Mother, while he is at his work in the neighbourhood ; I follow him across the fresh fields, early in the morning, to the *Ha*',[3] and heartily wish him a *useful* day. There is no other way of making a *pleasant* day, that I could ever hear of. That he finds employment in his honest vocation is a great

---

[1] Her son James having recently brought a bride home to Scotsbrig.
[2] Endure, have patience.   [3] Kirkconnell Hall.

blessing, for which I trust you are thankful. Tell him to *follow* his vocation honestly, not as a man-pleaser, or one working for the eye of man only, but as one forever under *another* Eye that never slumbers or sleeps, that *sees* in secret, and will reward openly. I hope and believe that this *is* his course, that he will persevere in it, let the wind of accident blow fair or foul; and so I can prophesy all manner of good for him.

. . . There is much loud thunder to-day, and a copious deluge of rain; of all which we hope to reap the benefit to-morrow; for the air was growing foully uncomfortable, and oppressive too; a sour east-wind, amid the sultriest brick-kiln heat, with dusts enough and vapours as we have them on these streets and ways. A day's rain washes everything above ground and beneath it; next morning we can "snuff the *caller* air," for it is there to snuff. . . .

This is a far larger Letter than yours, Dame; and deserves two in return for it; think of that, and of what you are to *do* in consequence. . . . That Scotsbrig residence, I think with you and have always thought, can hardly be permanently comfortable for our Mother; if it serve well for one year, that is all I hope of it: then other outlooks may have opened. In the meanwhile, Toleration, "the Act of mutual Toleration"! One can live without it *nowhere* on this Earth's surface.— Remember me kindly to dear little Prudence.[1] Tell her to mind her seam, and be considerate and wise, and grow daily wiser; and it will go better and better with her.—Jane, whose health seems better than of old and still improving, sends her love to all of you. . . . And so farewell, my dear Sister. Be true and loving!— Ever your affectionate, T. CARLYLE.

.   .   .   .

CXXII.—To his MOTHER, Scotsbrig.

5 CHEYNE ROW, CHELSEA, LONDON,
5th August 1834.

MY DEAR MOTHER— . . . Life here in Cheyne Row goes on in the steadiest manner; nothing to glory in; much to be glad of, and

[1] His youngest sister Jenny.

humbly thankful for. Our House is all settled and swept long ago, and proceeding at a fixed rate, our accounts all paid off; so we know in some measure what we have to look for. Living is really not *very* much dearer than at Puttock; one has a less plenteous supply in some things; but on the whole what it amounts to "ultimately" is no such grand matter, "after all." We calculated that we could live here, everything included, for £200, and seem as if we could for less. At all events there will be no more "fifteen pounds for fodder" or other provoking items of that sort to pay; but for one's money there will be real *ware* of some kind. In all other respects, as you at once judge, I am much better off, and feel habitually that here or nowhere is the place for me. Old Annandale itself seems lovelier than it ever did: often in the still sunset, when I am alone, it comes before me with its green *knowes* and clear-rushing *burns*, and all the loved ones that I have there, above the ground and below it; and I feel a sweet unsullied affection for it all, and a holy faith that God is there as here, and in His merciful hand is the life and lot of every one of us for Eternity as for Time. Unspeakably wearisome, in such seasons, were the light cackle of the worldly-minded: but indeed I am not much troubled with that. Once for all one should "set his face like a flint" against the idolatries of men, and determine that *his* little section of Existence shall not be a mad empty Dream, but as far as possible a Reality.

I have not written anything whatever for Reviews or Magazines since we came hither; and am not likely to write. In fact, it is rather my feeling that I should abandon that whole despicable business, and seek diligently out for some freer field to labour in. Nothing can exceed the hollow frothiness and even dishonest blackguardism of Literature generally at present: but what then? This is even the very thing thou art sent to *amend!* Mill's Review is to go on, about New-year's day next; there, it is possible, I may contribute something: but there too I wait till I see further before taking any very *fixed* hold. My former Book, that came out through *Fraser*, is happily at last all printed within these last days : I hope to send you, and some others of them, a full copy of it about the beginning of next month by the Dumfries Bookseller. You will have leisure to peruse and consider it; and finding it very *queer*, may not find it altogether empty and false. It has met with next to no recognition that I hear of in these parts; a circumstance not to be surprised at, not to be wept over. On the other hand, my American Friend[1] (you remember hearing of him at Puttock) sends me a week ago the most cheering Letter of thanks for it (with two *braw* American Books, as a present), and bids me go on in God's name, for in remotest nooks, in distant ends of the Earth, men *are* listening to me and loving me. This Letter, which did me a real benefit, and will give you (the Philosopher's Mother) great pleasure, shall be sent to you: I would send it to-day, but that I fear the frank will be already too heavy. The vain clatter of fools, either for or against, is worth *nothing*, for indeed it *is* simply nothing : but the hearty response of

[1] Emerson.

earnest men, of one earnest man, is very precious. Meanwhile I employ all my days in getting ready for the new Book (on the French Revolution), and think, if I am spared with health, there is likelihood that it will be in print, with my name to it, early in spring. I will do my very best and truest; give me your prayers and hopes! This task of mine takes labour enough: I am up once or twice weekly at the British Museum for Books about it; these are almost my only occasions of visiting that fiercely tumultuous region of the city, which is at least four miles from me. I walk slowly up the shady side of the streets; and come slowly down again, about four o'clock, often smoking a cigar, and feeling more or less independent of all men.

Several of our friends (the Bullers for instance) are gone out of town. We have made, at least Jane has made, a most promising new acquaintance, of a Mrs. Taylor; a young beautiful reader of mine and " dearest friend " of Mill's, who for the present seems " all that is noble " and what not. We shall see how that wears.

We are to dine there on Tuesday. . . . Hunt, nor the Hunts, does not trouble us more than we wish: he comes in when we send for him ; talks, listens to a little music, even sings and plays a little, *eats* (without *kitchen*[1] of any kind, or only with a little sugar) his allotted plate of porridge, and then goes his ways. His way of thought and mine are utterly at variance ; a thing which grieves him much, not me. He accounts for it by my " Presbyterian upbringing," which I tell him always I am everlastingly grateful for. He talks forever about " happiness," and seems to me the very miserablest man I ever sat and talked with. . . .

Coleridge, a very noted Literary man here, of whom you may have heard me speak, died about a week ago, at the age of sixty-two. An Apothecary[2] had supported him for many years: his wife and children shifted elsewhere as they could. He could earn no money, could set himself steadfastly to no painful task ; took to opium and poetic and philosophic dreaming. A better faculty has not been often worse wasted. Yet

---
[1] Condiment.   [2] Mr. James Gillman of Highgate.

withal he was a devout man, and did something, both by writing and speech. Among the London Literaries he has not left his like or second. Peace be with him.

Here then is the end, dear Mother! My kindest brotherly love to *all*, including Jenny; Jane is not here at the moment to add hers, but would grieve much if it were not habitually understood. All good be with you all!—Ever your affectionate Son, T. CARLYLE.

CXXIII.—To Dr. CARLYLE, Naples.[1]

5 GREAT CHEYNE ROW, CHELSEA, LONDON,
15*th* *August* 1834.

MY DEAR BROTHER—How long it is since I wrote last is not accurately in my memory; I know only that your last Letter has been in my hands, and indeed in my Mother's (to whom it was forthwith sent) above a fortnight; and that *my* last, which was all that remained due when you wrote, must be fairly digested by this time; so that now, on a day of leisure, another may

---

[1] Parts of this letter are given in Froude's *Life*, ii. 446-450, but with many notable errors and omissions.

be fitly despatched. The news of your welfare, your *Seelen-bekenntnisse*, your trustful brotherly affection: all this is ever one of the most solacing items of my lot. To address you in return, and impart my satisfaction and anxieties, with the assurance of having them heartily sympathised in, is also one of my agreeablest employments. Would you were here again! But May is coming, and with it flowers. By God's blessing you will be restored to us; not to wander, we will hope, any more.

There came a Letter from Alick very shortly after mine to you was sent away. All is in the usual way in Annandale; for we have heard again only yesterday from Mrs. Welsh who had seen Jean and Jenny at Dumfries: nay this moment, since I began to write, the Dumfries Newspaper arrives with the mark of safety on it. Alick represents our Mother as moving about a good deal on Harry, and keeping her health very tolerably: she does not seem altogether *hefted* yet, he says, at Scotsbrig: however, the new Daughter-in-law seems to be a reasonable young woman, well-disposed to do the best for all parties there : till a new Whitsunday at least there can nothing go very far wrong among them. Jamie and she, it would appear, are still fond as turtle-doves, and prolonging their honeymoon. . . . As for Alick himself, he writes in the middle of a wet abundant hay-harvest, and dates on two successive Sundays : he has signified by Letter to his Catlinns Landlord that unless they abate him £20 of the rent, he cannot keep the Farm longer than Whitsunday ; and so waits, in a kind of confusing uncertainty, the slow issue ; forecasting rather that he will *go*. I am sorry for Alick : he has a heavy burden to bear, and toils at it rather impetuously than steadfastly. There is much wisely-suppressed energy in him too ; but he feels, in general, that he is not in his sphere ; and has internally only an artificial kind of composure. . . .

As for myself, I go on here almost without adventure of any kind. All of us have tolerable health : Jane generally better than before ; I certainly not worse, and now more in the ancient accustomed fashion. I am diligent with the Showerbath; my pilgrimages to the Museum and on other Town-errands keep me in walking enough; once or twice weekly, on an evening, Jane and I stroll out along the Bank of the River, or about "the College," and see white-shirted Cockneys in their green canoes, or old Pensioners pensively smoking tobacco. I long much for a *hill*, but unhappily there is no such thing; only knolls, and these with difficulty, are attainable. The London street tumult has become a kind of marching music to me: I walk along, following my own meditations, without thinking of it. Company comes in desirable quantity, not deficient, not excessive, and there is talk enough from time to time: I myself however, when I consider it, find the whole all-too *thin*, unnutritive, unavailing, and that I am *alone* still under the high vault. All London-born men without exception seem to me narrow-built, considerably perverted men, rather fractions of a man. Hunt, by nature a *very* clever man, is one instance; Mill, in quite another manner, is another. These and others continue to come about me, as with the cheering sound of temporary *music*, and are right welcome so: a higher co-operation will perhaps somewhere else or sometime hence disclose itself.

> "There was a Piper had a Cow
> And he had nought to give her;
> He took his pipes and play'd a spring
> And *bade the Cow consider!*"[1]

Allan Cunningham was here two nights ago; very friendly, very full of Nithsdale, a pleasant *Naturmensch*. Mill gives me logical developments of *how* men act (chiefly in Politics); Hunt tricksy devices, and crotchety whimsicalities on the same theme: *what* they act is a thing neither of them much sympathises in, much seems to know. I sometimes long greatly for Irving, for the old Irving of fifteen years ago: nay the poor actual gift-of-tongues Irving has seemed desirable to me; and I have actually, as you shall hear, made my way through to him again. We dined with Mrs.

---

[1] The next verse supplies the meaning:

> "The Cow considered wi' hersel',
> That music ne'er wad fill her:
> Gie me a pickle pease strae
> And sell your wind for siller."

(Platonica) Taylor and the Unitarian Fox (of the *Repository*, if you know it), one day: Mill also was of the party, and the Husband, an obtuse most joyous-natured man, the pink of social hospitality. Fox is a little thickset bushy-locked man of five-and-forty, with bright sympathetic-thoughtful eyes (the whole face reminded me of Æneas Rait's, compressed, and well buttressed out into broadness), with a tendency to pot-belly, and *snuffiness:* from these hints you can construe him; the best *Socinian Philosophist* going, but not a whit more. I shall like well enough to meet the man again; but I doubt he will not me. . . . We walked home however, even Jane did, all the way from the Regent's Park, and felt that we had done a duty. For me, from the Socinians, as I take it, *wird Nichts*. Here too let me wind up the Radical-Periodical Editorship,[1] which your last Letter naturally speculates on. Mill I seem to discern has given it to this same Fox (who has just quitted his Preachership, and will, like

[1] Editorship of the short-lived *London Review*, founded by Sir William Molesworth, merged in 1836 with the *Westminster*.

myself be out on the world); partly I should fancy by Mrs. Taylor's influence, partly as himself thinking him the safer man. *Ebbene!* I can already picture to myself the Radical Periodical, and even prophesy its destiny: with myself it had not been so; the only thing certain would have been difficulty, pain and contradiction; which I should probably have undertaken; which I am far from breaking my heart that I have missed. I may mention too that Mill is so taken with the *Diamond Necklace*, he in a covert way offered the other night to print it at his own expense, if I would give it him, that he might have the pleasure and profit of reviewing it! Mill likes me well; and on his embarrassed face when Fox happened to be talked of, I read both that Editorship business, and also that Mill had *known* my want of it; which latter was all that I desired to read. As you well say, disappointment on disappointment only simplifies one's course; your possibilities become diminished, your choice is rendered easier. In general I bate no jot of confidence in myself and in my cause.

Nay it often seems to me as if the extremity of suffering, if such were appointed me, might bring out an extremity of energy as yet unknown to myself. God grant me faith; clearness and peaceableness of heart! I make no other prayer.

As to Literary work there is still no offer made that promises to bring in a penny; though I foresee that probably such will come, and, as they often do, all in a rush. Mill will want if his Fox concern go on; nay poor Heraud was here the other day endeavouring to bespeak me for a Periodical of his; for even he is to have a dud of a Periodical. Cheeriest and emptiest of all the sons of men! Yet in his emptiness, as in that of a dried bladder, he keeps triumphantly jingling his Coleridgean long-gnawed metaphysical cherry-stones, and even "makes a kind of martial music" for himself thereby. I do not remember that I ever met a more ridiculous-harmless froth-lather of a creature in all my travels. He lets you tumble him hither and thither, and cut him in two as you like; but in the cheerfullest way joins again, and is brisk froth-lather as before. One should surely learn by him.—The *Diamond Necklace*, I should have told you, has been refused by Moxon: shall I *let* Mill print it? I do not know, and really hardly care. As to Moxon I reckon that we are not only done with *this*, but with *all*, and need not for the present come into contact again. . . . [Fraser] has finished *Teufelsdröckh*, and paid me for it instantly (in all, £82 : 1s.); and got me 58 perfect copies (really readable pamphlets of 107 pages, and all made up without break), which I was yesterday despatching far and wide from his shop. Some twenty copies yet remain, which I am in no haste to dispose of. . . . The Book is worth little, now that I see it; yet not worth nothing, and will perhaps amuse you. I rejoice heartily in having done with it.—My grand task, as you already know, is the *French Revolution;* which, alas, perplexes me much. More *Books* on it, I find, are but a repetition of those before read; I learn nothing or almost nothing further by Books: yet am I as far as possible from understanding it. *Bedenklichkeiten* of all kinds environ me.

To be *true* or not to be true? there is the risk. And then, to be *popular* or not to be popular? that too is a question that plays most complexly into the other. We shall see, we shall try : *Par ma tête seule!*—Before quitting this of Literature, I must tell you, among numberless discouragements, of two most encouraging messages I have had. The first is from an unknown Irishman from Cork, or rather in Cork :[1] did I tell you of him before? The second is from that American Craigenputtock friend of ours,[2] from whom there came a Letter and Books lately. Both the two, in the most authentic and credible though exaggerated manner, cry out Εὖγε! for which I am heartily obliged to them. It is in regard to *Teufelsdröckh*, and they both make their objections too. The day of small things! For which, however, one cannot but be thankful. And so enough of my endeavourings and my cares and little pleasures : my good Jack has now as clear a view of [us] all as in a single sheet he could expect. We may say in the words of the Sansculotte Deputy writing to the

[1] Father O'Shea.   [2] Emerson.

Convention, of the progress of right principles: *Tout va bien ici*, LE PAIN MANQUE! Jane and I often repeat this with laughter. But in truth we live very cheap here (perhaps not much above £50 a year dearer than at Puttock), and so can hold out a long while independent of chance. Utter poverty itself (if I hold fast by the faith) has no terrors for me, should it even come.

I told you I had seen Irving. It was but yesterday, in Newman Street, after *four* prior ineffectual attempts. William Hamilton, who with his wife[1] was here on Saturday, told me Irving had grown worse again, and Mrs. Irving had been extremely ill: he too seemed to think my Cards had been withheld. Much grieved with this news I called once more on Monday: a new failure. Yesterday I went again with an unsuppressible indignation mixed with my pity: after some shying, I was admitted! Poor Irving! he lay there on a sofa, begged my pardon for not rising; his Wife, who also did not and probably could not well

[1] A sister of Mrs. Irving.

rise, sat at his feet, and watched all the time I was there, miserable, haggard. . . . Irving once lovingly ordered her away; but she lovingly excused herself, and sat still. He complains of biliousness, of a pain at his right short-rib; has a short thick cough which comes on at the smallest irritation. Poor fellow! I brought a short gleam of old Scottish laughter into his face, into his voice, and that too set him coughing. He said it was the Lord's will; looked weak, dispirited, partly embarrassed. He continues toiling daily, though the Doctor (Darling) says, rest only can cure him. Is it not mournful, hyper-tragical? There are moments when I determine on sweeping in upon all Tongue-work and Martindoms and accursed choking Cobwebberies, and snatching away my old best Friend, to save him from Death and the Grave! It seems too likely he will die there. At lowest I will go again soon and often: I cannot think of it with patience.

. . . Mrs. Welsh was up at Craigenputtock; it looks all very wild, and made her greet "*not that we were gone*": she had escorted thither a certain Indian friend who has (through M'Diarmid) taken the shooting, with right to *lodging*, for £10 a year: old Nanny M'Queen pays us other £10 for the Park and right of living in the House, with charge of taking care of it, and admitting any decent "gunner body" of that kind. Both sums I believe will be faithfully paid; and old Nanny is said to be the carefullest of women.... —Alas the paper is quite done. Attend me on the margins.—

I have not said a word about Italy; for indeed, my dear Brother, except you there is nothing there that my thought turns upon; and your position has in it the happy monotony (happy for your friends) of one at rest. Well do I understand those meditations of yours, those goings forth into the uttermost shores of being, those soundings into dim depths. Indulge not too much in them. For the rest, rejoice always that you have found footing; prepare yourself not only to stand on it, but to build on it. I wish much you had some more decisive occupation; but such is not appointed yet for a time. Meanwhile you are *not* idle, you are active as the scene allows; many future years, I trust, will be the better for this leisure. Have you *any* company? Tell me whom. Give me descriptions of them, and "how they *ack i' the vaarious pleaces.*"[1]—Do you know Thorwaldsen at Rome personally? This Rennie[2] seems to be intimate with him, and to love him well: he has cut a head of him, and has it here: the head of a man of energy and sensibility, with a *nose* of most honest simplicity. Go and see him, and try to get speech of him: a man of genius is always the best worth conferring with.

. . . Jane who is not very well this particular day sends you her sisterly love. She takes well with Chelsea, and seems to be cheerfuller than she was wont. And so, my dear Brother, here must I end. *Gehab' dich wohl; leb' heiter; lieb' mich.* May all good things be with you. —I must to Charing Cross where the Post is still open. *Felicissima notte!*—Ever your faithful Brother, T. C.

[1] Cumberland pronunciation.
[2] Mr. George Rennie, sculptor, and for a short time M.P., mentioned in *Reminiscences*, i. p. 70.

CXXIV.—To ALEXANDER CARLYLE, Catlinns.

GREAT CHEYNE ROW, CHELSEA,
28th August 1834.

... You are too indignant against Destiny : it is a fault of my own too ; in which my example has perhaps harmed you ; yet a sore fault it is, as I see more and more. Not Pride (from which that indignation, if we examine it, arises) but Humility, the *humbling* and down-pulling of that same Pride, is the lesson *we are to be taught*. Happy for us if we can learn it ; and so with wise submissiveness " bear our cross," whatever that may be, and *skirt* many an obstacle which we cannot *mount* over, which we would so fain *hurl* from us (were the arms strong enough) and utterly destroy ! Finally, my dear Brother, call, from the depths of your heart, on God to help you, to guide you in the way, for it is not in man to guide himself; and so with your eye on fixed heavenly loadstars, walk forward fearing nothing—for Time or for Eternity. Nothing! There is *work* on God's wide Earth for all men that He has made with hands and hearts ; and we, by His blessing, will seek it, and find it, should we go to the Transatlantic grass-plains for it. And so here will I end. You do not object to my advisings and moralisings ; you know that the feeling they spring from is of the deepest : I know you ponder what I say beyond what it deserves ; and, in any case, are cheered to consider that you have an elder Brother who in no chance or change can cease to sympathise with your weal or woe, and help you if it be in his ability. Forward then ! Steady and strong ! . . .

CXXV.—To his MOTHER, at Dumfries.

CHELSEA, LONDON, 1*st September* 1834.

MY DEAR MOTHER—It is long since I have been so much delighted with anything as I was with your affectionate, good-humoured, excellent little Letter: indeed, I think it was one of the blithest moments it gave me that I have had since I left you. Now at last I can fancy that I shall not want for Letters ; you, with the matter in your own hand, will duly think of my necessities in that way, and may at all times be depended on for punctuality. For I calculate that "having put your hand to the plough" you *will not* in any wise draw back! No, no. Let them rule you a piece of paper, or, what were better, make you a set of permanently ruled *lines*, and then, with a pen and an ink-bottle, you can at any moment tell me your own story independent of any one: were it nothing but "half a drop" it will be welcomer to me than any whole drop, or whole *flood*, that can come from any other quarter. You speak with so much hope and kindliness about everything, and take with such a cheerful patience all the changes appointed you (of which in late years there have been enough and too many), and ever are found waiting to welcome the new time, and make the most of it, with glad submission to the will of Him that appointed it, —I confess, my dear Mother, you might be a lesson and a wholesome reproof to the best of us. May the Father of all be thanked that it is so well with you! Nay, while He gives you that spirit, it can never be ill with you. Whatever can betide, for Time or for Eternity, is not

He there, the All-powerful, but also the All-loving, All-pitying!

I have endeavoured, from your description, and Jean's former one, to picture out your two Scotsbrig Rooms, with the red curtains and the new window; and fancy that in the pleasant season you will be very *braw* and not uncomfortable: when the winter comes, as it is fast doing, you must keep a good fire; and if the weather detain you from stirring out, yet I know your hand will not lie idle; and with work to do, one need not weary. Let me find you well, dear Mother, when I come back. And if I bring you a good *new Book* in my hand, will not you have that *new plaid dressing-gown*[1] ready for me! . . .

CXXVI.—To Dr. CARLYLE, Rome.

CHELSEA, LONDON, 21*st September* 1834.

MY DEAR BROTHER— . . . On the 16th August, there was a Letter in my Mother's own hand, which gratified me extremely: it is

[1] See *ante*, p. 157.

short, and in the heart of one from Jean ; I
think I will copy it for you :

"DEAR SON—After long and regretted silence, I may
thank you for your kind attention. You ask how we go on
at Scotsbrig: I am happy to say we do very well; they
are very kind to me, and Jamie rejoices to see us agree so
well. My health is better than when you saw me last. We
have shifted the large bed, and dyed the curtains red; they
are also up. We are putting a window in the little bedroom where I stay. Be easy in your mind as to me.
Commit me to the care of the Great Shepherd, who careth
for all that trust in Him. May He enable us all to cast
all our cares on Him alone for time and for eternity, and
seek His direction in all our undertakings. If so, I hope
well of your French Revolution and all other matters. May
we therefore endeavour through His strength alone to act.
—Peter Austin was in since I began to write : poor Glen
is no otherwise. Peter has been down with bark, the last
of it but one load: the wood is all gone long ago, as you
will have heard, without sending for the neighbours"
(alluding to Peter's greed about the Craigenputtock wood-
weedings). "What is Jane doing? I think she promised
to write me. I think I see her on the deck waving her
hand. I confess I was afraid. What reason of thankfulness have we that you got through all so well! Give my
best love to John when you write to him : he says much
about faith; tell him to seek diligently after the Author
and Finisher of it; and may we all have that faith that
worketh by love and purifies the heart. Let us pray for
each other; and though separated for a time let us try
to meet at God's throne of grace, where we are all welcome
with our most enlarged petitions. I had a thousand such

things to say; but let us both hope and quietly wait. I had a letter from Mr. Church, Kirkchrist, with the magazines with many thanks: I was to tell the Doctor, but this you will do for me. You will see by Jean's I came direct from Mary's, and left them well. Pardon mistakes.—Harry is plump and does well. 'Nothing more but half a drop.' —Your affectionate, MOTHER."

This is the whole Letter; written in a cramp but distinct hand, and with hardly any other difference than that of certain punctuations. The little piece, in its humble clearness, its genuine cheerful faith, and affection and simplicity, will speak more to you than some volumes. May God long preserve to us such a Mother; and make her declining days bright with a light which passeth not away! . . .

CXXVII.—To his MOTHER.

5 CHEYNE ROW, CHELSEA,
23d October 1834.

MY DEAR MOTHER— . . . In the meantime, I sit busy at my Book, which is the only thing I have any business to think of at present: it goes along not so badly; I have three little chapters of it fairly done, and so the *rusty wheel* is in motion; and I ought to think that like "a begun turn," it is half ended. When once I get fairly afloat in work, I do not care a farthing for all the obstructions of this Devil's den of a world, were it twice as bad. Thou too, as I say to myself, hast a small fraction of a gift: God has given it thee, the Devil shall not take it away! Unfortunately I cannot now run over to Scotsbrig, when I have got a little job done: but you see, I write; which is the next best; and by and by I *shall* run over too, and meet you again (if the good Providence permit), and tell you a whole bag of news. There is plenty of work here for me; and hundred thousands of more feckless characters than I make a living of it too: so I whistle up Johnny o' Cox, and fear nothing. They may use my poor *Revolution* well or ill, or not notice it at all if they like that better: it is a very indubitable fact that no service God meant me to do *can* remain undone; and should one not "learn therewith to be content." Jane rather fancies, however, that this will prove a more readable kind of Book: it shall be the best I, in these circumstances, can make it; and then if the people like to read it, we shall wish them great profit of it. . . . I am afraid, you make nothing or very little of *Teufelsdröckh*; which however I am very glad to know that you have got. . . . Do the best you can with it! Take it any way as a token of my love. By and by you shall get this "more readable" one.

Our friends now are all coming back: we were at Mrs. Austin's lately (who had been in Jersey, France, etc., and returns as affectionate as ever); we had Mill long last night; have seen the Cunninghams, etc. etc. We spend the evenings very comfortably without company too; reading for the morrow's writing; or even writing when the *task* is behindhand. The *bield*[1] situation of Chelsea is in our favour now, the October gusts can get no painful hold of us; our weather too has been dry and pleasant (till these late days), better I fear than yours. We see comparatively little of the Hunts for some weeks; they have sickness in

[1] Sheltered.

the house, and many sad cares: poor Hunt himself I think one of the most innocent men I ever saw in man's size; a very boy for clear innocence, though his hair is gray, and his face ploughed with many sorrows. I have met some new people too, not without worth; meet with nothing but regard and kindness from every one. . . . Lastly, we have removed upstairs this day; for I cannot write without fires any longer; and this is a larger room than either *half* of the ground-floor one, where we are obliged to shut the folding-doors in winter time:—so Jane sits here sewing, and I before her (at one of the three windows), and all is as comfortable as it ought. . . .

CXXVIII.—To ALEXANDER CARLYLE, Catlinns.

5 CHEYNE ROW, CHELSEA, LONDON,
24*th October* 1834.

MY DEAR ALICK—It is many a long day since you sent me the *scrape of a pen;* you are in my debt too I believe for one very long Letter (or more?), and still persist in silence. This is not right; though I know writing is a great burden to you, and from day to day some new thing or other is turning up to frustrate the purpose you may form in my behalf that way.—Well! I look for a frank to-day; and will send you this thin memorial of me: whether you answer or not, I shall know that it gives you pleasure, and never doubt that you send me (in heart at least) your thanks and best brotherly wishes.

We have a new winter at our door; all, as I fancy it, has been got under *thatch and rope* about Catlinns; not without an effort, as I often fancied when thinking of you on the wet harvest days. But the thing I have no means even of guessing here is what arrangement you have found, or whether any yet, with your poor needy and greedy landlords. Are you to leave that *Knowe-head* at Whitsunday; or have they lowered your rent so as to make it tolerable and payable? This last is perhaps the way I ought to wish it, so wasteful are all *changes*. However, I am very anxious to know.—In any case, be of good heart, my dear Brother: let no difficulties darken your mind, or beat down the vigorous energy that is in you. "To be *weak* is miserable," says the Poet Milton—*that* is the only misery for a man. I am a poor comforter, for I preach up nothing but toil, toil; yet such is the truth, if we saw it, for all men: and for all genuine men, is there not the sure hope of a *reward?* Persevere, then: "in due time ye shall reap if ye faint not."

What passes with myself here I have mainly described in Letters to my Mother, and others of them, which most probably you have seen. The world looks rough on me, but not hostile; I feel that I shall have labour enough, and what payment I ask from the world: meat and clothes. There is nothing like the *deep sulkiness* of Craigenputtock troubles me here: I see always that I am in the right workshop, had I but got acquainted with the *tools* properly; here I must stand to it; here or nowhere! My Mother will tell you that I am getting on with my new French Book: it is calculated that I ought to have it out about March next (that being what they call "a good time," the Parliament and Fashionables all on the spot): but whether I can keep my day or not will depend somewhat on fortune. I strive to be as diligent as possible in all senses and do my best. You have got the old Puttock *Teufelsdröckh* (I hear), the last I wrote near you; and will prize it on that account, I believe; it is *printed* there you see, and cannot now be burnt or lost; and so if there be any good in it, the world has it; if none there is little harm done. I find strictly *few* to admire it, but then actually a few; and great multitudes to turn up their eyes in speechless amazement.

I saw the fire of the two Parliament Houses; and, what was curious enough, Matthew Allan (of York, you remember) found me out in the crowd there, whom I had not seen for years. The crowd was quiet, rather pleased than otherwise; *whew'd* and whistled when the breeze came as if to encourage it: "there's a *flare-up* (what we call *shine*) for the House o' Lords." —"A judgment for the Poor-Law Bill!"— "There go their *hacts*" (acts)! Such exclamations seemed to be the prevailing ones. A man *sorry* I did not anywhere see.—They will have to build a new house; and it may produce consequences not generally foreseen yet.

Poor Edward Irving is at this moment, I believe, in Glasgow: the accounts I get of him (from William Hamilton) fill me with pain. He is in the worst state of health, and will not rest; threatened with consumption; it now at last begins to seem too likely to me, that the conclusion of all that wild work will be *early death!* Oh dear, what a tragedy is Life to most of us; often to those that seemed the luckiest! I know not what to do in this matter of poor Irving, and can for the present do nothing but grieve.

Alas, my dear Brother, here is the end of the Paper! There will be more franks going soon, and I shall afford you better measure.—Give our love to Jenny:[1] lovingly guide and encourage her in all right ways, as is your duty and engagement.—Little Jane I suppose is become a very "*conversical*" little *kimmer*[2] by this time: even Tom must be beginning to make his observations. Be thankful for them, and yet earnestly anxious: regard them as a gift and a

---

[1] Alick's wife. [2] *Commère*, gossip, companion.

solemn obligation. Write soon. May all good be with you and yours, my dear Brother!—I am ever your affectionate, T. CARLYLE.

CXXIX.—To Mrs. AITKEN, Dumfries.

LONDON, 24*th October* 1834.

MY DEAR SISTER— . . . I was very greatly pleased with the news your goodman so punctually despatched me; pray thank him in my name, and say I wish he would write soon again,—and improve in one particular only: in length. Other fault I have none to find with him. And now let me hope you are continuing to do well, and that poor little Sandy (poor little Newcomer!) complains of nothing hitherto in these strange new quarters he has got into! Poor little fellow! He is a Sandy the Second, or even Sandy the Third, of my acquaintance: may he prove no worse man than his foregoers, and a happier one! His Grandfather of the name had a hard battle to fight, but fought it, too, like a man; and so left the *best* inheritance for those he loved. I am often reminded of him here: there is a queer kind of *sub*-likeness to him in our good neighbour Leigh Hunt,—who also is one of the most elastic, unconquerable, innocent-minded mortals I ever met with.—But tell me how the little fellow gets on, and what he says to it. Very little yet, I fancy; he is too busy considering what a singular concern it is.

. . . I depend on you for writing to me, at any rate, if anything go wrong.—Tell me how all is; what James is doing; where his work lies; how he holds out against the spirit of Quackery which is in all trades, in his as well as mine. I wish I were not too far for sending you Books: but 5d. a pound Carriage is too dear for the most of them.— . . . The Parliament fire was noticed out of our back top windows, and I went up to it for two hours. The people had done speaking of it before next day was done: that is their way here. It was but a low confused mass of houses, and did not (the people complained) "make a *good* fire"! "Come now," they said at times when something flamed up, "that's not so bad though!"—Write to us, or make James write. Our best wishes and prayers are always with you, dear Sister.—Your affectionate, T. C.

CXXX.—To his MOTHER, Scotsbrig.

Saturday morning, 25*th* [*October* 1834].

MY DEAR MOTHER—The Frank came yesterday, but dated for to-day; so I finish it out, and take it up to Town with me, as I go to Fraser the Bookseller's to consult about scribbling matters; specially about a Manuscript, which a certain unknown well-wisher of mine in Liverpool has entrusted me with. Manuscripts indeed have been flowing in of late; so that at this time I have no fewer than *four* in my hands. It may be an honour, but is no profit: however, one cannot refuse poor people that petition civilly.

Along with the Frank, Mill sent me a whole pile of new Books, some of them I think almost specially *bought* for me: indeed nothing can exceed the obligingness of Mill; I had already as many Books of his as would load a considerable *cuddy-cart*;[1] all lent me for unlimited

[1] Donkey-cart.

periods ; a perfect outfit for this present enterprise of mine. So I hope, when I write next, it will be that I have got *done* with that " Taking of the Bastille," which is now my next task (or Chapter IV.) : yet it will not be without a hard *tuffle;* for if the reading of a *Shaiptur*[1] be so easy, the writing of one is another matter.

There was no *Examiner* this week ; Hunt bids me tell you that whenever one is missed, there will be *two* next week : he is a much-harassed, confused, poor man ; sits in the middle of a distracted uproar that would make many a one mad. I borrowed an *old* Paper from him, that you might not be altogether disappointed : he sent me one of January last ; ten months old ; which I should think is among the oldest that ever went by post. However, I marked upon it that you were to have a Letter next day. Whenever the two *strokes* are wanting, look strictly in the inside ; you will usually find some word ; though it is a thing I study to avoid when possible. The Newspaper should be at Ecclefechan ready

[1] Chapter.

for you after *Preaching :* but disappointments may occur too, for we are nearly two miles from the Post-office (one close by charges an additional twopence), and if it were a very wild afternoon, one might lurk within doors. . . . Janè has a little headache to-day, and sits reading here: she bids me send her kind affection to you all in the kindest words I can. She makes the breakfast herself (like the Tod running his own errand[1]) of late months, as formerly; and has, as poor Irving said, "always a little bower of elegance round her, be where she will": in truth, a shifty, true, gleg little creature, worth any twenty Cockney wives that I have yet met with.—Now write soon, my dear Mother: for *all* sakes take care of yourself. May the great Father ever bless and guard you! —Your affectionate,   T. CARLYLE.

CXXXI.—To Dr. CARLYLE, Rome.

LONDON, 28*th October* 1834.

MY DEAR BROTHER—About a week ago,

[1] The Tod (fox) runs his own errand best, is a Scotch proverb.—M. C.

your Letter, which had been rather longed for, arrived to make us a happy day; and even now, I daresay, it may be doing similar service at Scotsbrig; for I sent it off thither in a frank, with store of other news, last Saturday. Our Mother was very anxious about you, by reason of that Eruption of Vesuvius, which I had striven, probably with no full success, to convince her, did not much concern you. As you say, if we were not stupid creatures there needed not thunderbolts and volcanic explosions to teach us by what tenure we hold our life! Dangers deep as the Infinite Abyss environ us at all moments; nevertheless, till *our* moment come, we are preserved, and work as if in safety. One other remark I cannot but make, in reference to that fearful death that has passed so near you:[1] it is, How unfair we are in estimating our own lot. What a small though never so hearty joy we feel at this providential escape of yours, compared with what our endless sorrow would have been had the devouring

---

[1] The house in which Dr. Carlyle was living had been struck by lightning.

lightning buried you in that ruin! It is thus everywhere: we *strike our average* far too high, and at best, even if we be "very glad," are seldom "very thankful."—On the whole, however, one feels satisfied to know you fairly out of that Neapolitan Elysium-Tartarus; again safe and lighter of heart in a scene that you are more at home with: let us hope that your next great movement will be northward, across the Alps and sea, hither to Cheyne Row and Annandale! Meanwhile I need not exhort you again to do whatever you possibly can (for I know you are doing it) towards getting some professional occupation for your spare hours at Rome: there is no way in which one would like so well to know you employed, both for your present satisfaction and future interests. Never (as I have long felt) till a man get into practical contact with the men round him, and learn to take and give influence there, does he enjoy the free consciousness of his existence. Alas I have long felt this, and felt it in vain. Nevertheless there is a kind of inextinguishable hope in me that it *shall not* always be so; that once, for some short season, I shall live before I die. With you the prospect is much nearer and surer: if not at Rome, this winter, then here in England, say next winter, you shall actually try what force is in you to work in your vocation. The difficulties for us both, as we often admit, are great; but we will front them resolutely, and by God's grace they shall not conquer us. At lowest and worst, you have still reading, the power of study, reflection and observation to fill your winter with. The great thing is to take care of the *hours*, the *months* will take care of themselves. If there is anything still in Rome that you have not mastered according to your wants, think that you may not have another opportunity there. All this of Art, Pictures, Architecture, and so forth, I feel, were most sapless provender for my poor soul at present: at the same time I see more and more that there *is* something in all that; an indisputable element of our modern existence; which I could still wish (and some years ago could have much more passionately wished) to understand and make mine. On the whole, dear Doctor, I will give you up to your good genius; adding only my hopes, especially my wishes and prayers, which you always have. I like to hear of your Journal: there is always a benefit in that; were it only that in writing down things we are forced to think of them more distinctly. Go on, in all true ways, and prosper!

With regard to our British affairs, take the comfort of knowing that all is much as it was; and nothing worse than that. . . . As to London, the only news with us is that the new *Book* is fairly under way, and doing not so badly. The first three Chapters are finished; and now there is a kind of pause for a day or two before I start with the fourth, which may be headed "*Taking of the Bastille*"*!* One knows not well what to think of so singular an attempt as it is; for though studying rather zealously to avoid cramp phrases and all needless cause of offence, I feel at every sentence that the work will be strange; that it either must be so, or be nothing but another of the thousand-and-one "Histories," which are so many "dead thistles for Pedant-chaffinches to peck at and fill their crops with;" a kind of thing I for one wish to have no hand in. Jane rather thinks "it will do." So I struggle along with the best heart I may; and will, if possible, have the thing out in the course of spring. For the present I am busy reading all manner of Memoirs of Mirabeau; especially a late large work by a natural son ("*fils adoptif*") of his. If they have it in Rome (4 volumes are already out), you too might find it interesting. Mill got it, I may almost say bought it, for me, the other day: he is, as always, the most helpful of Book-providers (I have some hundred and fifty volumes of his even now!), and really seems to take a pleasure in assisting me. The *Diamond Necklace*, Fraser, after reading it, thinks ought *not* to be published till after the other; a judgment I rather agree with; though poor Mill, who had set his heart on "reviewing" it, is obliged to express the most tragi-comical regret.... As for *Teufelsdröckh*, I think he rather meets with approbation and recognition in his bound up shape: had the thing come out as a Book, it might perhaps have done something; yet, after all, so questionable a production is probably "just as well" in its actual middle-state of published and unpublished; it cannot be *lost* now, by fire or accident; afflicts nobody, and is ready if ever wanted.—The business of Literature (which indeed while occupied writing, I think little about, and care almost nothing for) looks not as yet more motherly *nutritive* upon me than it did. I think, if ever I am to live by it, I must have some vehicle of my own, and a public of my own: poor Leigh Hunt, with a three-halfpenny Journal, gets (as I understand) "eight guineas a week"; which for me were Potosi wages. The Chancellor is going to take off stamps. We must see about it by and by. A most questionable enterprise! But if the Ishmael is cast forth into the Desert, with bow and quiver, in his coat of wild skins, shall he not *shoot* such game as there is? Depend upon it, he must and will! In the meantime his task (and let that suffice him) is this *Book* of his: forward, and be done with that. *Das Weitere wird sich zeigen, sich geben.*

We are not without society here, from time to time; but still it is not of the rightly profitable sort. The men I want to see are such as could give me some glimpse of practical insight into the road I have to travel; of all which there is yet too little going. Indeed, many with any sense, or insight into anything, are singularly rare in this world: one ought ever to be thankful for "the day of small things"! Mill and one or two of his set are, on the whole, the reasonablest people we have: however we see them seldom (being so far off, etc.); and Mill himself, who were far the best of them all, is greatly occupied of late times with a set of quite opposite character, which the Austins and other friends mourn much and fear much over. . . . Fox the Socinian, and a flight of really wretched-looking "friends of the species," who (in writing and deed) struggle not in favour of Duty being *done*, but against Duty of any sort almost being *required*. A singular creed this; but I can assure you a very observable one here in these days: by me "deeply hated as the GLAR, which is its colour (*die seine Farbe ist*)," and substance likewise mainly. Jane and I often say: "Before all mortals, beware of a friend of the species!" Most of these people are very indignant at marriage and the like; and frequently indeed are obliged to divorce their own wives, or be divorced: for though the *world* is already blooming (or is one day to do it) in everlasting "happiness of the greatest number," these people's own *houses* (I always find) are little Hells of improvidence, discord, unreason. Mill is far above all that, and I think will not sink in it; however, I do wish him fairly far from it, and though I cannot speak of it directly would fain help him out: he is one of the best people I ever saw, and—surprisingly attached to *me*, which is another merit. Hunt is also a "friend of the species," but we make an exception of him; though nowise of the Doctrine as held by him: indeed I find my Cameronian rigour, and denouncement of all paltering, poltroonery and "crying for the want of *taffy*" has quite scared him into seclusion; and he comes now only some once in the fortnight, and gives us really a most musical evening (for he is far the most ingenious creature I speak with here), concentrating many visits into one: I never in my whole life met with a more innocent childlike man; transparent, many-glancing, really beautiful, were this Lubberland or Elysium, and not Earth and England. His family also are innocent. . . . We get no harm from them, and some little good. God help him and them! is our hearty prayer for them.—Allan Cunningham and his Wife come down, at long intervals; were here lately in the Scotch "fore-supper" style: good people in their kind, and friendly to us; incapable of close sympathy. I have mentioned Eastlake,[1] and that I saw him at Rennie's. The man (very inquisitive about Goethe, and otherwise intelligent and courteous) had rather pleased me: some three weeks ago a Mr. Cockerell[2] (an Architect, Brother-in-law of Rennie) came down very unexpectedly to ask me to meet

[1] Afterwards Sir Charles, and P.R.A.
[2] Author of the sumptuous volume on *The Temples of Jupiter at Ægina, and of Apollo at Bassæ*, in folio, London, 1860.

him again. My rule being to meet all honest persons, I went. . . . Eastlake is a man turned of forty, with bushy eyebrows and hazel eyes that have a glow in them : the rest of his face and figure is sympathetic-precise rather than better ; a rational man, raised a little above commonplace, and yet not far above it : I mean to see more of him. . . . The Austins are come home again and Hayward (the *Faust* translator, become *ein und etwas* rather suddenly) : we saw them all in full blow lately, talk without end, happiness, admiration (of Mrs. Jameson, and the "swarm that came out with the Annuals," as Mrs. Cunningham called that sort); and had occasion again to envy the "happiness of Commonplace;" not to say *le bonheur des sots*, for that were too strong here. These are all our associates I will hint at : are there not enough ? . . . T. CARLYLE.

CXXXII.—To his MOTHER, Scotsbrig.

CHELSEA, 20*th November* 1834,
Thursday night.

MY DEAR MOTHER—You are not to take this

for a Letter, but for a mere *off-put:* I am not getting the *Bastille* taken so readily as I expected; so having seen Buller to-day I begged a frank from him merely to say that we were all well, and that I *would* write. It will serve to keep your kind heart quiet about us, which may, not improbably, be disposed to misgivings in such bitter November weather.

The *Book* continues to form my grand occupation: sometimes I incline to fancy that it will prove not so bad a Book; at other times, it looks poor enough: but in either case, I *persevere*, and study to remember your old precept at the shearing: "If it were never so little *it'll no loup*[1] *in again.*" I have a great deal of reading to go through, and little arrangements to make about it, which consume time: but on the whole "one must just do the best he can." . . .

How are you doing in windy Scotsbrig, when it is so cold in *lown*[2] Chelsea? Many a time I think, If you have a good fire, and are keeping yourself snug within doors? Had one

---
[1] Leap.   [2] Windless, sheltered.

but the little magical glass the Fairy Tales speak of, whereby one could at any moment *see* those he loved, though never so distant! But I suppose, it is better as we are.

Our friends are all come back again, and there are meetings and conversings and callings enough. Mrs. Austin has introduced Jane to a very excellent-looking Scotch lady, who lives close by: a Mrs. Somerville, distinguished in the Literary world (very strangely for a woman) as a *Mathematician*. Far better than that, she seems to have a real fund of mother-wit, good sense and good principle: her husband is Surgeon to the Chelsea Hospital (comes from Kelso, she I believe from Fife); she is a woman turned of fifty, and has seen troubles, and seems to have learned from them. I hope she will be a small acquisition to Jane, who has little sympathy with the *flaffing* ways of the Cockney women, and does not esteem many of them much. . . .

Charles Buller is one of the sensiblest people I see : . . . [he] is going to make himself notable as the most decisive of Radicals: he has come forward with most abundant *promptitude* on this new occasion ; is to be President of a Public Meeting to-morrow night, to which I undertook to go as a dumb spectator (being curious to see such a thing) and probably shall go. You are likely to hear something of it in next *Examiner*. This grand change of Ministry appears to be taken very quietly here ; rather with surprise as to what it means, or how it will go on, than with any other feeling. For myself I am sorry about it, as about most *changes :* there will likely be a new Election of Parliament, the whole country thrown again into ferment; and as for the *ultimate* issue, Providence alone can foresee it. That it may well end in mischief, nay, in confusion worse than the Duke dreams of is but too probable. My work as heretofore lies quite out of it : I am an onlooker merely. God guide it all for the best ; and take pity of the poor blinded sons of men — whose ways the more I look on them the more surprise me. . . .

CXXXIII.—To his MOTHER, Scotsbrig.

CHEYNE ROW, *Monday afternoon*,
[1*st December*] 1834.

MY DEAR MOTHER—Three hours ago came this Letter from our good Doctor; which I know will give you pleasure, the rather as you have been anxiously waiting for it. I will not detain it a moment; but go to Buller, and (if he be at home) perhaps get a frank for it this very night. Jack you will find is all right; and settled for the winter at Rome.

As to myself I have not a moment's time to write; and do not mean to pay my debt to-day. That tough *Bastille* (which I have had work enough with) still holds out; but will be done in two days. There is, after that, another small *Sherra' muir*;[1] and were I over with that, I will treat myself—and you.

For the present, dear Mother, take my assurance that I am well, no less than busy.

[1] Much ado about nothing,—like the battle of Sheriffmuir (fought between Mar and Argyle 13th November 1715), at which no one was killed, and both parties thought they had gained the victory.

Let not your motherly heart be anxious about my health, or anything that concerns me. Depend upon it, I do *not* overwork myself, but study to take it moderately like one that had a *longish* spell of it to do: I am always happiest and best when in the middle of work; provided it will go on with me! Which, indeed, it will not always do. . . .

My dear Mother, you are growing a *capital* writer; positively you need nothing but just to go on, and make me quite independent of all of them: I will tell Jean, by the next frank, to get you a quire of *ruled* paper at Dumfries, and send it out: you may take a whole week over your letter; fill at your leisure, *to the very brim*; and let it be right sure of a welcome! I owe you some long sheets for your last kind little one; which I have still in my breast pocket, and make much of. What a blessing that there is such a thing as writing; that you have learned to write!

I went to Buller's Radical Meeting, and was greatly amused by it. The people were in deep earnest: some two thousand of them, mostly industrious-looking men, the better kind of operatives; many of them under thirty. The murmur of their assent or dissent, above all the kind of *bark* (what we Annandale people call a *goust* or *gollie*) coming from two thousand voices, at any sound or mention of Toryism and its insults, was grand to hear. It was bitter earnest with them; not so with me, who came thither as a mere onlooker, and did not care much which way it went. Toryism or Radicalism, it seems to me all things are going *to the howe pot*;[1] whether to-morrow or the day after is small concern. God is above all, and will work His own wise Purpose with it;—and support and save those who are worthy. I only hope, they will not get to absolute *breaking of crowns*; which indeed seems a thing no one apprehends.—In Wellington's shoes I would not willingly be: he thinks to rule Britain like a drill-sergeant; but will find it not answer. As bonny a man I have seen before now lose his head in such a business. God pity him, and all!

Plenty of company is here now; and in the

[1] Equivalent to the bottomless pit.

cool weather (which is wonderfully clear and dry) I can take long walks. Mill speaks of some [arrange]ment for sending me a daily Paper he gets: in that case, when [anything] special occurs, I can send you a Number. I fear you are short of good reading, when you take to poor *Schiller* a second time: tell me if you are. It were easy to make a better effort to get more for you, even from this distance. I could write to Ben Nelson to give you *share of his share* in the Annan Library: I believe he would do it at once with pleasure. Tell me, if it would be useful. There are stores of good reading there.

My own poor *French Revolution* struggles on as you see. It will keep me all winter: but if the people "read it when it is *irwitten*," or if it be worth reading, we will not complain. Mill's new Periodical is to go on; and I shall get work there if I want it: but for the present I rather *hold back*, till I see what sort of fellows they prove; what sort of terms they will offer me. I have much to learn here (for it is a most confused singular world this); but it is good that I have come to learn it: I feel no doubt but I shall *swim* in the water, did I once know the currents of it. *None,* when I see what *wights* are swimming! Fear nothing.

I have almost filled my sheet; for I could not send it away vacant: I fear I shall thereby lose the Post for this night; but Buller at any rate had little chance to be in. I will have tea, and then try him. It is four miles off; but I did not walk to-day on purpose for that. Goodnight, dear Mother! I see you in the Scotsbrig two rooms, with the gurly winds about you; but, I hope too, a little comfortable *black teapot* (a *witch* one) on the hob; and kind thoughts to your children that are far or near, and assurance that they send you the like. When will you write to me? I myself will not be long. Our kind love to Jamie and his Dame, to Mary, Jean and them all.—Ever your affectionate,

T. CARLYLE.

CXXXIV.—To his MOTHER, Scotsbrig.

CHELSEA, LONDON, 24*th December* 1834.

MY DEAR MOTHER— . . . Never was finer

winter weather than we have had here; hardly a drop of rain, hardly a day of *blustering*, and now it is the finest frost. We are come up-stairs now (into my writing room), which is warmer and cheerier: the under apartment is *two* rooms, with folding doors for making them into *one*, and answers best in summer. This is really a fine spacious place; as broad as your Scotsbrig big room, and somewhat longer; all lined with wainscot; a curiously carved mantelpiece, quite a venerable-looking old piece of *sufficiency;* with three windows, looking to the south-west, over the street, into potherb gardens, then houses, and (when the wind is blowing) *clear* blue sky. There are houses here, let at £300 a-year, not intrinsically better than this, or so good. . . .

I am fighting away at my Book; have got the *Bastille* all comfortably laid flat; and am *determined* (alas, I fear in vain!) to have my *First Section* finished on Saturday night. My progress is slower than I expected, and the work grows on my hands; so that I fear I must make two volumes of it. But if the quality be not *bad*, that will be no disadvantage.

We must "do the best we *can*." Do not fear my *over*working myself: I am very regular; get breakfast about nine; work till two; then go walking till *four;* and after dinner seldom work more, except reading and the like. The populous roads, parks and streets are very amusing to walk on: such a bustling flood of life. I have got me a *cloak* (of brown cloth, with fur neck), a most comfortable article, in which I walk, in sharpest weather, as warm as a pie: I have also a new hat; and on Friday morning am to have a new frock-coat (of very dark "rifle-green"): really a most smart man!—Poor Jane has got her foot burnt; the maid poured boiling water on it instead of into the coffee-pot, and so the poor Dame sits prisoner; but is getting better. Our maid, who accomplished this feat, is the best-natured, most laborious of *Pluisters*;[1] whom, after all, we reckon far better than a thief or *swingler*,[2] as many of them are.

No more to-night, dear Mother! I will soon write again; nay, perhaps still add a word

[1] Slatterns.   [2] Swindler (Yorkshire form of the word).

on the cover. Good be with you, dear Mother! —Your affectionate   T. CARLYLE.

CXXXV.—To Mrs. AITKEN, Dumfries.

5 CHEYNE ROW, CHELSEA, LONDON,
28th January 1835.

MY DEAR SISTER—I have been in your debt for a Letter, which came most acceptably, and which I did not at the time mean to owe you for so long: my delay, as I hope you have never doubted, arose from occupation, from want of news, from anything but want of care about you. I have an evening to myself just now, and, as I can hope also for a frank, you shall have the benefit of such opportunity.

It gave us great satisfaction to hear that you were safe, and had realised a little Boy, of whom we have learnt since from various quarters to entertain a hopeful opinion. Nourish up the little Alick with all diligence; that he grow to be a man profitable in his day and generation! Our work in it will be over by and by; and his be beginning. Mrs. Welsh saw you and him and James, and sent us word about it; she subsequently also sent to you for news (she told us), but your own Letter was just coming off. Or perhaps I am confusing all manner of dates here? For the truth is, I have sat so chained to my writing-table these many weeks; that much of the outer world often seems to me almost like a dream.

James, I think, has very likely done well to purchase himself a house. You will find yourself much more comfortable in a "bit *haddin*[1] of your ain for a' that"; indeed, I imagine the house is of itself far better than your present one: besides it tends to give the Goodman a kind of consistency in his Trade; and so I hope every way will turn to good. He has a fair proportion of business, I understand: "the hand of the diligent" had long ago the best word; and even in these times shall not be altogether foiled. I hope all that is favourable of you both; to hear that you live not as fools but as wise: that is the grand blessing for this world and for the next.

As to myself, having already told you of

[1] Holding, house.

sitting over my papers, and struggling with my evil genius there, I have hardly anything more to say that is important. My health stands out very tolerably, though it is the most unwholesome craft: it is true, I am faithful in walking and so forth, and we have generally weather one can walk in. I do not think I ever saw a year with less than *six* times as much rain: this is a far drier climate than yours, and the present season, moreover, has been unusually dry. In other respects, all goes as it was wont, or nearly so. We have a few friends that come about us, and might very easily have more *visitors* if not friends; but find no profit in that: the good are *thin-sawn*[1] everywhere, and perhaps not thicker here than elsewhere, though there are *more* to choose among. The quantity of *folly* in all shapes that one finds here is really amazing. Gabble-gabble in every kind under the sun except the *wise* kind: the reasons are "like two wheat-grains in the bushel of chaff." We must even let it go on, as it has done, and will do; it can, on the whole, "di' tha' naither

[1] Thin-sown.

ill na' guid." At lowest it is my happiness, as it was of that joiner friend of James's (whose name I think was Thomson), that if contradiction is like to drive one mad at any time, one can "take gey guid care; and aye mostly work in *a place by himsel'!*" I, by the nature of the case, mostly aye work in just such a place.—What the fruit of my working[1] is to be we shall not begin to know yet for seven or eight months; or perhaps for not as many years: that is the law of the trade, and one must just abide by it. I do the best I can, and shall pray to be thankful for such reward, or such punishment, as is appointed. One thing alone I am sure of, that if I live I shall *have done* with the weary job;—and then hope for another that may be easier and more profitable. Probably some of them have told you that the thing was growing on my hands, and threatened to become three volumes! I was to be done in February or March; and so, if I have it all fairly off my hands by the end of May I shall think it very tolerable. But *then*

[1] *The French Revolution.*

indeed, if the guiding Powers continue kind, Jack will be coming homewards, and we shall have a *gliff*[1] of Scotland again! It is by toil, and the vanquishing of trouble and obstruction, that man lives here below.

I need not tell you about our Elections and public matters; men have been parading all streets with Election Placards on long poles, or with two *poleless* Placards, one on breast and one on back, fastened with string; others have been busy singing Ballads, hawking Political squibs, etc. etc., of the like purport; to all which, I have said: Behold I have no care for thee! You too, I find, have had the pleasure of an Election, and Sharpe has got once more returned, though with difficulty. It seems to me there are confused times coming; times that cannot be furthersome to peaceable men. For these also, however, one must be ready. Meanwhile, they that are called to mingle in such work are not the enviablest; but rather they that can say to it, Go thou thy way, I go mine.

[1] Glimpse.

Allan Cunningham has been unwell, and I have not seen him for a great while, though often purposing to do it. He lost a brother here in Autumn, and seemed to suffer from it: his wife also has lost a brother resident here. They are *canny* people; of whom one gets, with some good, no chance of hurt. "There is a Dumfries Mason," Jane said, the first time she saw him; "better such, very considerably, than many a Cockney Literary Gentleman!"

My Mother has written me a Letter since yours, with nothing but good news in it. I fear always she leans to the *favourable side*. Your accounts of her way of doing, the look of her rooms, etc., are very interesting to me, and form the best of what picture I have made out respecting it. She says, last time, you had sent her a cake for New-year's gift. That was right. O be good to her: I need not bid you, I do believe. She has been a blessing to us; and, I trust in God, will long continue so. When I look over the world, and see what Mothers and Fathers the average have, I feel thankful for mine.—She said they had been singing at Scotsbrig; "Johnnie o' Cox" was sung too: I am right glad to hear of a song there. But now, *Missus*, I have a commission for you about that. Will you go over to any Stationer's shop, and buy half a quire (12 sheets) of *ruled* Paper (they have it ruled with blue ink, or can soon rule it); or if one has it not, go to another, and on the whole *get* it; and send it to my Mother for writing to me on. She wants nothing but straight lines to write a most sufficient slow hand; and unless you bestir yourself in that way, I see no chance of her securing it. Now will you look to that? See in packing it, that you wrap it well, and if possible lay it *flat* (in some Book if there be such a thing; or between two pasteboards); for otherwise it gets creased, and " becomes unpleasant."

I must write some more letters than this; and will not seal till to-morrow: you shall then have "time of day" again,—unless I am too hurried. We are going to dine with the Bullers, who have all taken up their abode in Town, and are very kindly disposed towards us. It is there that I expect a frank; for there will likely be a Radical Member or two present. Charles is becoming a notable in that department; a *liesh* fellow,[1] were he not so loose in the hinges!—Jane is sitting sewing here; she sends you both her kind New-year's wishes. Be happy in your quiet circle there; be faithful, diligent, undaunted. Love one another; bear one another's burdens: how much is there in that! Alas, we have all our faults, our infirmities, our blindnesses, and have much to forgive and be forgiven. God bless you, dear *Craw!*—Your affectionate Brother,

T. CARLYLE.

[In Mrs. Carlyle's hand.]

Carlyle has the impudence to say he forgot to send his compliments to Jenny, as if it were possible for any one acquainted with that morsel of perfections to *forget* her! Tell her I will write a letter with my own hand; and hope to see her "an ornament to society in every direction."

[1] Brisk, effectual fellow.

CXXXVI.—To ALEXANDER CARLYLE, Catlinns, Lockerbie.

5 CHEYNE ROW, CHELSEA, LONDON,
28*th January* 1835.

MY DEAR ALICK—It is long since I got you written to with any deliberation; I know not how long. I have been so busy; nothing but flying slips of paper, and blotting and scribbling all round me for week after week. However, now for the last eight days, I have been making a sort of pause; occupied only with reading and reflecting: so before falling-to again, I will send you a small word. You may well fancy, judging no doubt by yourself, that I am often, often thinking of you while no writing goes between us: indeed whither should my mind turn, when it has leisure to meditate, if *not* towards Annandale, where so much of my possession in this lower world lies? . . .

My Mother's last letter came the very day I had sent off a hasty scrap to her. The various postscripts and notices contained in that welcome sheet gave me a clear notion of

Scotsbrig, with the winter work you were all busy in: I was particularly glad to hear you had been down shortly before, and that "singing" had been going on among you. Long be the like among us! You cannot imagine how quiet and cheery all that looks from amid the confused din of this Metropolitan Monstrosity! Here, least of all places on Earth's surface, quiet never is; a raging and a roaring; all men hunted or hunting; all things "made like unto a *wheel*"—that turns and turns. I have grown greatly used to it now; and for most part walk the London streets as if they were peopled only with Images, and the noise were that of some Niagara Waterfall, or distracted universal carding-mill. There is something animating in it too; so that in my walks I generally turn Townwards, and go up through a larger or shorter circuit of real London Tumult (hereabouts we are not much noisier than in the stiller parts of Edinburgh, and in *our street* at ten at night and later there is no noise at all): for "man likes to see the face of man;" one's very dispiritment in these peopled spaces is nothing to the gloom of Puttock. My shortest turn (for I have various of various lengths) is to Hyde Park Corner; where I see quality carriages, six-horse waggons (horses all jingling with little bells), mail coaches, etc. etc.; and the Duke of Wellington's House, the windows all barred with iron (since the Reform Bill time), and huge iron railing twenty feet high between him and the street, which, as the railing is lined with wood too, he does not seem to *like:* there are carriages sometimes about his gate now; and I bless myself that I am not he. Let me mention also that a waggoner occasionally passes this door (of Cheyne Row), whose voice to his horses, "wey-ho!" infallibly brings me in mind of one I have heard 300 miles off and more.—Alas, *this* will never do; the sheet almost done!

Has the Catlinns business got itself settled yet? I was very glad to learn that there was some prospect of its soon being settled; and, on the whole, not sorry that you expected they might make it eligible for you to stay there. Staying is always best, if one can stay; there is such waste every way in removing; waste of time, of money, of habit and connections: "three flittings are equal to a fire." But any way you seem to take it in the right mood: that of courage and patient faith. There is no fear in that case. The world is wide, as you say; and there is a Heaven above us go where we will.—Make my respects to little Tom; and have him speaking a mouthful of Annandale Scotch when I come back: Jane I fancy is a strapping *hizzy* by this time, and able to bear her share in any dialogue. Be careful of them, poor Creatures; and above and before all things, study to train them in the way that they should go.

My own history here may be summed up in very few words. I have finished my "First Part," which may possibly make a First Volume; and am about beginning the Second and then the Third. On the whole, I am about *half* done; for a great deal of the stuff is laid in. I shall have a tough struggle however; all the way till the summer be come. Other work or thought I do not much occupy myself with: this is the day's task and is sufficient for the day. The hopes I have of it are not very high; though I piously believe with old Johnson that "useful diligence will at last prevail;" and calculate that several other shifts may open before then. . . . By God's blessing I calculate that the Spirit of Dishonesty *shall not* get dominion over me; nor the Spirit of Despondency, nor any other evil spirit; in which case all will and must be *well*. There are many people kind to me, and many that seem to think far more of me than I merit; but it is not in them I trust. On the whole, I do often feel as if all that hindered one were in reality a blessed furtherance towards something better. Let a man toil diligently; cast his bread upon the waters, he shall find it after many days.—But, alas, my dear Boy, the sheet is done. I will hope for another chance soon; and in the meantime pray you to bear in mind that *you* are now clearly my debtor, and that before the ploughing get too hot, you are actually bound to write to me. Send *all* manner of news, about yourself and household, about my Mother, about every one dear to me. My Mother said you had got her a "cask of good ale." It was right well done: I thank you as if you had given myself a puncheon. I hope you go and see her often; and will get her in motion again now when the days are lengthening. This spring weather brings me in mind of many things. Jane is gone to bed; or she would *expressly* send her love. She had a baddish time of it with that foot but is better now.—We have not seen Leigh Hunt for almost three months! There was no quarrel either: but I believe the poor man is very miserable, and feels shocked at my rigorous Presbyterian principles; in short is afraid of me! I pity him much; but think too, he is perhaps as well where he *is*, and I where I am. Good-night, my dear Alick! Love to Jenny and the Bairns.—Ever your affectionate Brother,

T. CARLYLE.

CXXXVII.—To his MOTHER, Scotsbrig.

CHELSEA, LONDON, 29*th January* 1835.

MY DEAR MOTHER— . . . I have told Jean to get you twelve *ruled* sheets of Paper at Dumfries, and send them out for my benefit: it appears to me, you need nothing but straight courses laid out for you to write as well as need be; you will be slower than some of us; but you can begin in time always, and fill your sheet independently of any of them. I have strictly charged Jean to look to the paper; so now it will depend on yourself.—The Letter you sent was very gratifying and cheerful: I could fancy you all there, assembled in peace and goodwill, and see all the marketing, beef-salting and other winter work going on. . . .

My own work here gets forward as well as it can. I am very anxious to be perfectly accurate (which I find to have been exceedingly neglected by my forerunners); the consequence of that is great searching and trouble; yet the thing when one is doing it ought to *be done*. Hollow work always shows its hollowness one day or other : all men in all places at all times ought to *decline* working hollow. As to the reception I shall meet with, there is no calculating, nor indeed does it give me almost any anxiety whatever. The people that judge of Books and Men in these days are a wretched people, without wisdom, nay, without sincerity, which is the first chance for having wisdom ; one is under the necessity of letting them babble out their foolish say, and heeding it no more than the cawing of rooks,—in whose sound, guidance is *not* for man or woman. If I write anything that has meaning [in] it such meaning *cannot* be lost, He that *gave* me the meaning will care fitly for it. I wish, however, I were done with it ! But I must stand to my tools first ; there is no other way. The trees will be all leafy, and the fields all *gowany* before I even see the end afar off; nevertheless through it I will be, if life and strength are left me. For the rest, dear Mother, be not concerned about my health suffering : I find it from day to day the *thriftiest* way not to overwork myself ; and really my health stands wonderfully well. You see I am at this very time giving myself a half-recreation of ten days. By the time you read this, I hope to be in full activity again.

The Bullers are come to live in London; Mrs. Buller thinks Charles's health will fare better, were she here to look after it. She is almost fearfully bound up in Charles; and I think if he were to die, would almost die too: it is not safe to lean so on aught earthly. Charlie, however, is really a good fellow, and rising in his sphere of life; yet one cannot well prophesy much of him, he is so flighty, not in his purposes, but in his fits of application. He and his mother and the whole of them are Radically given, to a very decided degree. That also is my humour, but I find little profit in speaking it out; *rebellion*, against authority of any kind, is always a barren matter, full of irritancy, of poor painful feelings which are more of the Devil than of God. We are to dine with the Bullers to-night. I have not been in the Town these three days, but took my exercise in delving the garden, of which I have got a quarter put in order again. You will judge what a dry soil we have by my delving at this season. It is indeed and has been the finest winter I can remember. . . .

CXXXVIII.—To his MOTHER, Scotsbrig.

CHELSEA, 17*th February* 1835.

MY DEAR MOTHER—I am afraid I do not keep my promise and purpose to you so well as I ought in the writing way ; it is the weakness of the ability not of the will. I sit here of late so very motionless over my task-sheet, that the world is almost foreign to me : I take no note of its ways; the flight of days and of weeks goes on unmarked, and I am astonished to find them departed. You get the Newspaper, happily still with its *two strokes ;* and will not be uneasy about me. Besides I think you know so much of my old punctuality as to be pretty sure that if anything really bad were happening, I would not keep you in ignorance. As to the *fash* of putting the Newspaper into the Post-office, that is literally nothing ; I go out to walk daily, and nearly always from choice go up towards the press of the Town (close *past* the Post-office) ;

the tumult of these, my brethren, sons of Adam, amuses me. How different from the lone musing stroll along the Glaisters Hill-side! I never think of that now without a kind of shudder at it; of thankfulness that I am away from it.— But indeed I ought to write to you more deliberately, and will (were this villainous Book once done): nay, there is hope that I shall see you again before very long, which will be far better!

Jack's letter when it came in reminded me that I had heard nothing from Annandale since the last time of writing to him; also that I had not written to you again as I meant.—He is well, the worthy Doctor, and talks of homecoming! That late illness of Lady Clare's seems to have been a trying kind of predicament for him; and I think he managed with great honesty and discretion; really very *well*. The "Homœopathic Medicine" he talks of is a thing the poor *Gomerals* are making a noise about here too: it is probably among the most perfect delusions of its day, as far as I can see into it. Neither for love nor for money let a man have *any*thing to do with delusions in any place or at any time!

Jack, I trust, will come back to us *grown* in many respects; I hope we shall all meet again, for the better and not for the worse.

As to my own proceedings here, they amount to almost nothing, except the slow but determined progress my poor Book is making. I *cannot* write it fast; I could write it fast enough, if I would write it ill: but that I have determined not to do—wilfully. It will be bad enough *against* one's will. O that I were done with it! But Patience! Patience! One must *go* on,—as we did at the Cressfield shearing: were it but a sheaf cut, it will not "*loup in again.*" Hurry after all is of no use; one does nothing of any weight by *hurrying*. Many a time I think of my good Father's method of working, how he went on "without haste, without rest;" and did in that way the very most, I must believe, that he *could* do. I am not so wise in my trade; which, indeed, is more difficult to manage wisely.

However, you are not to suppose that I work myself into ill health. No; I really am not under my usual condition in that particular;

rather above, I should say ; for I take *no* drugs now ; and, for example, yesterday I walked upwards of eight miles (to and from the Bullers' old house ; they are in a new one now, a mile and half nearer us) before dinner, and was not a whit exhausted. I am still in a *new* sort of health, not as I used to be ; nay I sometimes think, I shall get heartily healthy once more, and be a young brisk man—turned of forty! In my mind, I feel quite young yet ; and *growing*, as when I was eighteen : this is the greatest blessing. As to my outlooks here, and indeed as to the world and the ways of it, and *its* usage of me better or worse, I cannot say that my heart is distressed, or will distress itself about it : it is God's world, and I am God's worker in it ; well for me if I can *be* that! I seem to see better and better that I have not wholly mistaken my calling, in that point of view ; and as to the rest—*Good* is our Maker ; He will give us strength according to our burden.—Hitherto the look of Literature as a trade is full of the wretchedest contradictions ; nor do I see how any man that has more than meat to look for, and would *keep*, not a carriage, but a conscience, can do much good in it as a getter of money. I have not found it very blessed in the way of *ease* either as I worked at it: on the whole, if it do not show a fairer side, I will fling it from me, and seek bread *otherwise:* there is bread to be had elsewhere; and I will think my thought, and write it down (as the Heavens enable me), and ask only Heaven's permission to do that. Accordingly, I question if there is any man in London with as small a "fixed capital," who carries his head as free, and will take fewer *dunts* from man or thing than "one Carl*y*le[1] of Craigenputtock," worthy man,—one of whose *toes* is sore at this moment; which is his grand grievance. The truth is, dear Mother, I am *full* of my task, and see it getting on; and think that is more than perhaps His Majesty can say: for me it ought to be enough. The Book will probably bring me no money; but I can do without that; and were it done and my hands free, I can write an "Article" or two again. They say it is going to be a tolerable

[1] Carlyle objected to this pronunciation of his name.—M. C.

enough Book ; a queer Book, yes, a *very* queer Book. — Jane's foot is quite whole, and her health, I think, as good as it has been for long. We go on very quietly here: "indulge" in a cup of hot coffee at eight o'clock by way of breakfast : she then goes downstairs, and leaves me the room to scribble in till one or two ; then I walk or dig till four : dinner next of simple mutton chop and *'tatie;* a little music, reading, or by a time some solid friendly visitor (no *quack* is at the pains to come so far), and so at ten our porridge comes in, and "all is by" in a very innocent manner. . . .

Now, when is the ruled sheet to come ? I long to know all about you, how you are, what you are doing. . . . O what a blessing that you are still able to go on so well. That you have a reasonable, acquiescing, hoping spirit ! I thank you, dear Mother, a thousand times for the lessons you and my Father taught me ; they are more precious than fine gold. . . . Jane's love to you all. Good-night, dear Mother. —Ever your affectionate,

T. CARLYLE.

The *Examiner* comes irregularly to poor Hunt; sometimes (as last week) not at all: *that* is the reason, and not my neglect. Almost always you will get something on Sabbath; and sometimes on another day too. They can ask when they are at the village. All are talking politics here; not I: it is *nothing* to me.

CXXXIX.—To ALEXANDER CARLYLE, Catlinns, Lockerbie.

CHELSEA, *27th February* 1835.

... The Proverb says, 'Better a finger off than ay' wagging.' I will not regret that you are done with that *glarry*[1] business of Catlinns; that now all the world is all before you where to choose. There is a probability that farm-stock will not be much *lower*, at any rate, about Whitsunday; so your calculation, favourable for the present, may be found to hold good then: and thus with "private capital" rather increased, with health, and a free heart and conscience, you can *take the bent*[2] again. I wish I knew

---

[1] Miry, muddy.
[2] Take the open field, set out on new adventures.

what were really wisest for you. For a *wisest* thing there indubitably is; only we with our poor eyes cannot always discern it. I, in particular, so far off, so inexperienced in the whole matter, can give you no counsel that has more to recommend it than best intention. You do well to ask counsel of the Heavens, and man's Great Guide there. New enterprises are always best entered on in that solemn feeling of dependence: in various senses that I can see, it is truly written, "He that seeketh *findeth*."—On the whole, however, you are not to take *gloomy* views, for there is nothing to mourn at, to despair at: a serious cheerfulness; that is the right mood in this as in all cases.

It is my impression that you ought not to meddle again with farms, at least not this year, when the season is spent, and so much is discouraging in that direction. In fact, I rather still incline to conjecture that Farming is henceforth no good trade in Scotland or Britain; not a better trade than others; a worse than several. We have often talked over that matter: high rents, low prices; a hungry set of Landlords (for I believe they too are sunk in debt), a population which, whatever Newspaper "Prosperities of trade" and so forth may say, is (and ever must be) struggling deeper and deeper into destitution, and inability to purchase anything but Potatoes;—these, with the enormous competition, are fatal circumstances for farming. Farming in America were something,—on your own land! For the sky is bounteous there as here, and the sky's bounty is not there whisked away, as by art magic, into hands that have not toiled for it. At the worst I always look to America. Perhaps, as to Scottish farming, it is well that you are rid of that.

Nothing else suggests itself to me as so likely for you as going down to Annan. There is always, and must always be, a good deal of trading in grain and farm-produce; in the management of which, a man that *can* manage it with discretion, punctuality, energy, must find some sort of reward. What degree of reward it is at present, I know not at all, but you do or can learn; and as for your fitness to work in that way, I have always understood it to be very considerable, and that, if you would improve more and more in *Punctuality* (which is the soul of all commerce) it might decidedly become superior, and I know not how much so. But the danger all over Annandale (perhaps less in Annan than elsewhere) is that miserable habit of *maffling*,[1] in all senses of the word: you must guard sternly and continually against that. I have also noticed that you are too sanguine or vehement (which is also a fault of my own), and take in more work than you can accomplish: this is a great enemy to Punctuality (one so often fails, and gets into the habit of failing), an "enemy to verta"[2] in general. Lastly the whole breed of us have "a dibble of a temper." These, my dear Brother, are the things to be striven with, to be better and better subdued: it is really my opinion that you were then *well qualified* for that kind of industry, and might find yourself more at home thereby in Annan than anywhere you have yet been. There are really some trustworthy and regular-working substantial char-

---

[1] Trifling. [2] Virtue.

acters there ; with whom by degrees you would get into the proper footing, and find it profitable every way. I think they are the best people I know about in our county. The loose, the vague, the irregular that have no rule or plan of conducting themselves (of whom also there are plenty), you will naturally shun : there may be profit away from such ; *with* such it is not possible that profit can be.—Think therefore what you might earn by trading in (say) corn and meal, no farther than you already see and understand such trade. If it would suffice to support you, I think you might go with no hesitation, with alacrity. A house and park (cow's grass, at any rate) cannot cost very much ; and with no servant, and a wife faithfully disposed to do the best, and who will learn better and better to do it, you can be far more comfortable than heretofore (with such a set of *gillenyers*);¹ you may live there in a still but assiduously industrious way, putting your hand no farther than the sleeve will let : I think there

---

¹ Great, lazy gluttons (this is the meaning attached to the word in Annandale).—M. C.

is a fair prospect, that *fitness* for your employment would really bring recompense in it; better and better recompense as you grew fitter.—You see I have it all cut and dry for you, as if I knew it all. But you will not forget that I properly know nothing of it, as it practically, at the moment *is:* you will correct my theory when you find it and the reality part company. . . .

I may say truly, Clow of Land's[1] liking to *Teufelsdröckh* is a real satisfaction to me; among the more genuine I have had from that Book. That it comes home to an earnest mind, so far away from it in every sense, is proof that there is earnest stuff in it; and should and does please me much more than any flimsy Review-praise it could have got from any Critic now going. I unluckily have not one other copy, or the worthy neighbour should have it: perhaps it may be reprinted as a Book one day, and then (if it be in our time) we may have another chance. I feel pretty much inclined to believe that had it been published in that fashion at

[1] Clow, Alick's brother-in-law.

first, it might actually have *done*. Several persons do more than like it. My last Copy was solicited from me (through the Bullers) very lately by a Sir W. Molesworth, a young Squire, of Radical-Utilitarian temper, but solid English material; much to my surprise; for of *his* whole Philosophy *it* is subversive. He is the man who has given, to Mill's charge, £2000 (for he is rich enough) to set agoing that *Review* of theirs. The first number of it is coming out soon. As for the *French Revolution*, the worst fault of it is, it gets on so dreadfully *slowly*. I think otherwise it is better than anything I have done; for it rests upon a *truth*, upon truths; and if I had done *my best* with it, I will very cheerfully tumble it forth to let the world do *its* best or its worst: Fraser has it advertised as "getting ready" in his next *Magazine* number.

The party we had at the Taylors' was most brisk, and the cleverest (best gifted) I have been at for years: Mill, Charles Buller (one of the gayest, lightly-sparkling, lovable souls in the world), *Repository* Fox (who *hotches*[1] and laughs

[1] Fidgets.

at least), Fonblanque, the *Examiner* Editor,— were the main men. It does one good; though I buy it dear, dining so late: towards eight o'clock!—I have also seen Southey the Poet (at another Taylor's, where is one of the finest old women ever discovered: a Miss Fenwick from Northumberland) :[1] Southey is lean as a harrow; *dun* as a tobacco-*spluchan* ;[2] *no* chin (I mean the smallest), *snubbed* Roman nose, vehement brown eyes, huge *white* head of hair; when he rises, —all legs together. We had considerable talk together: he is a man positive in his own Tory Church of England way; well informed, rational; a good man: but perhaps so striking for nothing as for his excitability and irritability, which I should judge to be pre-eminent even among Poets. We parted kindly; and might be ready to meet again. He lives at Keswick (in Cumberland there); thinks the world is sinking to ruin, and writes diligently. There are few sensible mortals anywhere: I suppose the best stock of them might be looked for

---

[1] For an account of this lady, see *Autobiography of Henry Taylor*, i. 52 *et al*. [2] Tobacco-pouch.

here. We do not see many people; yet enough for our purposes; and could see more. The Bullers are very agreeable; *old* Charles was down yesterday, and played a game at chess with Jane: I like him ever the better were he not so *deaf.* But, on the whole, there is nothing I find more profitable than to be left alone with my *French Revolution.* " They can da' tha naither ill na' guid!" You can fancy me sitting there in the old scribbling way, as you have seen me at Puttock; except that the *outrake*[1] is so inexpressibly different and cheerfuller here: into the very throng of the sons of Adam and the business they have. The *noise* long since has become indifferent to me: *here* at any rate we have no noise; but at night are as still as you.... Good night, my dear Brother! may God guide you and bless you! My love to little mute Tom, to talking Jane, and to the Mother who lovingly watches them, —and shall make tea for me yet.—I remain, ever your affectionate Brother,

T. CARLYLE.

[1] Airing, walk.

CXL.—To Dr. CARLYLE, Rome.[1]

CHEYNE ROW, CHELSEA, LONDON,
23*d March* 1835.

MY DEAR BROTHER—Your Letter came in this morning (after sixteen days from Rome); and, to-morrow being post-day, I have shoved my writing-table into the corner, and sit (with my back to the fire and Jane, who is busy sewing at· my old jupe of a Dressing-gown), forthwith making answer. It was somewhat longed for; yet I felt, in other respects, that it was better you had not written sooner; for I had a thing to dilate upon, of a most ravelled character, that was better to be knit up a little first. You shall hear. But do not be alarmed; for it is "neither death nor men's lives": we are all well, and I heard out of Annandale within these three weeks, nay, Jane's Newspaper came with the customary "two strokes," only five days ago. I meant to write to our Mother last night; but shall now do it to-morrow.

[1] Two short extracts from this letter are printed in Froude's *Carlyle's Life in London*, i. 30, 31.

Mill had borrowed that first Volume of my poor *French Revolution* (pieces of it more than *once*) that he might have it all before him, and write down some observations on it, which perhaps I might print as Notes. I was busy meanwhile with Volume Second; toiling along like a *Nigger*, but with the heart of a free Roman: indeed, I know not how it was, I had not felt so clear and independent, sure of myself and of my task for many long years. Well, one night about three weeks ago, we sat at tea, and Mill's short rap was heard at the door: Jane rose to welcome him; but he stood there unresponsive, pale, the very picture of despair; said, half-articulately gasping, that she must go down and speak to "Mrs. Taylor." . . . After some considerable additional gasping, I learned from Mill this fact: that my poor Manuscript, all except some four tattered leaves, was *annihilated!* He had left it out (too carelessly); it had been taken for waste-paper: and so five months of as tough labour as I could remember of, were as good as vanished, gone like a whiff of smoke.—There never in my life had come upon me any other *accident* of much moment; but this I could not but feel to be a sore one. The thing was *lost*, and perhaps worse; for I had not only forgotten all the structure of it, but the spirit it was written with was past; only the general impression seemed to remain, and the recollection that I was on the whole well satisfied with that, and could now hardly hope to equal it. Mill whom I had to comfort and speak peace to remained injudiciously enough till almost midnight, and my poor Dame and I had to sit talking of indifferent matters; and could not till then get our lament freely uttered. *She* was very good to me; and the thing did not beat us. I felt in general that I was as a little Schoolboy, who had laboriously written out his *Copy* as he could, and was showing it not without satisfaction to the Master: but lo! the Master had suddenly torn it, saying: "No, boy, thou must go and write it *better*." What could I do but sorrowing go and try to obey. That night was a hard one; something from time to time tying me tight as it were all round the region of the heart, and strange dreams haunting me: however, I was not without good thoughts too that came like healing life into me; and I got it somewhat reasonably crushed down, not abolished, yet subjected to me with the resolution and prophecy of abolishing. Next morning accordingly I wrote to Fraser (who had *advertised* the Book as "preparing for publication") that it was all gone back; that he must not *speak of it* to any one (till it was made good again); finally that he must send me some *better paper*, and also a *Biographie Universelle*, for I was determined to risk ten pounds more upon it. Poor Fraser was very assiduous: I got Bookshelves put up (for the whole House was *flowing* with Books), where the *Biographic* (not Fraser's, however, which was countermanded, but Mill's), with much else stands all ready, much readier than before: and so, having first finished out the Piece I was actually upon, I began *again* at the beginning. Early the day after to-morrow (after a hard and quite novel kind of battle) I count on having the First Chapter on paper a second time, no worse than it was, though considerably different. The bitterness of the business is past therefore; and you must conceive me toiling along in that new way for many weeks to come. As for Mill I must yet tell you the best side of him. Next day after the accident he writes me a passionate Letter requesting with boundless earnestness to be allowed to make the loss good as far as *money* was concerned in it. I answered: Yes, since he so desired it; for in our circumstances it was not unreasonable: in about a week he accordingly transmits me a draft for £200; I had computed that my five months' housekeeping, etc., had cost me £100; which sum therefore and not two hundred was the one, I told him, I could take. He has been here since then; but has not sent the £100, though I suppose he will soon do it, and so the thing will end,—more handsomely than one could have expected. I ought to draw from it various practical "uses of improvement" (among others not to lend manuscripts again); and above all things try to do the work *better* than it was; in which case I shall never grudge the labour, but reckon it a goodhap.—It really seemed to me a

Book of considerable significance; and not unlikely even to be of some interest at present: but that latter, and indeed all economical and other the like considerations had become profoundly indifferent to me; I felt that I was honestly writing down and delineating a World-Fact (which the Almighty had brought to pass in the world); that it was an *honest* work for me, and all men might do and say of it simply what seemed good to *them*.—Nay I have got back my spirits again (after this first Chapter), and hope I shall go on tolerably. I will struggle assiduously to be done with it by the time you are to be looked for (which meeting may God bring happily to pass); and in that case I will cheerfully throw the business down a while, and walk off with you to Scotland; hoping to be ready for the *next* publishing season.—This is my ravelled concern, dear Jack; which you see is in the way to knit itself up again, before I am called to tell you of it And now for something else. I was for writing to you of it next day after it happened: but Jane suggested, it would only grieve you, till I could say it was in the way towards adjustment ; which counsel I saw to be right. Let us hope assuredly that the whole will be for *good*.

I told you there had been a Letter from Dumfriesshire. Mrs. Welsh writes to us oftener, with full news of everything (our Mother *was* at Templand, did I tell you?) : but she is still in Edinburgh, though soon returning now. Alick on this occasion was the correspondent : I had written to him just three days before, so that his Letter would be put into the Post-office and mine taken *out* by the same messenger ; I wrote again very soon after. He has actually done with Catlinns. It was let by auction on the day advertised ; to somebody for £12 less than his rent : that somebody I suppose is *glarring* and ploughing over it (poor fellow) in these very days ; and Alick marches at Whitsunday *first*. He wanted much to have counsel : I could give him little except in general ; farming seemed to me also a thing he was probably as well done with ; Annan and some kind of grain-dealing there looked the likeliest. It seems to me not improbable that he will try himself there: he was to see Ben Nelson about it, he said; his tone of temper was good; cheerful, and *determined* to have another fly at it. He will perhaps find himself much better situated in that way of life; there is better society to be had there; more of interest; a freer field in several respects. He seemed very grateful for your Letter; charged me to send you his thanks over and over again. I hope we shall see him in Summer, doing better.—Our good Mother added a little postscript; in the same meek cheery temper they are all in: Jean was to get her some ruled paper at Dumfries; with the aid of which she might really write a very reasonable Letter.—I get a daily *Globe* Newspaper from Mill (he leaves it in masses, every two or three days, at a shop in Knightsbridge): copies of this I circulate among them far and wide: one or two weekly to my Mother; who also pretty regularly gets the *Examiner*, furnished me by Hunt (whom for the rest I do not *see* once in the month), though I myself sometimes *omit* to read it. The aspect of Politics seems to me the wretchedest ; and happily there are several people here who never open their mouths on that subject. I have sent a Newspaper or two to poor Johnstone at Haddington ; to Arbuckle,[1] to Glen, etc. etc. There is little other good in them : only we felt rather ashamed that Whiggism was all out a week before we knew it, down here in our village stillness!—Peel apparently will be out soon too : and then ? *Des Sottises !*

Your practice at Rome is literally of the profitableness that all good work is of : for this world, Nothing. Never mind, my boy; take more of it if it offer. . . . I believe Doctorship here to be at as miserable a pass as well could be : " Homœopathy " the ready road to fortune in it ; *quackery* as from of old abounding. There are two grand Homœopathists I find : Doctor Quin, and Doctor Bel'uomo (Beautiful Man !) an Italian. Mrs. Buller has taken into it : finds the most *astonishing* relief, etc. etc. : Austin has paid off Quin. *I* could interpret all Mrs. Buller's wondrous cases-in-

---

[1] Dr. Robert Arbuckle, a friend of Dr. Carlyle.—M. C.

point: the old story of imagination and nerves, *Fantasiestücke!* Dow of Irongray[1] worked a *miracle* even: it is the *food* of quacks.—This, however, I fancy is the thing to be striven against everywhere by the true man of every craft. I trust (if God will) we shall meet "before June be done": I with my Volume finished, you with your Travel; and then we shall do our very best to decide on something wise. A journey to Scotland among the first things,—on foot! . . .

Our visitors and visitings are what I cannot give you account of this time: not that they are many; but that the sheet is so near full. One Taylor (Henry Taylor, who has written a *Philip van Artevelde*, a good man, whose *laugh* reminds me of poor Irving's) invited me to meet Southey some weeks ago. I went and met Southey. A man of clear brown complexion, large nose, *no* chin, or next to none; care-lined and thought-lined brow, vehement hazel eyes; huge mass of white hair surmounting it: a strait-laced, limited,

[1] Minister of Irongray.

well-instructed, well-conditioned, excessively sensitive even irritable-looking man. His irritability I think is his grand spiritual feature; as his grand bodily is perhaps leanness and long legs: a nervous female might shriek when he rises for the first time, and stretches to such unexpected length—like a lean pair of tongs! We parted good friends; and may meet again, or not meet, as Destiny orders. At the same house, since that, Jane and I went to meet Wordsworth. I did not expect much; but got mostly what I expected. The old man has a fine shrewdness and naturalness in his expression of face (a long Cumberland figure); one finds also a kind of *sincerity* in his speech: but for prolixity, thinness, endless dilution it excels all the other speech I had heard from mortal. A genuine man (which is much), but also essentially a *small* genuine man: nothing perhaps is sadder (of the glad kind) than the *unbounded* laudation of such a man; sad proof of the *rarity* of such. I fancy, however, he has fallen into the garrulity of age, and is not what he was: also that his environment (and rural Prophethood) has hurt him much. He seems impatient that even Shakespear should be admired: "so much out of my own pocket"! The shake of hand he gives you is feckless, egoistical; I rather fancy he *loves* nothing in the world so much as one could wish. When I compare that man with a great man,—alas, he is like dwindling into a contemptibility. Jean Paul (for example), neither was he *great*, could have worn him as a finger-ring. However when "I go to Cumberland," Wordsworth will still be a glad sight.—I have not been fortunate in my Pen to-night; indeed for the last page I have been writing with the back of it. This and my speed will account for the confusion. Porridge has just come in. I will to bed without writing more; and finish to-morrow. Good night, dear Brother!—Ever yours!

Tuesday, 3 *o'clock.*—My dear Jack, I have not gone out, being so busy with this First Chapter: congratulate me, I am *done* with it already! I will now walk with this up to Charing Cross after dinner; which will still do.

Jane has been out all morning, and could not write a postscript: she is in now, and sends you her sisterly affection,—would like heartily, I do know, to read *Manzoni* with you again.— . . . Mill also has written this morning to say that he cannot think of so little as £100: we must abide by that nevertheless, I fancy. . . . Lord Jeffrey, most likely, is in Town at present: he will probably call here, but *not*, surely, with much rapidity. He has my true wishes; and I (theoretically) have his: but we *cannot* help one another. Our Mother has never said anything of Teufelsdröckh; but I learn from Alick that Clow of Land is *very* fond of him! A certain Sir W. Molesworth (a Radical Utilitarian M.P.) also "sent for a copy." Oh that I had more paper! But we shall *meet* if Heaven please. . . . Adieu, dear Jack! finis here. Will you and Dr. Brunn[1] walk to *Pasquin* (do actually) and make my compliments to him.

[1] Of Coethen, an intimate friend of Dr. Carlyle.

CXLI.—To his MOTHER, Scotsbrig.

CHELSEA, 25*th March* 1835.

MY DEAR MOTHER—I purposed writing to you two nights ago, as you might perhaps notice on the Newspaper; but a little man came in, and occupied the whole evening I designed for you. It turned out, however, to be "probably just as well": for next day there arrived Jack's Roman Letter; which now can go along with mine to make the bargain better. We are, as Jack says, very lucky; and should be thankful that we hear from one another so regularly. I will only wish now, since *you* have delayed so long, that our Letters may not again *run into one another's mouth:* however, in that case too, I will send you an answer the sooner, and make matters straight again.

Jack, as you will see, has nothing but good news for us: the best is that he is (we can hope) on the way to see us all again, "by the end of June." I answered him last night; and could not but, among other things, agree with him that it were as well if his Travels ceased after that : he will have funds for attempting a settlement somewhere ; and, if he see any feasibility, ought to do it. The money he speaks of will be sent forward as the last was ; I will give you notice of it, and you will have to go to Dumfries ; which, if Harry be in any condition, will perhaps do you no harm. As for that question about whether you got the *annual* (or interest) regularly, I could make no answer ; but hope you do. If you do not, pray apply, and make the people pay up. I never learned either whether the houses at Ecclefechan were got satisfactorily repaired, or how the rents come in : you complain of nothing ;—but have doubtless complaints that you *might* make ; and which I ought to know of. In the meanwhile, dear Mother, what a satisfaction for me is it to know that you are one of these that look not either to Houses in Ecclefechan, or any House or Possession on this poor Earth for your comfort and stronghold ! I know well that there is nothing but *such* a faith that can render this Earth and her stinted allowances endurable, nay matters of thankfulness for one. The cheerful wise way in which you adjust yourself to so many vicissitudes, and are always seen to be yourself in the midst of them, should be a lesson to me and all of us.

I had some occasion lately for a portion of your faith; in a most unexpected *accident* (what we call *accident*) that befel me; of which I delayed writing till I could not only say that I *would* get over it, but that I had got over it. Be of good cheer, therefore, as to that: it is all right (and for the best, I am persuaded); and you shall now hear about it fully. To sum up all in a word: the *First Volume* of my poor Book is utterly destroyed! Mill, to whom I had lent it to read, and write Notes on (for he is skilled in that subject), and who was full of admiration for the bit of work, had left it carelessly out in his house: some of the people saw it lying; tore it up as waste paper; and when he noticed it, there were only some three or four fractions of leaves remaining. He came hither to me, in a state looking not unlike insanity; and gasped out (for he could hardly speak) his Job's news. I am very glad that I got it borne so well; for it was a hard thing. It never got the better of me; and by next morning the bitterness of it was all over; and I had determined that there must be a finger of Providence in it; that it meant simply I was to write the thing over again *truer* than it was. My little Dame stood faithfully by me too, and was very good and brave. Having finished out the new Chapter I was upon therefore, I resolutely turned back to the beginning again; and have this day finished the First Chapter of all a second time, certainly no *worse* than it was; a thing that gives me great comfort, for I now find that I *can* do it; of which, before trial (so *irksome* was the business), I had no certainty, except in the determination to "*gar* myself do it." "Dinna tine[1] heart, therefore; if thou tine heart, thou tines a'!" I do really believe the Book will be the better for it, and we shall all be the better.—I must not forget to say that poor Mill next day sent a passionate entreaty to be allowed to pay me, what money could pay; to which I, as to a reasonable thing,

[1] Lose.

acceded; and so he sent me soon after a Draught for £200,—which however I returned that same day saying it was just *twice* the sum due. I have seen Mill since, and we talked of it; he this day sends me another Letter still wishing I would stand by the original sum, or some intermediate one : but I had explained to him that £100 was fully my expenses during the time of writing the thing; and so I fancy we will still adhere to that computation; for if any one had asked me to throw the writing into the fire, and said, What would I take? I could have given him no definite answer— except that I would be *ill, ill indeed* to deal with. In this rather handsome way, has the matter been brought to a bearing. One other thing I proposed that it should never *be spoken of* (except to you and Jack and the kindred) till it was all made good again.

So that you see, dear Mother, I have no chance to *earn* my Dressing-gown this summer: but you will give it me on trust I daresay? My whole object now is to get the lost part made up again by the time Jack may be expected : I will then throw it by for a while, and take it up afterwards; perhaps write some part of it beside *you*. It really was going to be what I reckoned a reasonably good Book (and a Part of it I still have); neither will it, one may think, the *rebellious heart* being once subdued to work quietly at it, be *worse* than it was; but *better*, for I know it better. You cannot think what a comfort the feeling that I am doing an honest work in God's creation, whether I be ever paid for it or not, gives me: I have not been as contented for many years. The great uproar of London is a great beautiful moving Picture for me: I say to it, with the greatest goodnature, "Go thou thy way, I am going mine." There is no blessedness in the world equal to that.

Besides, I ought to say, we are not ill off, or ill-used in any way, but really *well*. I suppose we have a little circle of society here, considerably better than His Majesty's, or his Grace of Wellington's; for it consists of really superior honest-minded men and women (most rare, as the world goes); and the respect we are held in there could *not* be procured by running the brightest Gig in nature, or spending daily "a Mill and a Mains."[1] One ought to be really glad of *this*;—but glad above all things that one *could do without it too.* "Mind thy own trade!" That is the great secret: the others can "*da' tha naither ill na guid.*"—When we meet (as I trust the good Providence will permit) I will tell you all about our people: we have made acquaintance with a very excellent woman, since I wrote; a Miss Fenwick (from the North Country, Durham or Northumberland originally); an oldish woman, with a deformity in the spine, but otherwise really rather good-looking; I often say that she is the wisest person, male or female, I have fallen in with in London: I am very sorry that she is but a kind of visitor here (in the house of one Henry Taylor, also a very worthy person), and is going off to Devonshire or some whither in April. At that house, Jane and I lately saw Wordsworth; reputed the greatest Literary character at present in England: a good kind

[1] "A Mill and a Mains" = a small estate.

of man; but "alas, gude wife, nothing *but a fluff o' feathers*"[1]—when you come to *weigh* him! We were very glad however, if not to see him, yet to *have seen* him; and so returned content. — But in truth, we have *not* much society; very nearly I think what is about the right stock. Night after night we can sit here, quite still, over our Books or Papers, and find it a not unprofitable night; and then when a rap comes, one can with the better conscience prepare to welcome it. Besides at any time one can *go* out and see somebody. It is very different from Puttock; which indeed I never think of without feeling that we did well to leave it.—For the rest, you must not think, dear Mother, that I am overworking myself: I assure you, no; I walk as regularly as possible, disregarding the foul weather, and all the rest of it: the birds are singing in the Parks, or I have people to call on; it is all very pleasant even if one do nothing but look at it. My health is surely not worse than it was but better.

[1] An eccentric old minister in Dumfries, buying a live fowl, weighed it in his hand, and used this expression.—M. C.

This afternoon I went to Charing-Cross Post-office (which keeps longer open) with Jack's Letter: whom should I meet tripping along in Pall Mall? My Lord Jeffrey; just arrived two hours ago! I was heartily glad to see the little man; gladder, I think, than he to see me (for that Astronomy Professorship sticks with *him*, not me): however, he got my card, and will be down before returning Northward to his Judgeship again. He was looking gray and dusty: "ye may depend on't," as an old Roxburghshire woman said, "forty years maks a great odds of *a girl*,"— or boy either.—Another still queerer fellow I saw not long ago in Hyde Park. It was a bright day, and the quality were all out driving and coursing; as I came down through the thing, one figure struck me: a lean rib of a creature, buttoned in white greatcoat, his head and even his hat *lost* within the collar of it (which stood out a foot or more from his neck); eyes winking, under-jaw projected, whole face puckered into wrinkles; the whole going on at a kind of ineffectual high-trot; it was "our ain Hoddam, Sir;"[1] General Sharpe, member for those Burghs! I actually burst into laughing, though grave enough before.

Alas, my dear Mother, the Paper is done; and this wretched Pen has been so thriftless!— I wrote to Alick; Jamie would get a Note, and for you only a piece of paper. I long to hear what Alick is deciding on. Tell him to keep up his heart; for better days are coming: also to write to me by his earliest convenience (whether he have decided or not). My love to Jean, Mary, to Jenny whom I fancy still with you. Have you got the ruled paper? I did expect a Letter; and of course now do more than ever. Tell me all that you are doing: how you stand this wild spring weather. I have nothing for it but to believe in Jean's *two strokes;* which are most welcome weekly. If your weather is no better than ours, the ploughers must be at a bad pass: everything

---

[1] The minister of Hoddam, out catechising, asked a boy, "Who was the first man?" and received an unhesitating reply, "Our ain *Hoddam,* Sir!" (meaning the Laird of Hoddam, General Sharpe. He was elder brother of Charles Kirkpatrick Sharpe, antiquarian and friend of Sir Walter Scott).—M. C.

is drenched here (only our subsoil is all *sand*) ; and March *dust* is none, only March *glar*, what you like. It is among the rainiest springs I remember. Do you care about the *Globes?* I can easily send you a better share of them ; but I doubt whether you would get them oftener than weekly, and then they are so old. Charlie Buller often writes the *big print* part : all that has any *fun* in it is by him. It is thought these poor Ministers will soon be thrown out ; a thing which I for one neither pray much for nor against. They are [a] set of poor shambling individuals, they and their opponents ; and nothing but "*Lonsdale* coming" to "*sittle them aw*"[1] is to be looked for.—Jane is up to bed ; or her *expressed* affection would have been sent to you all. She is livelier and better than formerly ; has *been mending my old dressing-gown!*—Now, do write to me soon, and tell me *how* you really are, and so much, much that I want to know. Good night, my dear Mother. God be with you!—Your affectionate,

T. CARLYLE.

[1] See *supra*, p. 80.

CXLII.—To Mrs. AITKEN, Dumfries.

5 CHEYNE ROW, CHELSEA, *9th April* 1835.

MY DEAR JEAN—Your Letter arrived the day before yesterday ; and to-day comes the Newspaper, with James's *two strokes*, always welcome. There is a frank going off to Mrs. Welsh, which will carry so light a sheet as this : so I, having *slurred-over* rather than done my day's task, will answer you ; preferring that to my due daily walk ;—for indeed I have to walk some five miles into the Town, to Tea this evening at any rate ; and that ought to suffice. You shall hear what I on the spur of the moment can tell you ; and in the first place that all goes in the old way "tolerably well," which we ought rather to account "very well," as the world wags now.

There is none of my Scotch Correspondents that gives me so authentic a picture of things as you do; wherein I can see the *wrong-side* too, with its seams and thrums (as every earthly thing has a wrong-side), and know that it is all authentic. If you wrote a smaller hand and wrote oftener, I should have no quarrel with you. Our dear Mother seems to be going on in moderate health at least, and moderately well every way : I hope [to] see more minutely *how*, in the course of this present Summer. What Jenny and she *do*, or how they get along in that new Scotsbrig world, I still very imperfectly make out. The "new relations," poor little things, are right welcome into this evil Earth : may they find it a place if not to be at ease in, to be busy in *wisely!* That is always possible for all men. I can see "James of Scotsbrig" tolerably from what you say ; and reckon that the opposite Parties are arranged there on the *proper* footing. So Alick has about engaged with the Howes! I do fancy it may be the best thing he could do. He must write to me soon, and tell me how it is arranged. Say to him from me that all will yet be well ; that the faithful man was *never* yet beaten ; if he stand to himself the Heavens stand by him ; the troubles they afflict him with are actually but *trials*, to try what stuff is in him, and bring it out.

Of James and you nothing but good accounts come to me. Know this always, my dear friends, for a very truth, even as it stands written in your Bible: "The *fear of God* is the beginning of wisdom." Let a man reverence that Unseen Highest; feel that "he is ever in the eye of his Great Taskmaster," and it shall be well with him.—You are perhaps no worse for the present that you have little society; unless your neighbours can teach you something, or strengthen you or be strengthened by you in some useful way, you are as well to let them go their *gates*, with your good wishes. Have *nothing* to do at any time with malicious, false, idle, or God-forgetting people! Good is the company of four bare walls compared with that of these. By degrees, however, you will find more or less of real worth in several that you must be thrown in contact with. One never gets much good of society, or even much favour from .it, I think, till once one have learned how easily it can be *done without:* as for him that *leans* any of his weight on it, he leans on a broken reed.

Mind thy work, honest man; and let the world mind *its*,—or neglect it.—I suppose you go into that new house at Whitsunday: I shall fancy you as more comfortably situated there. Be "busy," whether "bare"¹ or not; and there is no fear of you.

Did you send out my Mother the "ruled sheets"? I rather fancy not; for she has never filled one of them yet. But indeed perhaps she still expects some notice about Jack's money; of which I have still none to send: so soon as I get any, I will put the matter under way, and send word; you will likely get your Visitor then. In the meantime send word that you have heard from me, that we are all well. I fear my Mother is too much vexed about that Manuscript mischance. Tell her, the thing shall be for good: I will actually make it better than it was, if I can; nay I think it *will* be better, though I get along very toilsomely. Do not speak of it to anybody till I am fairly done; then we will speak. I hope Jack will come safe, in good time, and

¹ Proverbial: "*bare and busy.*"

that I shall be *done* when he comes. I never had as long a spell of writing; and could like well enough to take my ease a while: but alas, bairn, I have "the Bastille to take" a *second* time, so unlucky am I! For the rest, my health, etc. is not to be despised. . . .

There were great quantities of things to write about, tea-parties, and societies and people; but the sheet is so near done! A small circle of good people seems to be gathering about us here: we might have a much wider one, if we wanted to get *people* merely. We are to lose Mrs. Austin: her husband is in perpetual ill-health and depression here; so determines to go to Boulogne in France, where he was once better, and leave all: employment, society, and what not. I feel she will be a loss to us: for herself perhaps it may turn out a gain; she had got to be that unfortunatest thing in nature, a "London distinguished female," and this is the handsomest chance she could ever have of walking *out* of such froth-element; which otherwise would have *cast* her out, when her day came. She is a good woman; and will be far better when she becomes *un*distinguished again.—My little Lord Jeffrey interrupted me since I began this Letter; coming down to inquire if we were "happy." He is here for some weeks, enjoying his vacation: a nimble little individual, whom I wish heartily well to, but have no farther trade with, I apprehend, except in the "Fine-day, Sir" manner. His ladies are with him; but their way is not our way.—Allan Cunningham's Brother was here last night: he wrote a Book about New South Wales; is a most modest, intelligent man, with much simplicity and a kind of *blateness*;[1] we give him a bowl of porridge and friendly greeting, and he goes his peaceful way. I have had much "going out" with other people for the last fortnight; but am as good as determined not to go out again for six weeks; but stand by my work, which is the only thing that turns to aught.—"Sandy Donaldson" is here from Haddington; but I was out when he called yesterday: Jane is going to dine at his Brother's some day; I "decline from eet."—Of

[1] Bashfulness.

public news I suppose you get enough from M'Diarmid. The Peel ministry are all out since yesterday; what will next be done, his Majesty is revolving in that wise head of his. To walk over to Hanover and leave them to *seek* a king, were for him the wisest thing.— Did I forget the two strokes on the *Globe?* Or rather was it not sealed with some *internal* wafer; the sign that it contained writing; which you did not find, *so* cunning was I? I will not forget again, I hope; while the *liberty* to do it is continued one.—Will you send our kind love to Mary, our hope that her little Mag is better? I sometimes send her a *Globe* too, and would do it oftener: but that I think it costs her a halfpenny, which perhaps it is scarcely worth.—I had a Letter from Burnswark lately, which I was very glad of, and mean to answer soon.

Jane comes up to say that it is far more than time I were off! For it is after dinner now (so long did his Lordship detain me); also I have smashed asunder an old Dumfries Barrel (which came with furniture, and has stood with lumber) since that. Our piece of garden is all dug, and has wall-flower blossoms, plum-tree blossoms, vines budding, and much *spearmint*. It is bright beautiful weather; I have sat for a week without fires; wind is west, and we are clear as azure.—God bless you, my dear Sister; you and your Husband and Child! —Ever your affectionate Brother,

T. CARLYLE.

CXLIII.—To his MOTHER, Scotsbrig.

CHEYNE ROW, CHELSEA, 20*th April* 1835.

MY DEAR MOTHER— . . . I am struggling along with my second-edition Manuscript, in the best spirit I can. The second Chapter is done again; after a really tough battle; and the Third goes along much more sweetly. I was seized with some kind of bilious humour, which exhibited itself mainly in the shape of *Stupidity*, the most inconvenient shape of all for me; so that I had my own *ados;* and would have run over into Annandale (and given it up for a while),—had I been near enough! There came further a most extraordinary succession of *Parties*, which with the talk and tea of them wore me quite down; till at last I stuck up, and refused to go out *anywhere*, even to the simplest cup of tea; and lay at home, resting in the evenings, with the full conviction that to get on with my work was the only good for me, and better than tea-ing with Queen Adelaide. . . . So I got through the business; and am now afloat again, and going on, as I said, far more prosperously. It requires really great Christian virtue to hold patiently by this sad work: but I shall get through it before long, and be all the better for such trial of my patience. Sometimes I think it will be better (as surely on the whole it must be); but sometimes too I think it *worse:* and then what a thought is that! Every one of us is buckled into his harness, and *must* on, be the road smooth or rough. You need not, my dear Mother, let it "come into your mind like fire" that I am working too hard! I assure you, no; I take it very deliberately; even on a principle of *thrift;* for always *Too-much* to-day produces an overbalancing *Too-little* to-morrow. But I have stood long to it, and shall be glad enough to have a little rest in Annandale. . . .

It is getting close upon supper-time, and I am weary of stooping and driving this assiduous Pen. How much more convenient were it, had we word of mouth! But we should be right grateful for the Pen too.—I will give it up for this night, while the play is good, I think. Except supper *starken*[1] me a little, and I be tempted to resume. Good-night, my dear Mother; may all that is Good be round you always. . . . —Your ever affectionate,

T. CARLYLE.

CXLIV.—To his MOTHER, Scotsbrig.

CHELSEA, *Tuesday, 12th May* 1835.

MY DEAR MOTHER—You will learn without regret that I am *idling*, or nearly so, for these last two days. My poor Work, the dreariest of its sort I ever undertook, was getting more and more untoward on me; I began to feel that toil and effort not only did not perceptibly advance

[1] Strengthen.

it, but was even, by disheartening and disgusting me, retarding it. I gathered my papers together, therefore; sealed them up, and locked them in a drawer, with the determination not to touch *them* again for one week from that date. I flatter myself it was a very meritorious determination. A man must not only be able to work, but to give over working. I have many times stood doggedly to work; but this is the first time I ever deliberately laid it down without finishing it. In fact, it is the strangest thing I ever tried that of re-writing my first Volume; one must vary his methods according to the task he has: take it gently, take it fiercely; you cannot tickle trouts in the way you spear whales. On the whole, it has given me very great trouble this poor Book, and Providence (in the shape of human Mismanagement) sent me the severest check of all: however, I still trust to get it written sufficiently: and if thou even *canst* not write it (as I have said to myself in late days), why then be content with that too: God's Creation will get along, exactly as it should do, *without* the writing of it. At all events, my head shall settle itself, and my face clear itself in the pure May air of these days: I shall then be readier for this work, or for whatever else. There are other proposals hovering about me; but not worth speaking of yet. The "Literary World" here is a thing which I have had no other course left but to *defy*—in the Name of God! Man's imagination can fancy few things madder; but me (if God will) it shall not madden. I will take a *knapping*-hammer[1] first.

Meantime see what cheer comes to me from over the water! This is another Letter of the American's;[2] introducing a Friend; whom we expect this night at tea. The good Yankees seem smit with some strange fatuity about me; which will abate in good time. Fraser, whom I saw yesterday, has no hope that an Edition of the Book[3] would sell here: so they must just provide *themselves* with copies, these worthy souls. Nothing gives me such in-

[1] A hammer for breaking stones used in mending roads.
[2] From Emerson, dated 12th March, introducing Mr. Henry Barnard.—See *Correspondence of Carlyle and Emerson*, i. 47.
[3] *Sartor Resartus.*

dubitable satisfaction about any of my Books as one fact always: That *I* have done with them. That blessing was nearly all I expected from this poor *Revolution;* and, alas, that is not so near as I expected. However, we will have patience. You can read this good Emerson's Letter, and put it by the other; and tell nobody of it: to you it will give real pleasure, and that perhaps is the chief good of it.

Everything is confused here with the everlasting jabber of Politics; in which I struggle altogether to hold my peace. The Radicals have made an enormous *advance* by this little Tory interregnum; it is not unlikely the Tories will try it one other time; they would even *fight* if they had anybody to fight for them: meanwhile these poor Melbourne people will be obliged to walk on at a much *quicker* pace than formerly (considerably against their will, I believe), with the Radical bayonets pricking them behind; and so whether the Tories stay out, or whether they try to come in again, it will all be for the advance of Radicalism; which means revolt against innumerable things, and (as I construe it) Dissolution and Confusion, at no great distance, and a Darkness which no man can see through. Let them take it, and the thickest skin hold longest out! Everybody, Radical and other, *every* body here tells me that the condition of the Poor people is—improving! My astonishment was great at first, but I now look for nothing else than this: "improving daily." "Well, gentlemen," I answered once, "the Poor, I think, will get up some day, and *tell* you how improved their condition is." It seems to me the vainest jangling, this of the Peels and Russells, that ever the peaceful air was beaten into *dispeace* by. But we are used to it from of old. Leave it alone, permit it, while God permits it. And so for work and hope—else whither![1]

CXLV.—To his MOTHER, Scotsbrig.

CHELSEA, *Thursday, 4th June* 1835.

MY DEAR MOTHER—As I shall probably have a chance for a frank to-night, and am

[1] A portion of this letter is given in Froude's *Carlyle's Life in London*, i. 37.

not likely to do much good at working for the present, I propose paying off some epistolary debts, and send you in the first place a little hint of our welfare, and way of procedure. Alick has written us a Letter, which came yesterday; assuring us of your continuance in moderate health, which was the best news we could get out of Scotland. They are all flitting and bestirring themselves, jumping hither and thither; it is now just about a year since we were at the same work: people have many *fitches*[1] (as I once told Jemmy Bretton) "before they get to the *crown-head!*" Let us all be grateful that we have still some strength to carry us on, and are not deserted of Hope, and even of Guidance, if we will ask it well.

Last time I wrote, you heard that I had laid by my work for two weeks: I have taken it out again since that, but have been making (at least so far as *black on white* goes) very small way in it. I have had such a long spell at the business, and then was so tumbled over

[1] *Moves* at the game of Draughts.

head in that sorrowful loss of the Manuscript, I feel as if there were nothing more profitable for me than to rest a while, and gather new *smeddum*[1] for assaulting it again under better omens. Not much will be done, I think, till after I have seen you in Annandale. I have great doubts about many things connected with this Book of mine, and Books in general; for all is in the uttermost confusion in that line of business here : but, God be thanked, I have *no* doubts about my course of duty in the world ; or that if I am driven back at one door, I must go on trying at another. There are some two or even three outlooks opening on me, unconnected with Books, about which I cannot write to you yet with any distinctness : one of these regards the business of National Education, which the Parliament is now busy upon, in which I mean to try all my strength to get something to do (for my conscience greatly approves of the work as useful); whether I shall succeed herein or not I cannot with the smallest accuracy guess as yet. Another out-

[1] Force.

look invites my consideration from America : I have another long Letter from Emerson,[1] and plenty of Yankee good-wishes, and a project chalked out for passing a winter over the water, and *lecturing* there! Something or other we shall devise : in the meantime I let it all lie round me shaping itself; and shall probably have fixed on nothing till after we meet, and have a *smoke* together, and get the thing all *summered and wintered* talking together freely once more. It is an awful Distraction this huge Babylon of a City ; and yet there are many kind persons and circumstances in it ; and I do not doubt I have gained much instruction, correction and profit in it, during this twelvemonth ; and behold still, thy servant is *here*, ready and disposed to do the best he can.

Mrs. Austin, who went away some two months ago, writes to us yesterday in very bad spirits, that her Husband, poor man, is no better, is even sicker for the time. We are

[1] Of 30th April 1835.—See *Correspondence of Carlyle and Emerson*, i. 52.

very sorry for her, very sorry for *him*,—who is one of the faithfullest men living, but driven almost desperate by the *lying* dishonest world he has had to live in. One *should* not be driven desperate (for this is the place of *hope*); yet a man may easily be excused sometimes for going that way.

A new young figure, and with him a new family of acquaintances have risen on us: the young man is very clever, and true and kind-hearted; his name is John Sterling: he has written a very superior Book [1] (some years ago); and strangest of all, is a Clergyman of the English Church. His Mother and Jane are about "swearing an eternal friendship." John himself sent me the other day three full sheets and a cover, of criticism on *Teufelsdröckh;* expressing amazement, admiration, horror—all in sufficient quantity. I really like the youth rather; and shall rejoice when he comes to London permanently (for as yet he re-

[1] In 1833 Sterling had published *Arthur Coningsby*, a novel in three volumes, indicating "ambitious aims in literature."—See *Life of Sterling*, part i. chap. ix.

sides in the country and only his people are here). . . .

To-night we are invited to see the great Agitator O'Connell! Unless it be wet, we intend to go: it is at Mrs. Buller's; one of the meetings called a *rout*, or huge multitude of people all elbowing one another. You shall hear of it on the cover, dear Mother; for I hope to send you a few finishing words tomorrow. My blessings till then! T. C.

CXLVI.—To Miss JANET CARLYLE, Scotsbrig.

CHELSEA, 4*th June* 1835.

MY DEAR JENNY — Alick, writing to me yesterday, mentions among other things, that you are *shorted*[1] (as he phrases it) because I have not written. Can it be possible your good little heart has got so far out of its right movement as to be *angry at me!* I do not believe a word of it. The utmost is (and this I had overlooked), you feel that your sisterly love was clear and active towards me; that I,

[1] Grown short of temper.

by not writing expressly on the matter, have as good as slighted it as of no account. Dear little Jenny! it is not unnatural, but perfectly erroneous. Young woman was never farther *wrong*. As you would *know*, were you here with your own eyes to see. My dear Sister, let no such notion now or henceforth enter your kind little heart. Depend upon it, such come of the Devil (though in a disguised shape), and ought to [be] dismissed back to *him*.

I have a kind of headache, and cannot write further to you to-day. It would give me very great satisfaction indeed to know accurately what you are about, and how you go on. I hope to see farther and clearer into it all, when I come back; which, though the Doctor has not written yet, I trust will not be distant now. Alick says you are going to the Dumfries Schools again over Summer; a step he seems not to be very sure of. Certainly, if you hope to *learn* something that will be profitable, there is nothing more advisable than to go. Nothing that a human creature can do is at all times so inevitably right as to *learn something*. There-

fore go, my dear Jenny, if it so seem to thee.
. . .—Remember me to Jean and James when
you see them : I trust I am not in their debt
as to Letters ; at all events, tell them that if
they *shorten* upon me, it will be the greatest
injustice ever done to any man. And do not
you *shorten*, my dear little Bairn ; but *lengthen*,
and know that if you take anything amiss, it
is for mere want of seeing how it really was ;
that of all delusions Satan could tempt you
with, that of wanting my brotherly affection,
now and always while we inhabit the Earth
together, is the most delusive. Oh that is *not*
true, and never can be. — Finally, my dear
Jenny, I must for this brief time be going.
Keep diligent, cheerful ; ready to improve the
passing hour, and make the most and best of
it. Jane sends you her true love. May all
Good be with you always !—Your affectionate
Brother, T. CARLYLE.

CXLVII.—To Dr. CARLYLE, Paris.

CHELSEA, 15*th June* 1835.

MY DEAR BROTHER— . . . I must tell you

something about some of our new *people*. Did I ever mention the name of the Sterlings to you? John Sterling, a man about your own age, remembers you once at Shooter's Hill : he has written Novels since that (one Novel rather, by which I came to knowledge of him at Craigenputtock); has taken up a Coleridgean Christianity, for better or worse, and even gone into orders, become an actual preacher; and, what in these circumstances may astonish, takes greatly to me! A whole retinue of curious persons belong to him : in his hand a glass which shows us many more. His Father is Irish; the redoubted Sterling of the *Times* Newspaper, really a very notable man; who flies greatly about this place—for the time. Finally one "Mr. Dunn," an Irish Clergyman, "who refused a Bishoprick" (for Athanasius' sake), one of the *best* men I ever looked on; whom I hope to show you. . . . How I saw O'Connell one night (at Mrs. Buller's rout) and Peninsular Napier and multitudes of notable men and women; and said almost nothing, and thought very little : all this with much like it I must leave (till meeting!), for my paper wanes.—Let me mention only that Sterling has sent me (from near Hastings, where he resides as yet) a vituperative expostulatory criticism on *Teufelsdröckh* of *thirteen pages;* that the Americans have sent an order for "fifty or a hundred copies" of the same poor Book, and could only get three (and threaten to reprint it); finally that these surprising Yankees invite me in really pressing terms to come over to them this very winter, and "lecture" on *any* subject, with assurance of success! As the Book-trade seems to me utterly over here, I have really been meditating that proposal: but I will decide on nothing till *we* have compared Notes. There is also a thing started here, about "National Education," and a Parliament Commission, for which I will try and am trying; however, it is distant yet. You have now enough on our posture and speculation and non-action here: Oh when will you *look* at it *selbst!*

As to Paris commissions, I now find, considering it close at hand, that there are almost none, or altogether none. If you could get me a good *cheap* map of France, to be pasted on a wall here, I would take it; also a map of the old Isle de France or modern Departement de Seine (in which Paris stands), I would welcome : but I think D'Eichthal tried once before, and could not. Take you therefore no special trouble with it. A pianoforte score of *Ça-ira* I want rather more : the *Marseillaise* we have got here but not the other : ask a little after it. Tell D'Eichthal that his two Quartos on the *Collier* (Diamond Necklace) are here; and a thing written from them, as will be seen one day. . . .

Will you go to the Rue du Faubourg Saint-Antoine, and see if you can discover a certain Tree there; an Elm, planted (as Tree of Liberty) in the Federation of 1790? I am told, *it* is still growing, though few know it now : I feel a real interest in it.—Will you inquire if there is *any* Book on *Danton* worth reading, new or old? I heard of one last year (a Novel), but concluded it was nothing.— Were you ever out at Versailles? I had laboriously to get an idea of it. Go to the Hôtel de Ville and look at the *Lanterne* (corner of the Place de Grève): I am told it is still there. . . .

And so finally, my dear Boy, send us news that you are safe in Paris; that you are coming home to us! We shall sit on the watch for you: at the latest hour of the night, how welcome will your knock be, how glad we, looking over the window, to find that it is Doil! May the good God grant us this blessing. Come and let us front the world together, Boy, some way or other. I begin to as good as despise the world, and will like it all the better for that: it has *terrified* me long enough; and shall not again. What is *it?* *Schall und Rauch:* the Reality is *under* it, and beyond it. Adieu, dear Brother. Our prayers are with you, always: come soon and safe.—Ever your affectionate,   T. CARLYLE.

CXLVIII.—To ALEXANDER CARLYLE, Annan.

CHELSEA, 1st *July* 1835.

. . . I wish I had any good word that I could

write for you here, my Boy, to encourage you in your new struggle, which I often picture to myself with interest and anxiety. There is little good going I think for many an industrious man as times are. It is a sore struggle, and poor wages; with little outlook of its mending, in our thank.[1] . . .

To me, I confess, when looking at this country and the perverse state it is in, one of the best refuges, though somewhat of a stern one to take, is the one you alluded to in your Letter: America, and "over the water" to — food for one's toil! It is really a great blessing of Heaven that there *is* land under the Sun where the husbandman's hand will bring him corn for his ploughing; a country which God's sky stretches over, even as here, and where man's perversion has not stept in to say "Thou that tillest, let another reap"! You remember in old years I used always to dissuade from America; neither am I yet any adviser of it, where extremity has not arrived: but the longer I look and live the less questionable does it

[1] As we think.

seem,—I might say, the more inevitable for thousands and millions of European men. But in the meantime you must play "hoolly";[1] be *canny* and patient till you see well what Annan will do for you. There must be many kinds of business going on there, at one season of the year or another; and strange will it be if you are the unfittest of all for all of them! Keep clear-headed, clear-hearted; be as *cheerful* as is possible for you : meeting all men with the look of peace, tolerance, and even trust: whatsoever is to *be* seen will show itself, and you will clutch at it deftly enough if it look suitable. And so God speed you, my dear Alick! Take a pen and write to me what you are about : the mere telling of it over to me will make it plainer to yourself. . . .

CXLIX—To his MOTHER, Scotsbrig.

CHELSEA, 19*th July* 1835.

MY DEAR MOTHER—As the last Letter must have brought you little but unpleasant news,[2] I

---
[1] Softly, gently.
[2] Namely, that Dr. Carlyle's return was indefinitely postponed.

had it in contemplation, of late days, to write to you again, that if my news were not of the best, they might be more frequent; for I know well it makes you happier to hear from me when my news are not positively *bad.* Luckily yesterday there came this Letter from our Doctor; which will make my sheet better worth its carriage. Jane is gone out to "a Music Party" with the Sterlings (whom I think I mentioned to you; very kind people, who come out to us often of late) : she will not be home till late ; I have sent the woman to bed, and have the house to myself. I thought once of getting on a little with my Book-writing (on your old principle, which I always remember, "that it will not *loup in again*"); but a better thought suggests itself that I shall do more good writing for Scotsbrig than for the world at this late hour; the rather, as I *did* my bit of task to-day, in some manner, and have little force in me to resume it. You shall have therefore what is going; till "the Wife" come home, and send me to sleep.—I regret greatly that my Letters to you have not been so deliberate, radical and complete as they should have been : but you will fancy all manner of excuses for me ; which indeed I am not without right to ; such "driving from post to pillar," and unsatisfactory hoping and being disappointed, working and being idle, have I had for a good while now. The burning of that Manuscript has proved hitherto about the very ugliest job I ever had to deal with, in innocency: but I shall get through it too, and without *doubt* (if I be wise) it will prove for good, and not evil. I am at work again, as you will guess; and more at ease with myself.

Jack has hardly much news from Munich, except the assurance that he is well and thinking of us : which is always welcome intelligence. . . . Before I forget, let me tell you about that money, which he wants sent to you. It will be too late the first Wednesday ; but on Wednesday next after that, which I think is the 29th day of the month, you will find it waiting for you. Ask for "one hundred and forty pounds" payable to yourself " Mrs. Margaret Carlyle." James Aitken will go with you, and manage it exactly as the last was done : enter it on their receipt-books in the name of Dr. Carlyle, Rome, with interest payable to *you*. James can clap a "*right*" somewhere on the next Newspaper, and I shall be satisfied. The interest will "keep you in tobacco"; which is better than doing nothing at all here.

I fancy you may possibly be up in that side of the country then, at any rate. Mrs. Welsh informs us she has sent for you to Templand, which I hope you resolved to go and visit again. She was for you "a couple of weeks" with her; but that can be as the spirit moves yourself and her when there. At all events, however, I hope you will go. She is to come up hither, and will bring us news of you. Tell her if she still hesitate, that she *must* come; there is no other resource for it. Jane is quite off the thought of coming this year; and as Mrs. Welsh proposes visiting London some time at any rate, there is surely no time so suitable as this. She must bundle, therefore, and get under way.

How long is it, dear Mother, since I now

had a scrape of a pen from you? Not one of them has written to me; were it not for the two scratches of Jean's hand weekly, I could not know what evil might not have befallen one or all of you. I will not blame *you;* for I know it is the ability not the will that fails: nevertheless do set about it, with your own hand, you there; it is only difficult not impossible. I want greatly to know how you get on in your two Scotsbrig Rooms; how your health is; what you are employed with,— whether my winter coat is spun; and a thousand things. You must really write.—M'Diarmid says there is very bad hay-weather; so I must imagine James and men weltering occasionally, not in the best humour, among wet swathes. Let him be patient and canny; it might have been worse.— . . .

You have heard that I am working again. I prosper considerably better than formerly; and see the weary *day'rk*[1] growing gradually a little less. By Heaven's favour, I shall

---

[1] Task, literally day's work (oftenest used in the form of "darg").

be through it; and surely not forget it for a long while! Nay, if I can have it done, as I first proposed, before coming off to Scotland, that will really be far better. I go jogging on, at any rate, according to ability; and no man should ask more of me. —My health is decidedly better than it was. Indeed, this Summer, which has been so unthrifty for your fields, has answered me and our streets much better than last did : there is always wind blowing, breath to be had ; the pavements seldom get *burning* hot; one can quite readily endure it. The Summer has been changeable ; but we have evidently a third less of *rainy* weather than you. Sometimes I do not go out at all till the evening ; and then a *long* roam over "the Parks"; a beautiful region, one of the main "temporal blessings" of these parts. Hyde Park itself is a fine expanse of smooth sward, with noble clumps of oaks and other towering wood ; I should think nearly *three times* as big as all Scotsbrig farm. You can think what a comfort that is, close upon the dusty streets. Wellington's House is at the corner of it, two miles from this. We went into it (having got an "order," by favour of the Sterlings) to see the furnishing out of the Tables for his grand Waterloo Dinner, which he gives yearly: it was the richest thing to be seen anywhere; more gold-plate, vases and splendours than I shall ever have occasion for. The Duke himself was visible for a moment; a tough-looking old steel-grey figure; really "one of the tightest old quarry-boys in the whole Howe-rigg." Since that, I saw a grand Review in Hyde Park, where the veteran was again. The people ran round him (when it was all done) huzzaing; at which he seemed to me not unlike *greeting;*[1] he lifted his hand refusingly from time to time; was *chewing* with his toothless lips; nostrils inflated, colour going and coming: I felt kindly drawn towards the old man. He is honest I do think, in his fashion; he had fought his way round half the terrestrial Globe, and was got *that* length; and at no great distance (from him and me) lay—Eternity too! —The old King came driving to the ground,

[1] Weeping.

near where I was standing: he was in regimentals with a most copious plume of feathers, so that while he sat all shrunk together in the open carriage, you saw little else but a lock of feathers, and might have taken our Defender of the Faith for some singular species of *Clocker*[1] coming thither. On dismounting, he showed an innocent respectable old face ; straddled out his legs greatly (which seemed weak), rested on his heels, *stiddering*[2] himself, and looked round with much simplicity what they wanted next with him. The Review itself was a wheeling and marching of foot and horse, several thousands ; a flaring and a blaring from trumpet and drum, with artillery-vollies, sham-charges, and then a continued explosion of musketry and cannon from the whole posse of them, like a long explosion of Mount Ætna : all very grand.

And so enough of clatter! Jane should be here now very soon, or should already have been here: at all events I am tired. I declare there she *is!* Exactly at the right moment!

[1] Clucking hen.   [2] Steadying.

Down to open!—(The Sterlings sent their coach, and I heard wheels).

20th July.—MY DEAR MOTHER—There is little to be added to-day, after the copious details of last night, cut short in that way, in the nick of time. I meant to write a fraction of a Note to Jean at Dumfries: tell her so, and to take the will for the deed. I cannot do it to-day; my work is all lying about me, not progressing in the best way, and I must go out with this to have it franked, and also for the sake of a walk. Tell her further that I know not whether she is in my debt or I in hers; but I *desire* her to write to me, and *soon.* Remember us kindly to Mary; say that I hope to breakfast with her yet this year, and eat of her *banna*'.[1] What is Jenny doing? Is she at Dumfries?—Have you ever been at the Sea-bathing yet? You are more convenient now than ever; I am persuaded it will do you good. —If you see Graham tell him that I meditate writing, and regret that *writing* is the only way

[1] *Bannock*, cake.

of communicating between us.—Now write, dear Mother! Take care of yourself; keep up your heart, and I will not *tine* mine. God be with you, my dear Mother!—Jane sends her loving regards to all of you.—I am ever, your affectionate, T. CARLYLE.

CL.—To Dr. CARLYLE, Geneva.

CHELSEA, 10*th August* 1835.

MY DEAR BROTHER— . . . The news you send us are as satisfactory as we could hope. *Your* resolution is taken; wisely, as I think: other persons, and other things, will resolve themselves as they can. My prediction again begins to be that your next route will be *homewards*. Heaven send it, safe and soon! It is quite right what you determine about going idle. Nothing can reward a man for doing nothing! The significance of life is a doing *something*. One gets food and lodging, and is found *living* this way or that, with what *Thatkraft* one has realised, with what *deeds* one has done therewith. I feel more and more of a settled humour in that particular. Much I can even *thank* that it has been so kind as grow the worst possible; it will take its way, and I shall know what is mine. There seems to me not a "chance," but a perennial behest and invitation for such workman as you, in this place: if the place do little for you, you shall do much for the place. Men are sick and distracted, bewildered, bequacked, bedevilled: come and help them if you can! All men's works are as *nothing* (the very *Iliad* and Gospel of Saint Matthew will one day *not be*); and yet, in *all* true work, there is such an *everlasting something*. Let the vanity be killed out of us, were it with whatever pain; let us go on working, in patience, in the name of God.—These things we shall yet peaceably speak of and *do*, if it be God's will. . . .

Since the day your Letter last but one came, I have sat by this desk (with a holiday on ending a Chapter, or so); struggling at that unspeakable Task. I trust, I shall never in Time have such another. Occasionally it has been disagreeable beyond speech. The best of it is, however, that except one (longish) chapter and some two days of another, it is *done!* The thing is worse, not very much worse, than it was ; but anyway it will stand again on paper, and I shall *crow day;* relieved from the unspeakablest load. At the time of your return to us (would we saw that!) I hope to have finished ; to be ready to rejoice in all points! There is then a period of recreation and vacation ; afterwards, a steady spell (of work that I *know* the nature of) ; and so the Book is off *my* hands,—and *on* the hands of whosoever has business with it. Sometimes I think it possible the world may take notice of the Book ; sometimes, no notice : either way, my contentment is great, had I it but *done.* Literature, after that, must go its way for a while : I, expecting simple Nothing of it, shall not be disappointed. *Hoffentlich* there are other ways of living ; other way of dying there at lowest is. *Es geh' wie es gehen will!* . . .

I had a Letter from Boston in America, with the signature "George Ripley";[1] full of

[1] The founder of the Brook Farm establishment, one of the characteristic outgrowths of New England Transcendentalism,

the most enthusiastic estimation ; really a good feeling ill-expressed, struggling for expression : *Teufelsdröckh* he calls " a crying out of the heart and the flesh for the living God"; one of the chief Signs of the Era, etc. etc.; and withal bids me by the name of Brother, go on in God's name, and falter for no man. Ripley seems to be a Clergyman of some Church (I think Emerson mentioned him to me): his Letter gave me no comfort at the time, it seemed so overdone; but it does now occasionally some, when I think of it. There was a pamphlet (of his writing) sent too : but it has not come to hand ; W. Hamilton is getting it for me, from "the St. Katherine Docks" and Packet ships there.—I have sent my other Americans, Germans, etc., almost all on their travels : your Elliot never came or sent sign.—We had a visit from the good Mr. Dunn (Irish Clergyman, *Nolo-Episcopari*, whom I spoke of): you are pretty sure to like him, and he you. John

which served Hawthorne for the groundwork of *The Blythedale Romance*. Mr. Ripley became afterwards well known as the literary critic of the *New York Tribune*.

Sterling has taken a house in Bayswater; is to be here very soon. That also, I imagine, is a future friend for you : there never came athwart me a man of a finer, open, guileless, all-hoping, lymphatic-sanguineous temper; one fears only that his Church-profession may prove questionable in these times; that his very life (he so headlong, excitable, his element so confused) may not hold out with him. . . . Henry Taylor we still see occasionally; a wholesome Northman, full of stubborn English stuff, of the slow, quiet, almost dull sort, yet which is not dull. I read his "Poem"; feeling that the *man*, though he could write no poem, would not have written No*thing:* as it proved. Allan Cunningham has not come across me for some weeks, but is well: his Brother the Doctor was with us the other night (the Sterlings, who came also, admired his *talent pour le silence*); a simple, quiet man; Nithsdale mainly, though he has been four times round the world. Hunt sits near us, radiating good wishes; seldom comes, for reasons known to himself. He is one of the cleverest men I ever spoke with : but unfortunately *Cockney-bred;* let him *gelten in seiner Stelle.*—Here is a *rap* at the door! I suppose I must leave you.—It was only worthy Mr. Dunn and his Wife come to ask us to Tea on Friday night: Jane was out; and they went in a minute. I finish my pellmell rubbish-cart of news, by telling you more specially whither Jane is gone. To Marlborough Street, to the Bolognese Contessa's (*degli Antoni* whom I told you once of), for an Italian Lesson! She volunteered to teach the poor Countess and Chauntress (and even Enchantress, for she is that too) a mouthful of English; but the degli Antoni insisted on *first* teaching *her* Italian (a most necessary preliminary); and so they go, Jane learning with amazing rapidity, but still in *una confusione siccome nella Torre di Babele!* That *Torre di Babele*, enounced with the right musical accentuation (for I too heard it), still sings in my ears, and has made me laugh a score of times.

I shall not succeed in gathering up this poor straggle of a letter now. I am in haste; and the day is hot, hot. We have suffered abundantly from heat and drought, these late weeks. The Parks are brown, bare as an old scratch-wig; give dust if you stamp on them; are rent into cracks. Our springs have not failed; but they say it is not so, in the South, where the people (as in Picardy, Normandy too) are ill off that way. Many a day, I do not go out at all till sunset: this day I have fled into the back-room; a bed-room (intended to be yours!); I look out on trees, grown dingy, but still trees; the sun, roasting, gives me a headache on the other side of the house. In Scotland they complained of *wet* not long ago, and did not know their mercies. . . .

I fear Jane will not be home in time to give you any postscript: her love you may authentically regard as sent. She is ill off at present about servants: the one we had (who suited very well) had to go off to Deptford, to wait on a sick mother, and is not like to come back. Jane has written to Miss Donaldson to get her an East Lothian one, and ship her hither. They are a miserable set of persons here: I often say (in my haste) " I would rather be my own servant once for all, and have done with them,"—living Diogenically. It is really *true;* but not quite convenient at present.—I like very well the temper you are in towards your Lady and all that *Umgebung.* It were sad to part otherwise than in friendliness and handsomely at lowest. Take patience where you are : it will soon be done. You are not to go by Paris ? If you did go, would you inquire among Printsellers for Vernet's *Caricatures* (I cannot tell you *which* Vernet;[1] but they are all during the Revolution ; of dresses, etc.: referred to often by Mercier) : I have searched here on all sides, but none knows anything. If there is such a *Collection* of Caricatures, I would give say £2 for it, poor as I am. If not *collected,* stray ones might perhaps be got. I find the whole French Revolution *new* to me in a manner, when I bring it actually *home.* The Thing *happened,* was visible of one form or the other : he who paints a Fact and Truth,

[1] Charles Vernet issued, under the Directory, a long series of studies of contemporary costume and character, among them *Les Merveilleuses,* and *Les Incroyables,* which illustrate vividly the strange dress and style of the revolutionary time.

paints something.—But now, my dear Jack, I must be off: my very head is getting sore; dinner is near ready, and the paper done. You can get no margins this time. God be with you, my dear Brother! Come safe home to us, and soon!—Your affectionate,   T. CARLYLE.

. . . . . .

CLI.—To Dr. CARLYLE, Munich.

CHELSEA, 23*d September* 1835.

You are doubtless longing, my dear Brother, to have another Letter from me; and will open this at Munich, I hope, safe and sound, with considerable impatience. I have not delayed wilfully; but only till I could send you decisive news. This is literally the first day, in which I could have specified my future whereabout in Time and Space, for the nearest Future, with any kind of completeness.

Though you are a sharp-tempered man, Jack, like the rest of us; yet I know you certainly for the placablest of *all* men: so I doubt not whatsoever of natural wrath you felt went fairly up the chimney with that sacrificed

Letter, and there was again peace between us, nay better peace than before. Well when a small holocaust of that kind will do the business!—I did not write in irritation against Her Ladyship or indeed anybody so far as I remember; but expressed in such words as came readiest the deliberate permanent opinion I had been led to form of her from such imperfect data as I had. If my reading was wrong, I recant it not only willingly but joyfully. To you at any rate such defence of your rather skittish and peculiar co-partner in this wayward business is very creditable: continue forever to take the *best* view of all mortals which your understanding will admit; nay it is often also *truer* than the surly one. But, for myself, all buckram grows more and more a kind of weariness to me: there perhaps has not been these two thousand years or thereby any mortal to whom man stood more completely as an *unclothed animal* than he (unluckily and luckily) does to me. It makes a strange world of it for one; and gives and will give one work enough: for often the buckram *crackles* amazingly when you treat it like mere cloth.—However let me tell you my history.

[1] First then, by the real blessing and favour of Heaven, I got *done* with that unutterable Manuscript, on Monday last. . . . The work does not seem to myself to be *very* much worse than it was; it is worse in the style of expression, but better compacted in the thought: as it goes through the Press I may help it somewhat. On the whole I feel like a man that had "nearly killed himself accomplishing *zero*." But *zero* or not *zero*, what a deliverance! I shall never without a kind of sacred shudder look back at the detestable state of enchantment I have worked in for these six months, and am now blessedly delivered from. The rest of the Book shall go on quite like child's play in comparison: also I do think it will be a *queer* Book; one of the *queerest* published in this century, and *can*, though it cannot be popular, be better than that. My Teufelsdröckh humour, no *voluntary* one, of looking "through the clothes" finds singular

---

[1] This paragraph is printed in Froude's *Carlyle's Life in London*, i. 55.

scope in this subject. Remarkable also is the "still death-defiance" I have settled into; equivalent to the most absolute sovereignty conceivable by the mind. I say "still death-defiance;" yet it is not unblended with a Greek-fire of Hope, *un*quenchable, which glows up silent, steady, brighter and brighter. My one thought is to be done with this Book. Innumerable things point all that way : my whole destiny seems as if it lost itself in chaos there (for my money also gets done then, etc. etc.) ; *in chaos, which I am to re-create,* or to perish miserably, — an arrangement which I really regard as blessed comparatively. So I sit here and write, composed in mood ; responsible to no man or to no thing ; only to God and my own conscience : with publishers, reviewers, hawkers, bill-stickers, indeed, on the Earth round me ; but with the stars and the azure Eternities above me in the Heaven. Let us be thankful!—On the whole, I am rather stupid ; or rather I am not stupid (for I feel a fierce glare of insight in me into many things) ; not stupid,—but I have *no sleight of hand.* A raw untrained savage ; for every trained civilised man *has* that sleight, and is a bred workman by having it: the bricklayer with his trowel, the painter with his brush, the writer with his pen. The result of the whole is : " one must just do the best he can for a living, Boy." Or in my Mother's phrase, never "tine heart,"—or even *get* provoked heart, which likewise is a danger.

But am I coming to Munich? Dear Jack, I have meditated considerably on that; and have figured out all your brotherly love and sorrow ; but after all I find, things being accurately weighed, my spirits, our cash, it is *better* for me and a kind of duty, to go to Scotland rather. Our poor Mother has had a most disappointed summer ; I promised to go and see her yearly while I could : God knows whether it may be *long* possible : I feel that I must to Scotland, and leave you far away. Besides I say to myself, If you are coming home in November (in a month!), what good were it? On the other hand, if by any unforeseen chance, poor Jack should *not* get home as he expects, I hereby engage that after this Book is done, I will cheerfully set out to see him, towards any point of Europe! I give you that promise; and mean, if needful which I hope it will not be, to keep it to the letter. The Book might be done in March : alas, it is not likely *so;* but we will hope and try.

My arrangement then is this. I went yesterday into the city to inquire for Scotch conveyances; I found there were smacks to Leith every Thursday and Sunday, a steamboat to Newcastle every Tuesday : I have as good as resolved in favour of the next Sunday smack; it is cheapest (the whole charge only £2); the accommodation *best*, as all agree and my own experience agrees; the sea-air promises blessed freshness to me; I will smoke and sleep for the four or five days we sail;—and finally there is the Mail to Dumfries that very night you arrive in Edinburgh. I write to my Mother announcing this, to-night or to-morrow. I feel as if I could fling my trunks on board, and then fling down myself, and *sleep*. I will have a dip in the Solway yet; *see* what they are all doing; and return a newmade man to my

winter's work before November set in. To
give you a better notion of it, you are to
understand that Mrs. Welsh is here: so that
Jane, whom it otherwise would not suit to
travel at this season, can still have the best
company in my absence. Mrs. Welsh has
been here some three weeks, and spoke of
returning in November. She does not take
very much to London or its ways; but seems
happy enough to be beside her Child again.
She has told me much about my Mother and
Jenny, whom she had up at Templand before
her departure: they were the happiest party;
jaunting, cuddycarts, Mrs. Glendinning, etc.
etc. — Poor Jane has been very unwell;
especially ever since her Mother came, when
she seemed as it were to give way; and broke
down into the most violent series of headaches
(with colic too) she has had for long. The
hot weather had withered us all up: I never
lived-through (*erlebte*) such a two-months for
weather; the stew and smoulder was as the
breath of kiln-drying, choking and palsying:
one felt as a certain Irishman told us he did at

Munich, one summer, "as if the spine were all gone; as if one were a serpent trying to *stand* on its tail." That is happily all over now, and we have even wet weather (still most grateful, by contrast); the Parks are springing up again like leek-beds: the little Dame will do well enough now. Especially, she says, as the Manuscript is over too! We have moreover had trouble on trouble with servants: two Irishwomen in succession, each half-distracted, though in different styles of distraction, filled up the series; the latter of whom, jingling down plates on the tea-table (for she had gone, an ugly woman too, with the face of a Polar Bear all week), and shattering the female and even the male nerves by it, had the luck to *explode* me upon her (just last night) at that fatal instant, and in two instants more was packing up her duds for march,—being desired "in God's name and even in the Devil's name" either to do that, or conduct herself like a rational creature, and preferring the former alternative. She is gone, I lit the fire this morning, our two Mistresses became their own housemaid; and we have perfectly a Heaven-on-Earth since. Shifty Jane has already found a *little* girl of suitable promise, who will come at four o'clock; and I am to try my whole industry, and bring some kind of damsel from Scotland with me. Nothing was ever more miserable than the arrangement of that universal relation, Master and Servant, here at this time. *Society*, of all kinds, in fact seems rapidly rushing towards unknown changes and consummations. We, meanwhile, have got a quiet house; and I have declared, what I deliberately feel, that I will rather get some small apartment, and sweep it out and arrange it for myself with my own hands (as my brave Uncle Tom did) than be bedevilled with *such* a set of unfortunates any more.—I have said nothing about our society etc.; which, however, you [can] fancy much as it was, only thinned somewhat by desertions to the country. The only new man I have seen is one Craik from Fife who "desired my acquaintance," and has made it, through Miss —— ... whom Jane had brought over from Edmonton to spend a few days with us. Craik is a solid fellow; edits "the Printing Machine," and otherwise bakes bricks for the Diffusion Society, with an honest oxlike strength and steadiness, not unworthy of praise. . . . Dunn the Clergyman sees us more and more, and loves us, himself loved: you will call him one of the best men you ever met with. They have all great favour for me, and tolerance really wonderful. Lastly *il Conte Pepoli* comes hither every Wednesday night, with Italian for Jane; with *Babelic* speculation, reading of Dante and so forth for me: a really superior sort of foreign product; vivacity, decision, grace, even harmony (for I have read some of his verses); a very entertaining man. We had a great burst of bravura together, over that class of Damned Souls in Dante, *A Dio spiacenti ed a' nemici sui*,[1] precisely "the respectable people" of this present generation of the world! Dante says, *non hanno speranza di morte, they* have not the hope to die! A grand old Puritan this Dante; depth and ferocity without limit; implacable, composed;

[1] Hateful to God and to His enemies.

as if *covered* with winter and ice, and like Hecla, his interior is molten fire!—Of Mill, Sterling, and others—nothing. Mill's Review is called the *London Review*, makes no figure or way, and will in all human probability, *trake*[1] by and by. . . . Now write you, my Boy, the instant you get this; to Scotsbrig: there will still be time, though we are farther apart now. I hope and indeed believe there is nothing wrong in *this* address. I shall delight to fancy you a free man, were it in your "own hired dog-hutch"—like Jean Paul. Do not regret me, my dear Brother; we shall meet when the time is, and be the gladder to meet.—My health, for I had forgot it, is really not at all bad; I have appetite, strength; want sleep a very little (fail of it I mean), am sensitive, irritable; I have often been far worse after work. Annandale will make me new again. God bless you, dear Jack! *Auf ewig!*

T. Carlyle.

. . . You can tell Herr Schelling when you

[1] Perish.

see him that he has more friends here than he wots of; that the thing *he* has thought in his solitary soul has passed or is ready to pass into many souls, of British speech, and do its work there. "*Not* like water spilt on the ground"!—You would hear of Dr. M'Crie's[1] death? *Ein Tüchtiger ist hingegangen.*—It seems to me always you ought to meet Teufelsdröckh in some of the Coffee-houses of Munich! Do they meet at *that* one yet,[2] and drink beer? —O'Connell is the *dining* man of this recess, as Brougham of last. He *schmaust und plaudert*—through the world.

[Postscript in Mrs. Carlyle's hand.]

DEAR JOHN—Headachy and without Domestic you may figure I am not in a promising frame for writing even so much as a postscript; but I can at least give you my kind love, and my Mother's best remembrances, under my

[1] Rev. Dr. M'Crie, author of the *Life of Knox*, etc.
[2] Carlyle said that the *Grüne Gans*, as well as Teufelsdröckh's lodging and watchtower in the *Wahngasse* (see *Sartor*, book I. chap. iii.) were places at Munich which his Brother John, after his former stay there, had described to him.—M. C.

own hand. God bless you. I hope to be well now that the weather is cooled and the accursed disaster repaired.—Your affectionate,

[J. W. C.]

CLII.—To his WIFE, Chelsea.

HOWES, ANNAN, *Tuesday, 6th October* 1835.

MY DEAR LITTLE WIFIE—There has been a longer delay in writing this time than I anticipated; and now at last if I would not again disappoint thee, I must write without deliberation, with the smallest possible convenience: I expected to be back at Scotsbrig last night, and to write there (as indicated in the Newspaper) with all fit means and appliances; but the weather, as it usually does in these weeks, proved rainy; I stayed with Alick, and must write here at his desk, or be too late for the post. You know what sort of thing writing here is! This Pen, for example, *marks;* but if it do not mark there is no tool other than an old razor for mending it: *Sic de cæteris.* However, I have a room to myself, a good fire and a locked door, kinder welcome never met man than that which meets unworthy me : so with or without much coherence, in the middle of the squealing of contented or discontented children, and the moist blustering of October winds, in view of the old steeple of Annan, with trees, grass and *mugworts* (that would delight Leigh Hunt) more immediately at hand, I dash you off some fractions of Autobiography as I can.

The journey to Liverpool I shall retain for long winter evenings. Garnier I fancy would call and say he saw me safe in the Coach : you can fancy that I lumbered along, much-enduring, and got to port some time within the twenty-four hours. Literally *to port:* for our so-called " Liverpool Mail " proved to be properly the " Chester Mail," and took us some twenty miles of roundabout ; landing us at last in the surly *gloaming* (for the day had been wet) on the bare stones of the Dock ; out of a steamboat namely ! There is no end to the deceptions of men and coach-keepers ! However, the grand question was now, What to do ? I was dusty, unslept, sulphurous ; Maryland Street as I calculated would be just at dinner ;

we were far from it; far from the Carlisle Steamer, the times or seasons of which no man there could tell me of. With Porter shouldering my luggage, I wandered to Steam-Offices; to a wrong Inn; finally to the right one (in Dale Street), learned that the Boat would verily sail at three in the morning; got hot water and a bedroom; intent to brush myself there, and, spending the evening with Uncle, sail, asleep or awake, at the given hour. I was *wae* exceedingly to open thy little red poke[1] with shaving tools, and find it all so right and orderly; Mother and thou sitting probably at tea 200 miles from me. Bagmen surveyed me as I ate my beefsteak and drank my thimbleful of brandy; I set out forthwith for Rodney Street and Maryland Street. A long way; and a dim one, compared with the London ways. In a dingy street an elephantine figure stalked athwart me; I said, " Dr. Carson!" it grunted affirmation; told me in a grunting somnolent tone what turns I had to Rodney Street; then lumbered on along its way without

[1] Bag.

other salutation or good-night. Heavy Bull of Bashan, thought I, retire to thy crib, and proper sliced turnips with chaff await thee there!—At last behold me in Maryland Street; the goodman welcoming me in his own openhearted brotherly way, the good lady making me tea with toast and "Irish honey," little Johnnie surveying Aunt Grizzie's[1] present; all hands blithe to see me; all things attainable there; only not the one thing needful, rest. Tower-of-Babel Johnstone and his Daughter came directly, or were already there: Dr. Arbuckle was soon sent for, and came. The good Doctor told me he was just leaving Liverpool and Europe: his romantic, mysterious source of supply (which he now made no mystery of) had dried up; and invitation to Maragnan (near Pernambuco, a Cotton-station in South America) had been sent him, to practise among the English and Portuguese there; which invitation he had accepted; he was to sail in a week! I could not blame him; but that too was a *wae* feature of the night. The

[1] *I.e.* Mrs. Welsh's.

young Ladies sang and played ; the old gentlemen and young drank red wine, ate shrimps and other supper, and all laughed as I talked : at length, after midnight, I arose and said to Arbuckle that he positively must then and there take charge of me, get me stuck in some lockfast place ; or should he even tie a shot to my feet and fling me into the Mersey brine : for one way or the other *sleep* was grown utterly indispensable to me. You may fancy the friendly obtestations, outcries and preventives, all which I had resolutely and with brevity to wave aside. Arbuckle led me through streets and confusions, I got bills settled, got porters, passed through mountains of cotton-bags with sleepless watchmen on the top of them ; on through Dock police, etc. etc. to the Carlisle Steamer ; and there under the void night with a heartfelt invocation to God to bless him, I took leave of the good Arbuckle, —probably forever in this world. We were sad enough both ; but so the Powers would have it. Sleep, after some jerkings and startings, rushed down on me ; drowned all snorings, etc. etc.; I awoke at my old hour of six; reeling in my drawer-bed, with the glad feeling that we were at sea, and must either get home soon or be drowned. I fasted; for we were all sick; the weather (for some hours) wet and gusty: finally after adventures and *misshanters*[1] (for I had fallen asleep, and they sailed *past* Annanfoot with me, etc.) I got safe to poor Mary's in the suburbs of Annan at nine in the evening. It was Roodfair day; all were at Dumfries, and she was alone: the kindest of little women. In spite of rains next day, Alick and I got to Scotsbrig at the hour of sleep; they put me into a dry snug bed; I ailed nothing but headache and *sniftering;* and, next morning, having "indulged in a cup of *castor*" I began rapidly to recover. I have done literally nothing since but go on with that; and so here I am, not at all entitled to complain much.

To tell you what they are all about would take long space. My Mother is well and cheerful beyond what I could have fancied. They have converted those two upper rooms

[1] Misadventures.

into a really comfortable, quite brisk-looking apartment, *far* better than we ever saw them : Jenny is the most assiduous little handmaid and all goes along as smooth as oil. I have heard much about Templand, Hugh and the Cuddy. I had much to answer about you and Mother. Jamie's Wife seems a fine *sonsy*[1] natural lass, with good sense ; whom any one can easily live with: there is a rocking of cradles, a quackling and lullabying in all these houses : one generation passeth away and another cometh ! Jamie lost "half his harvest" last year by bad weather ; has much in jeopardy at this moment : but holds on without complaining. Austin is the most diligent pacific of men, but can hardly, if at all, gain a subsistence in this Burgh, so wretched are the times. The result of Alick's jobbing is a *loss* of something near £20 ; neither does any prospect open on him : he seems clear and considerate, however ; and looks I think mainly towards Upper Canada for next spring. A resolution of painful character, yet which I cannot dissuade. Austin also in-

[1] Comely.

clines that way, though Mary is still very averse. They should both go I do think, and together. God guide them! The feet of men are sore shackled in this pilgrimage. — The playthings and presents were all joyfully welcomed; the young brood may now again point to this and the other novelty, and say again, "It was my Aunt's, the Leddy's at Lun'in:" they are a thriving brood, and will be *wealth* in America. I have seen Ben Nelson (last night), grown very hoary, and his Boy more taciturn than ever; also Waugh, writing "New Theory of Medicine," "Commentary on the Revelation;" rusty, dusty, confused of utterance; apparently in decided state of insanity. All is so sad, *spectral* here: yet it falls on me like healing oil to be *let alone*, to see greenness round me, to hear neither "shrim-m-mps" sung out, nor wheels grating base thunder, nor Cads quacking "*Bennk! Bennk!*"—I have written to Nanny Macqueen for my saddle; Harry is in stout muscularity and can go, though lazily: to-morrow we should be in Dumfries, if the weather will. I have also seen Cousin Tom (Frank's Tom) a *nice* youth really.

But now, dearest Bairn, how art thou thyself? Many a time I fancy; but could not hope to know till after I had written. Your Newspaper came, welcome: you would get one from me the same Saturday, then another you will get, then this. O I do hope you are a little quieter, stronger. I do hope that wretched pilgarlick *peesweep* " Sereetha "[1] is off, and something a shade better in her stead! Know at any rate for some comfort that I have (which was my errand hither yesterday) all but hired you a Scotch Servant, to come home *with* me. Do you remember the Toll-woman near Grange, whom we had no penny for? I am nearly sure this " Marion Hay " is her daughter. My Mother and they all think *she* will answer, if any will: her people are douce good people: she has lived two years as Cook (I think) with Mrs. Tom M'Turk, also about the same space with Little of Cressfield, they want her at Gillen-

---

[1] "*Sarah Heather*" (the little serving girl mentioned before), who so pronounced her own name.—M. C.

bie ; she prefers London, at least London *wages*.
I came yesterday as I said, and saw the *cratur ;*
she is keeping house for her Brother, a Baker
here ; Mary had found her out,—almost against
hope, for Betty's Daughter *could* not come,
though leaving Moffat. Well ; the lass is of
slight nimble figure, with a rustic simplicity of
intelligence and good humour in face ; *can* and
will wash, sweep, scour, cook, and do *all* things :
I must carry her to London (she has a. Brother
there, a shopman) : that will cost £2 : 10s. : her
wages must be £5 the half-year without perqui-
sites ; if we or if she want to be off at the end
of the first half-year, she returns *half* of the
£2 : 10s., and goes her ways. I will inquire of
Miss Little of Cressfield to-day ; meet the girl
again on Thursday, and hire her if it seem
good. My own private notion is that she is no
first-rate servant, more like M'Turkdom than
Chelsea ; yet it is indubitable that Cressfield
and others have wanted her back again : her
goodness of character and temper (or rather I
should say *nature*, for there may be quickness
of *temper*, in that face) seems well proved : she

wants no tea-money, beer-money, carpets, etc. etc.; and the chance is that as compared with any we have had, she may be a very jewel. I endeavoured to make all plain to her; especially to an elder *gled* [1] of a sister that had come with her: the creature looked innocently in my face, with a kind of trustfulness : for a year I do incline to suppose she may do. Shall I take her then ? I see no other that I can do. She seems some twenty-four years of age; an attachable creature ; may be handy, orderly (the probabilities are that way) is certainly submissive, lively and modest : better than most women. What can I do (let Miss Little testify or not) but take her, and be thankful ? *Nicht wahr ?*

This business of the Lass then being in a fair train, I must speak to you of *Harry*. Harry ran away, and flung off my Mother (*not* blamably), he has performed other beautiful feats (they are really wise and laughable) : my Mother will take him again from Alick, who has been feeding him on bought hay all this time : but the result of the whole is, he is not

---

[1] Kite.

of use to any of them here. Now an ancient Blacksmith near this house, a man I remember of old, has seen him, and fallen in love with him; a man "extremely kind to horses": he will give the value for him, and keep him hopping about in the easiest kind of employment in his old days; therefore, I ask, were it not well to sell him to the ancient Blacksmith? Say Yes, and it shall be done: say No, and I will try to do some other way. The result in money can be but some £5: but perhaps there were no smoother old age to be provided for the poor beast, than even this same, which offers itself. Write: about this; and O about so many other things! *without* delay. O Jeannie! My fingers are all as black as a crow (for our inkbottle is a phial), and my head itself is not of the clearest, and I had so many hundred things to speak about; and to think about unspoken! Keep thy heart up, my brave Lassie: it shall be well!

Probably you see John Sterling; to whom remember me *brüderlich* . . . kindly to Mill, and to Pepoli, if they come, as I hope they do.

Many true wishes were to go from *these* regions to Jane; but I have my door locked. Their love to us is all they have; but they give that freely. Kiss your Mother, and say that means my love. Love me, my dear Lassie, and fear God; and I swear by Him there shall nothing go ill with us. God bless thee ever, my Dearest.—Thy own, T. C.[1]

CLIII.—To Mr. HENRY INGLIS, Edinburgh.

SCOTSBRIG, ECCLEFECHAN, 21*st October* 1835.

MY DEAR INGLIS—No Letter that can come from me in my present mood and position, will be worth the reading, much less the paying for; nevertheless I had long ago determined to write to you when I should arrive here; and now something almost like a call of business (though, alas, on my part only begging business) impels me to do it. In the dullest of all humours, soliciting from the Heavens and the Earth no higher blessedness than to be let alone, I accordingly stir myself up, as it were in spite of

[1] Mrs. Carlyle's reply to this letter is in *Letters and Memorials*, i. 33.

the Devil and the Flesh. The probability, or even the certainty is, I shall profit by it myself: if you suffer, pray bear it like a Martyr, as you and all men are, or ought to be. . . .

I have fled hither some three weeks ago out of Din and Confusion grown insupportable; to rest me a little here; to look once again, were it only with the feeling of a *revenant* (all too ghost-like verily) on the scenes one inhabited when alive. In that Brick Babel, where all goes with such breakneck speed, *all* from the Cab-driving on the streets to the way of thinking, of existing within doors and within hearts, you grow after a certain length of time to feel as one whirled with inconceivable velocity on an immeasurable whirligig, for what purpose you cannot so well see; whereby you in a fit of desperation (as some I have known *do*) at length go and fling yourself into the River; or else, which is the milder and surely preferable method, retire for few weeks into the country; as I have done now. My wife has her mother with her; and with more or less patience waits my return. Did you notice on a newspaper that I hoped "to see you soon"? The truth is, I did calculate on going by sea and Edinburgh, to wait, with you mainly, there one night: but smacks and steamboats proved all ineligible; so I fled by Liverpool rather. Literally a flight; for no sleep rested on my eyes; and I felt as if retreating from the *höllische Jagd*, as properly it was. In another fortnight I must be back.

I have been exceedingly busied and bustled in that Babel: apparently to little end. A task I had set myself of writing on the "French Revolution," would not prosper much, met the sorrowfullest mischances, and is yet far from done. A first volume, the fruit of five months' hard toil, was lent to a friend, and by him too carelessly, *sent up the chimney*, as kindling for fires! This is literally *true*. The task of *re-writing* it lasted six months; and was the ugliest I ever had in life, or expect ever to have. It is done, however; and if the Heavens keep me alive six months longer, the rest of the Book shall be done; after which my outlook into the future, as it were, *terminates*.

Literature in London is madder than Bedlam: nevertheless true it remains, that God made this Universe and not the Devil; wherefore a man ought to possess his soul in peace if he means peacefully; and hold himself ready for turning to the right hand if his way on the left hand prove all too foul. Pray only that I may be able by and by to send you a copy of the Book! Who knows but it may prove almost a *unique* in Edinburgh. It seems more and more as if there were no one but yourself with whom I had any sympathy there, any call for sympathy. One should love his brothers; but finds it easier at some seasons to do it in the *cryptophilous* way, giving or receiving no sign. In London there is much to *over*look (if you would keep your temper), but also somewhat to *look* at and dwell on: in regard to companionship and social position among my fellow men, I was never elsewhere so well situated, indeed never elsewhere *situated* at all. We must take the evil with the good.

But amid these generalities, let me not forget the speciality, "call almost of business," which brings you in contact with them to-day. The question is, Do you fortunately want a Law Clerk? Do you know any reputable Law-practitioner that does? There is a young Cousin of mine, of my own name, who longs greatly for such a situation; who, I imagine, might really fill it well. He was in an "office" in these parts, but the Attorney died; and Tom is now in the Sheriff's Establishment at Dumfries, working without wages, for improvement merely. Improvement he does want (being still only nineteen or twenty), but also some frugal means of living. A place in some Edinburgh Lawyer's office, if not a W.S.[1] then some inferior kind of man, would meet all his wishes for a year or two. He is actually a modest, intelligent, very well-conditioned youth this Cousin of mine; of industrious, methodic habits; clear, even penetrating, for his years; likely one might say to make a superior kind of clerk; and, if he live, a superior kind of man. For the rest, owing to circumstances it seems to me as if a more than usual charge of

[1] Writer to the Signet.

him were laid in *my* hands; father and mother are gone; he is, apart from his qualities, one of the loneliest young creatures now living. Alas! I fear you can do nothing in this kind for him; yet it seems my duty to *try;* if you *can*, nothing is surer for me than that you will with true readiness. I remain here till the beginning of November (first *week* probably); after that the address is the old one, which you know.

As it is dubious whether you can even make out the handwriting of this, I will not soil more of the white paper with such work; but let you go. May good be with you and not evil, my Friend! Forget me not while we both pilgrim on this side the Moon. It is a solitary kind of world; yet it is a world; and I imagine had a Maker;—as the other also, and all others, will probably be found to have.

Farewell, and love me, T. CARLYLE.

CLIV.—To Mrs. AITKEN, Dumfries.

CHELSEA, 4*th December* 1835.

. . . As to myself I have really been but in a feckless sort of state these last two or three weeks; sitting at my desk once more, but with a degree of helpless ineffectuality that might surprise one. The *liver* is not right within, nor the heart; nor is the world right without. Little would tempt me to fling that thrice unfortunate Book of mine, even at this advanced stage of it, *cleverly* into the fire, and *so* have done with it. However I do *not* take that rash method; I, as you have heard, *take a blue pill* rather, and wait for better days. Like the man I one night heard on Leith Walk: a drunken individual whom he met growled out indignantly, "*Go* to H——, sir!" To which the other, in a frank historical tone, replied, "G——, I'm gaun to *Leith;*"—and have not convenience for the expedition just now! Let not me be less judicious. In fact, I have scrawled and *glarred* some portion of my poor Book but brought nothing whatever out in a clean shape yet. It is what James would call "laying it," perhaps the other finer parts of the process will follow in due course. I must be quiet, quiet: it is a *canny* way of working, not the right-forward main-force way, that will serve me in this case. The Book, be it worth nothing or worth something, shall, if Heaven please, be finished. After which it seems possible a radical reform, at any rate a radical change, in my figure of life may follow. I am grown or fast growing entirely wearied of much; especially of this perpetual pining in sickliness, in the mean painful enchantment (for it is very much that) of nameless woe and dispiritment. Nameless and needless; for I am not bound to it: one can live otherwise than by ink (and *poison* as it proves); otherwise, were it even by breaking stones on the highway. I believe myself to have at bottom a very *healthy* frame of body, for one so sensitive; and soon surely, or never, I ought to think of getting in possession of that. Let the whole world sing or say what it will, the course that has led a man into continual *ill*-health is a *wrong* course, and Nature herself surely warns him aloud to quit it. The only thing to be prayed for however, in this matter, is that you *keep your temper*, cheerful heart, and such clearness of eye as there is! If one gets *enraged*, he flings all topsy-turvy; and *is*, and produces round him, a mere "Tchaw-os."[1] . . .

CLV.—To Miss JANET CARLYLE, Scotsbrig.

CHELSEA, 23*d December* 1835.

MY DEAR JENNY—No letter could be welcomer than yours, bringing favourable tidings as it did, at the time when we were apprehensive that something was wrong with you. It is the first letter you have sent us; but must be the beginning of many. Do not spare us with letters: it will improve your handwriting, and be every way a good exercise for yourself, were there nothing more; and to us always, the smallest contribution of news will be welcome as flowers in May. Just do as you have begun doing: write down whatsoever comes readiest to hand; not minding whether it be well-worded or ill-worded; understanding only, with clear assurance, that the minutest piece of intelligence you convey from those two upper rooms, in *any* kind of words whatsoever, will be

[1] Chaos, so pronounced by a schoolmaster near Dumfries —M. C.

welcomer than all rhetoric could make anything else. . . .

As for me the principal news is that I have got another Chapter of that weary Book finished, better or worse. I felt rather feckless, dispirited, confused : but the thing went off when I roused myself; I found with joy that I could still go along writing as of old. A long task is still to do ; but it is all natural work now; no writing of *burnt* stuff, which latter surely is the miserablest of all human trades, enough to break the heart of a man. I am in better health than I was ; and will go on "*cannily*," well remembering John Ritchie's admonition : " The *slower* thou rides," etc.[1] It is in my favour too this fine hard weather we have; a ringing black frost all round ; I saw the people to-day skating on the pond of St. James's Park, the noses of all persons *blue;* gardeners, etc., thrown out of work will soon be begging, " Pity the poor *froze*-out Garden*as!*" It is winter fairly.

[1] " Thou may depend on't, the *slower* thou rides the *quicker* thou'll get to thy journey's end " (this to a man riding a mere skeleton of a horse, likely to die if urged on).—M. C.

People are to eat "Christmas Dinners": there are *walls* of beef, that might be built into beef-*stacks*, and such multitudes of dead turkeys, etc. etc., as fill one with amazement. . . . The paper is done, dear Jenny; and makes but a poor return for your full sheet. You will have more elsewhere, if not as mistress, then as bidden guest; for Jane is busy on my Mother's behoof at this moment. Take care of yourself, my little Bairn; take care of our dear Mother, who is near you, more dependent on you than on any of us. "Do not shorten but lengthen;" and believe me always—Your affectionate Brother,
T. CARLYLE.

CLVI.—To his MOTHER, Scotsbrig.

CHELSEA, 24*th December* 1835.

MY DEAR MOTHER — I walked over to Charles Buller to-day, and got this frank, which will be lying ready for you on Saturday, or whensoever, after that, you call. It was my promise that I would drop you a word so soon as anything *clean* came upon the sheets of the Book; and a little chapter being got into that state, I keep my word. John's Letter, spick-and-span new the other day, and full of nothing but welcome tidings, is so much *beyond* bargain. You will find him very well; better off, I think, than any other of us whatsoever at this date; and fixed there till April, when we may again cherish the hope of seeing him, should all go well. He has even Practice, it would seem, and has made 420 *francs* (or Ten-pences) by that, about £20, better very considerably than making nothing. I *had* written to him; and my Letter would be in his hands some two days after his own came off. I think I shall wait now, having nothing that presses to tell him, till I hear again.

I got your three words, my dear Mother; and was right glad of them, in the absence of more. I assure you I will be "canny"; nay I must, for a little overwork hurts me, and is found on the very morrow to be quite the contrary of *gain*. I have many a rebellious troublesome thought in me (proceeding not a little from ill-health of body); but I deal with them, as I best can, and get them kicked out.

Pride! Pride! as I often say. It lies deep in me; deep, deep, and *must* be beaten out, were it with many stripes. If this Book were done, I feel all but quite clear for giving up Literature as a trade, *whatsoever* other I fall to. But for the present all this is neither one thing nor another to me. On, on with thy work! that is the one commandment; sufficient for the day!—I see many good people here; and have indeed many a blessing, were I in the mood to make right use of them. The young Clergyman John Sterling comes very much about me; and proves by far the loveablest man I have met for many a year. His speech always enlivens me; shortens the long walks we sometimes take. There is no day almost but I walk: the streets, even when there is none with me, are amusing to look on, one does not readily weary.—I do not go much "out"; never to dinner when I can help it. Tea, again, suits me well enough: you take *your tea at home*, then fare out about seven or eight o'clock, drink one other cup of *jute*,[1] have some talk, often very rational and

[1] Weak tea.

pleasant, and come home unharmed. I saw the Bullers that way one night; also Mill lately (who has been ill of some kind of fever); John Sterling with whom I saw that Evangelist the good Mr. Dunn; etc. etc. So passes the day in labour, the evening in some sort of amusement or light employment.—There is a Paper in the last *North American Review*, headed "Thomas Carlyle"; which treats of *Teufelsdröckh*: it is extracts mostly; good-natured, rather stupid: you will see it by and by. The man says, if I will come to America, I shall be sure of a welcome, etc.: America we will leave as the *last* shift; so long as the bowls will roll here at all in a tolerable way, I will keep on this side the water. It is a queer thing Writing, in these days: you send a written sheet away from Craigenputtock, and the answer to it comes back by and by over the Atlantic Ocean. They seem very good sort of people these Yankees, —at least to me.

Dear Mother, how do you *fend* in this hard weather, these short days? Do you keep a rousing fire from the new coal-box? Mrs. Welsh has the Book for you. The days will always be growing longer after *this* ;—and times generally, never doubt it, will alter and even mend! We have the whole world to turn ourselves in; and it is the Almighty's world.—It will be another new year before you hear from me again. May the worst of our years be over! Good be with you and all of us, through this coming year,— through the endless Eternity which it brings us a step nearer.—You must very kindly remember me to Graham when you meet him, and say I will write, were I farther on, a little. My respects to that speechless Infant, brotherly wishes to his father and mother. Jenny is charged with my messages to Alick. Do not forget Mary and her household: she can also tell Ann Cook's[1] people that the lassie is well; hardy as a Highlander, full of assiduity, good-nature, and wild Annandale savagery, which causes the Cockney mind here to pause astonished. Broader Scotch was never spoken or thought by any mortal in this metropolitan city. Adieu, dear Mother.—Yours wholly, T. C.

[1] Ann Cook, the maid at Chelsea.—M. C.

CLVII.—To ALEXANDER CARLYLE, Annan.

5 CHEYNE ROW, CHELSEA,
18*th February* 1836.

MY DEAR BROTHER—I was much shocked to-day on opening the Newspaper to find in it a brief announcement that your little Margaret had been taken from you last Saturday. Apparently the call had been very sudden; for Jean, writing to me the week before, said nothing of any illness.—I remember the gleg-looking little creature in its Mother's arms; and feel sorrow for you all. It was not to know the good and evil of Life, poor little child; but to be called hence and cut off, while yet but looking into the world! The course of human destiny is "fearful and wonderful" ever as of old. Alas, one can say nothing, *nothing;* —except, if it so might be, what the wise have submissively said before us : " The Lord giveth and the Lord taketh away; blessed be the name of the Lord !"

I trust neither you nor Jenny will give yourselves up to unavailing distress, or lament beyond measure. Some natural tears are due and unavoidable; the innocent ways of such a being, briefly lent us, will plead painfully in the parent's bosom : but what then ? Is not *all* Human Life a shadow ; and whatever lives fast going down to Death ? We shall *all* be gathered thither ere long : "we shall go to them, they will not return to us."—My dear Brother, I feel how vain all words are ; whatsoever I could write would fall useless, where the stroke has fallen. It will show only that I grieve in your grief, and feel as a Brother for what befals you ; which is the little all that man can do for man.

I had thoughts of writing to you these several days ; but this sad occurrence hastens me : though I have no time or composure to write anything, I send you this Note of Remembrance ; with Jack's Letter, it will not be worthless to you.

. . . I think in general we have "a wide world," though full of impediments, and must set our face handsomely to it. For myself I cannot be said to fear anything, or almost to hope anything from this old country of ours. Things have grown so utterly contradictory and impracticable round me that I have, as it were, retired within my own citadel, and very quietly bid them welter their way, and do, in short, whatsoever it is their pleasure to do. By the grace of Heaven, I mean to keep my own senses clear, my own heart free and ready; and innumerable cobwebs shall be nothing but cobweb to me. But on the whole surely my position here is a very strange one,—as indeed is usually appointed for the like of me. Many men honour me, some even seem to love me; and withal in a given space of time I shall have no bread left here. So we must go and seek it elsewhere then? Clearly go, were it to Jerusalem (as our brave Father used to say); and seek cheerfully — whatsoever is allotted us. All things are tolerable, all losses but the loss of *oneself;* which latter is *not* entailed on us.

But after all there is a brighter side of possibilities; and much may be better than we think. For this also we shall hope to be ready, to be thankful; and to do wisely with this too. . . .

Jane is sitting by me, rather better than she has been of late. She has been plagued with colds, etc., all through winter; never very ill, yet never well. She bids me send you and Jenny her affectionate remembrances and sympathies. I expect you will write soon. God bless you and yours, dear Brother!

T. CARLYLE.

CLVIII.—To Dr. CARLYLE, Munich.

CHELSEA, 23d *February* 1836.

MY DEAR BROTHER— . . . There is no bad news anywhere, except one article which will be less so to you than it was to me, who knew the little subject of it. Alick's youngest child, a fine gleg-looking little creature, named after our Mother, is dead; of measles; rather suddenly, I think: but the news is quite laconic as yet, only marked on a Newspaper. Poor people: sorrow never fails long. I sent Alick your last Letter in a frank, with some words of sympathy; all I had to give. — There was shortly before that a Letter from Jean, testifying to our Mother's continued health, and the general welfare : Alick's trade, it was guessed, would prove unexpectedly successful : they were all well then, and stirring. I added a Note for my Mother ; whom I fancy on good grounds to have one bright hope, that of seeing the Dr. soon. — Jean hinted in a kind of ambiguous way that Jenny was likely to be wedded "in two months." . . . And so our Mother will be left solitary ; and rapid Time will have brought another change. But fear not: our brave Mother will take it well ; and with the heart she has never be left desolate. Jemmy's Wife and she seemed to do very handsomely, and she has the rest about her. Her Houses too, on which her income depends, were like to get into a better train : Baker Park, a very 'sponsible man, was about bargaining for the large House next year, and perhaps even taking the whole set of them under his own charge. That Village of Ecclefechan, which I passed through, once or twice, gave me the strangest unearthly feeling ; very sad, very ugly, yet not without a grandeur even a sacredness in the middle of such squalor. What is Eternal Rome, Jerusalem, or Nazareth itself, but a *temporary* set of huts and habitations, where Being begins, and is, and then is not — under God's *unchanging* Heaven? Alas, I often feel as if Hades itself were slight change to me, from this fearful and wonderful mystery of a World; surely no greater Miracle it were,—past finding out. Let us bow down in the dust; and in silence (since for the present one has no *words*) feel with the old wise, "though HE slay me, yet will I trust in him." *Hier steh' ich; kann nichts anders; Gott hilf mir!*—On the whole, I often meditate on Christian things; but find as good as no profit in talking of them here. Most so-called Christians (I believe I should except the worthy Mr. Dunn) treat me instead with jargon of metaphysic formulas, or perhaps shovel-hatted Coleridgean moonshine. I admire greatly that of old Marquis Mirabeau (though he means it not for admiration) : *Il a* HUMÉ *toutes les formules!* A man *should* "swallow" innumerable "formulas" in these days ; and endeavour above all things to look with eyes. —But whither this all? Unfortunately, almost nowhither.

If I tell you that my poor scribble, after above a week of rest, is again under way, and doing what it can, you must not grow weary of me and it: I have next to nothing else at present that seems to belong to me in this world. Whether the Book be good or be bad, it will to me be blessed in that one point,—in its end. Yet after all, it is only my impatient temper that makes me so speak: for the poor thing, full of faults as it can be crammed, will have a thought or two, a genuine picture or two; and so *not* be worthless: what more would I? The best news is that I hope to have the Second Volume fairly off at the time you appoint for returning: could all answer, how joyfully would I take my interregnum of vacation with Doil! We would walk together, to Hampstead, to Dulwich, to all places; and be happy in the spring sunshine. Let us wait, and hope.—Mill's new Review making small way, they have purchased the old *Westminster*, and will join that with it; on which occasion Mill, though he does not like to speak urgently, wishes very greatly that I would give him "a few Articles." I will think seriously of it : a hundred pounds of money might be earned ; my Third Volume waiting, not the worse for waiting. On the other hand, — but indeed I have no "other *hand*," or economic guidance of any kind here ; and go along, through boundless "quackery and triviality," in the peaceablest armed - neutrality *without* any. We shall see, we shall see. Dr. Bowring wrote to the tyrannous French Minister : " Sir, I am calm, but energetic."—Good-night, my dear Jack : the supper came (two lines ago) ; Jane wearied is off to bed ; I too am drooping with long day's work. Adieu. . . .

INDEX

"ABBEY, a laird in the," proverb, i. 325 *note*
Advocates' Library, ii. 88
Aitken, James, marries Jean Carlyle, ii. 129 *note*; mentioned, 194, 230; his son, 229, 254, 255
Aitken, John (Carlyle's uncle), oversees the alterations at Craigenputtock, i. 70, 95, 105, 118; letter to, ii. 69
Aitken, Mrs. *See* Carlyle, Jean
America a grand remedy against the worst, ii. 93; Carlyle receives encouragement from, 199: his hope in, 279: is asked to lecture in, 332 : is assured of a welcome in, 390; advantages of emigration to, 335
Anderson, James, death of, i. 178
Animal magnetism, essay on, by Dr. Carlyle, i. 152, 201
Arbuckle, Dr., ii. 294; a sad parting with, 368, 369
Arnott, Dr., Napoleon's physician, i. 57 *note*
Art, but a reminiscence, ii. 123; "sapless provender," 236
Arundell, Mr. Hunter, ii. 121 *note*
Austin, James, marriage with Mary Carlyle, i. 288 *note*; mentioned, ii. 160, 371
Austin, Mrs. Charles, first acquaintance with, i. 319, 320; personality, 321, 323; tea with, 380; friendship with Mrs. Carlyle, ii. 25, 223; mentioned also, 314, 326

BADAMS, Dr., Carlyle's regard for, i. 277; illness, 307; visit to, 351, 354; death of, ii. 127, 134
Bankruptcy Court, Carlyle applies for Registratorship in, i. 358
Barjarg library, ii. 121
Barnard, Henry, ii. 321 *note*
Barnet, Bessy, goes with the Carlyles to Chelsea, ii. 127, 138, 169, 171
Becker, Dr., i. 91, 112, 119; death of, 386
Bel'uomo, Dr., ii. 294
Belisarius, French print of, ii. 178
Bell, James, death of, i. 210
Bell's Life, characterised, i. 207
Biliousness shall not part a wise man from his purposes of wisdom, i. 108, 163; ii. 317, 318
Blacklock, tenant of Craigenputtock, negotiations with, i. 46-54, 106
Blackwell, his Homer, ii. 141
Blockheads, charity for, i. 184
Boisserée, Dr., i. 122 *note*
Book-trade, bad condition of the, i. 17, 21, 338; disturbed by the Reform Bill, 353; ii. 9, 82, 100, 103, 172; at its lowest ebb, 183

VOL. II   2 D

Bowring, Dr., i. 261, 265, 318; quoted, ii. 399
Brewster, Dr., canvassing for a professorship, ii. 78; mentioned, i. 14, 17, 18
British Museum, Carlyle invited to visit, i. 322; secures a reading-ticket for, 336; ii. 200
"Brook Farm," ii. 347 *note*
Brougham, Lord, Carlyle solicits his influence, i. 82; alarmed at Carlyle's exotic predilections, 88, 89, 103; a possible Cromwell, 270; mentioned, ii. 364
Buller, Mr., i. 120; ii. 10, 285
Buller, Mrs., her affection for her son, ii. 270; her *rout*, 328, 331
Buller, Charles, borrows MS. of *Sartor Resartus*, i. 391; characterised, ii. 10, 261, 270, 283; Member for Liskeard, 79; most decisive of Radicals, 245; his Radical meeting, 248; his articles in the *Globe*, 309
Bulwer, i. 388
Burke and Hare, murders by, i. 188, 375
Burns, Gilbert, death of, i. 57 *note*
Burns, Robert, Carlyle's article on, i. 157, 163: maltreated by Jeffrey, 168, 187: Goethe's interest in it, 239
Byron, his satanic poetry, i. 362

Cagliostro, ii. 95, 99
Ça-ira, Carlyle wishes for a pianoforte score of, ii. 333
Campbell, Thomas, ii. 139
Carlyle, Alexander, Carlyle repays loan from, i. 5; renting Craigenputtock, 34-43, 58 *note:* goes there with Carlyle, 46; new farm-house, 162, 170; losses and giving up of farm, 219, 223, 258, 264, 265, 286; loans, advances, and gifts to, 58, 66, 106, 117, 146; lends to Dr. Carlyle, 341; at the smithy, 206; manner of life, 177, 367; intends to marry, 71; his wife, 250; his daughter, "Jane Welsh," 354; at Catlinns, ii. 38, 67, 204: leaving it, 277-292; at Annan, 311; looking to Canada, 335, 371; emigrates, 93 *note;* too indignant against destiny, 216; characterised, 287; returns to Craigenputtock, 156; death of children of, 84, 392-395
Carlyle, James (Carlyle's father), a copy of *German Romance* for, i. 23; ill-health, 250, 251; cannot learn to be old, 210; at Craigenputtock, 177, 240; "not ashamed to live, nor afraid to die," ii. 37; death of, 11-19; Will, 38
Carlyle, James (youngest brother), "Maister Cairlil," i. 99; visits Craigenputtock, 161, 381; marriage of, ii. 125; characterised, 159; his mother's home with, 125, 137, 194, 204, 220, 371, 396
Carlyle, Jane Welsh, ii. 175; marriage, cheerfulness, and thrift, i. 1-11; postscripts to Carlyle's mother, 14, 19: to his brothers and sisters, 44, 65, 101, 171; ii. 261, 364; strongly bent on the Craigenputtock project, i. 139; studies German, 61; gives Carlyle a ring, 85; ill-health, 90, 125; ii. 7, 212; "I will take better care of her another time," 380; living dietetically, 384; better health at Craigenputtock than in London, 39, 40, 43, 61, 95, 97, 100, 101, 102; advice on courtship, i. 97; aunt's illness, 137, 142; surveying all things, proving all, 155, 223; contented at Craigenputtock,

175; learning Spanish with Carlyle, 176; to decide about removing to London, 311; Carlyle's love for, 311, 312; a friend found for, 320; why should she not *write?* 323; letter from Goethe, but none from her, 326; "talent for silence," 322; housewifery, 349; arrives in London, 352; delights in good talk, ii. 25; "Despairkin," 139; a new friend, 200; "worth any twenty Cockney wives," 233; her foot scalded, 253; destruction of *French Revolution* MS.; "my little dame very good and brave," 301; breaks down after the MS. is rewritten; studies Italian; trouble with servants: Carlyle to the rescue; visit from her mother, 359-361; Carlyle finds a servant for, 373-375
Carlyle, Janet (youngest sister), i. 288; ii. 161, 196, 328, 385; marriage, 396
Carlyle, Jean (third sister), visit to Edinburgh, i. 99, 109, 125, 146; at Craigenputtock, 155, 205, 213; taking a *front* rank, 254; returns to Scotsbrig, 345; marriage with James Aitken, ii. 129 *note;* books lent to, 130; letters of Carlyle to, i. 98, 251, 376; ii. 129, 187, 229, 254, 310
Carlyle, John, of Cockermouth (half-brother), ii. 18
Carlyle, Dr. John Aitken, at Carlyle's wedding, i. 2; visits Edinburgh, 27; going to Munich, 73; in Holland, 79; at Munich, 104, 115; Carlyle offers aid to, 124: advises what to observe, 134; anxiety over, 159; afflicted in spirit, 166; "sally against the French," 174 *note;* article on German medicine, 190; on animal magnetism, 152, 201; in London, 214, 304; advised to write, 218; his hard struggle, 272, 273, 276; Jeffrey's kindness to, 280; advised not to live by literature, 291, 292; Carlyle's sympathy for, and kindness to, 244, 292, 294, 296; Jeffrey's loan returned, 297; physician to the Countess of Clare, 310; characterised, 350; his *bonhommie*: "we all love him, and have good reason," ii. 110, 111 *note;* at Florence, i. 363; at Rome, 378, 382, ii. 11; at Naples, 31, 234; lonely spiritual meditations, 33; returns to England, 109 *note;* medical advice to Mrs. Carlyle, 121; settled at Rome for the winter, 247; troubles with the Homœopathists, 272; at Paris, commissions from Carlyle, 333; at Munich, 338, 353; sends money to his mother, 338; at Geneva, 345; offended at a letter from Carlyle, 354; some localities in *Sartor* taken from his descriptions, 364
Carlyle, Margaret (Carlyle's mother), her all-pitying disposition, i. 12 *note;* visits Edinburgh, 109-112; returns to Scotsbrig, 124; visits Craigenputtock, 143, 215, 288; her late husband's settlement, ii. 38; one of Goethe's poems sent to, 46; described, 73, 157; lives with her son James, 125, 130, 194; writes a letter to Carlyle, 217, 219, 220; ruled paper for, 248, 260, 268, 308, 313; Carlyle's picture of her at Scotsbrig, 251; Dr. Carlyle sends money to, 338; her lessons more precious than fine gold, 276; improvement in her affairs, 396

Carlyle, Margaret (eldest sister), illness, i. 172, 189; her death: lies enshrined in all our hearts, 254, 255
Carlyle, Mary (second sister), characterised, i. 25, 68, 70; marriage with James Austin, 288 *note;* at Annan, ii. 155; household, 160; Carlyle visits, 160, 370, 371
Carlyle, Thomas, marriage and settlement in Edinburgh; would give sixpence to see Dr. Carlyle *ut cum fratre, ut cum medico;* forswears tobacco for three weeks, i. 1-6; mine the best of all wives, 11; *German Romance* published, 20; "we go to church and read a sermon to the household," 14; "long ceased to expect happiness," 21, 22; many visitors, 17, 19, 29; "at homes," 29; daily life, 27, 28; kindness to his wife, 19; no occupation, 21; good news from Annandale better than all the wit of Poets, 25; invites sister Jane to Edinburgh, 99; his mother's visit, 109. Calls on Jeffrey, 30; might meet Sir Walter Scott, but is "little careful of such introductions," 30, 31; writes for the *Edinburgh Review*, 62, 107: editorial hacking of his *Burns* article, 168, 169 *note;* visits to and from Jeffrey, 157, 163, 232; begins a novel (*Wotton Reinfred*), 27, 121: it prospers indifferently, 62; intends writing on Tasso, 90; on *Werner*, 90; other review articles, 163; "becoming a sort of literary man," 107. Letters and presents from Goethe, 64, 226, 228, 229, 239: the seal for him, 278; asked to write a *Life of Goethe*, 216; thinks of wintering at Weimar, 221; on Goethe's death: "to me a kind of spiritual Father," ii. 29; articles on Goethe, i. 26, 39, 163. Thinks of removing to Craigenputtock, will Alick come and *farm?* both Jane and I very fond of the project, 34, 38-40: visits it and negotiates with tenant; anticipates happiness; advances money to Alick, 45-56: pays rent; repairing and furnishing; a smoky chimney, 94-117; preliminary visit with his wife; illness and death of his wife's aunt, 136-144; removal from Edinburgh: taking possession of Craigenputtock, 147-150: a winter storm, 231, 252: Arcadian beauty and stillness, 289: stillness of the moors, 175: more like Hades than the Earth, 339; builds a farm-house, 162; death of "Larry," 284; buys a gig, 228; impromptu visit to Templand, 231; "ebb tide with us all"; Alick's losses; new tenant of farm, 264-267; regrets Alick's leaving, ii. 2. Dr. Carlyle advised to visit Germany, i. 73: what to observe there, 134: at Munich, 104: his struggles in London, 272-276: hints for an article on *diet*, 246: on *Animal Magnetism*, 152, 201: anxiety about him, 159. Application for professorship at St. Andrews: the result, 114-149; application for professorship in the London University, 76, 82, 162: Brougham's influence, 88; Glasgow professorship proposed, ii. 89. The *History of German Literature:* to be cut up into articles, i. 206-225: Lardner proposes to

publish it, ii. 379, 389; a *Life of Luther* "shall be the best book I have ever written," i. 221; various papers sent to Fraser, 227; the St. Simonians: a significant attempt to rebuild the old dilapidated Temple with deals and canvas, 326-329, 363, 364; intends to translate *Faust*, 262; Taylor's *Survey of German Poetry*, 242-245, 322; *Sartor Resartus* (then Teufelsdreck) first mentioned: "looking almost as if it would swell into a book": sent to Fraser, 238: by all means to be got back: can give a second, deeper part, 235, 271; going to London to find a publisher, 261, 300; in London: MS. refused by Longmans: accepted by Murray, and in printer's hands, 303-337; Murray returns it: its further ill-luck, 353-365: is locked away, 391: letter offering it to Fraser, ii. 103-108: it appears in *Fraser*, and meets with the most unqualified disapproval: "all extremely proper," i. 210. To his wife, from London, 1831: alas no letter has come for now almost a week; write twice a week, that was the arrangement ever till we *meet again;* work for me here and I shall have strength given me to do it; Jeffrey too busy with politics for private talk; Jack engaged as travelling physician to Lady Clare; Irving wishes me to remodel and edit *Fraser;* would you like to come to London, and pass the winter here? 306-315; money for the journey; calls on Bowring; tea with Dilke; "you will like Mill";

Mrs. Austin "the most enthusiastic of German mystics"; "disciplekins"; what if Goody should shew other talents than those for silence; alas a letter from Goethe, and none from Goody; coronation of William IV.; sees the procession, reflects upon it, and bursts into laughter; too hazardous to settle permanently here; eight months of hardest toil will hardly be accepted "without fee or reward," 316-330; things you are to bring; the poor *tin mull* bought by Goody for three half-pence, more loved than a golden one; British Museum Library; Glen; "dream that I am kind to thee, happy or not"; my purpose to commence periodical writing (that I may live thereby); visits the *Mint;* Irving's miracles; "Heaven send thee safe and soon." To his mother: Jane will be journeying to Scotsbrig; I am uttering a sort of "gathering cry" to remind us all of one another; earnestly expecting Jane; "*forward her on her way*"; will write to you regularly through the winter, 331-349. Man walks on the very brink of unfathomable abysses; farming a bad trade, but what trade is better? Napier trusts to me for a striking paper: *Characteristics* "a sort of second *Signs of the Times*": Napier prints it, but finds it inscrutable, 355-387; a Registratorship in one of the New Courts of Bankruptcy; dines with Fonblanque: a "pleasant discursive sitting"; necessity of employment for peasantess and princess: difficult to find it, thus Swing burns ricks, Byron writes Satanic Poetry; Literature now our only symbol of the Highest, and German our only Literature; a gay breakfast with young Diplomatists; people are all in anxiety about the Reform Bill; have got little good of Irving these two months: his extravagancies, 359-371. Generosity to his brother Alick; Jane not very strong, now better, ever assiduous, clear, and faithful. This is my birth-night, my thirty-sixth. Brotherly counsels to his sister Jane; a sketch of our situation here. My good Wifie not so well as I could wish: will take better care of her another time, 372-380; fogs and climate of London; no Cholera reached us yet: its progress: poor Dr. Becker dead of it; hears of Mr. Strachey's death; paper on *Johnson*, and on *Diderot* on the anvil; no right vehicle for one's thoughts; Hayward's good offices as to the *History of German Literature;* contemporary British Literature a mud ocean in which however there is stilting; not the faintest symptom of preferment except that of being maintained alive for writing my best indifferent prose, 385-393. To his mother: grateful to his parents for his training; painful to see the poverty in London; of the Ettrick Shepherd, Jeffrey, Buller; Jack's letter too full of Roman antiquities. Tell my father that I love and honour him. Take care of him that I may find you both well, ii. 8-11. Death of his father, 11-20: testamentary disposal of his estate, 38; "Honour thy father and thy mother": doubly honour thy mother when she alone remains, 30. To Dr. Carlyle (written from Craigenputtock, 1832); "Nothing singular, much about our usual way, thank you"; I approve of the spirit abounding in your late letters, but the mind too much occupied upon itself; "turn outward;" *Grübeln* is a paralytic fascination; you should not be so solitary, scrape a talking acquaintance with *any* one rather than none; be alive; "the noble faculty of Healing," 31-36. Jane is better than in London; am apt to be stupid, but do the best I can; *Funeral Oration on Goethe* and *Corn Law Rhymes* written; beginning *Essay on Goethe;* articulate speech I hear little, my sole comfort and remedy is Work! Work! many blessings too, a kind true-hearted wife; this is even a beautiful place, and may serve for a *workshop* as well as another, 36-40; a visit to Scotsbrig; gunners come for grouse avoided; serves on a Jury at Dumfries; *The Gig demolished or Pride gets a fall;* mends the harness; interest in a servant-boy; cholera at Dumfries: why fear it? "Death's thousand doors have ever stood open," 43-71. Maclise's drawing of, in *Fraser*, 25, 108; goes (in 1833) with his wife to Edinburgh, rents a furnished house, 71; visit from Mrs. Welsh and niece, 91; reading in the Advocates' Library, with appetite sharpened with long abstinence; Edinburgh village-like after the roaring life-floods of London: cannot remember that I have heard one sentence with true meaning in it uttered since I came hither; not so comfortable a roomy life as at Puttook, 78-95. Letter dated from Templand: visits Scotsbrig; *Diderot* printed; *Cagliostro*, one of the most distorted bad things (not to be *false*) I ever wrote: payment of these two, near £100, my present disposable capital; hopes *Sartor*, cut into slips for *Fraser*, will bring about £200; have much reading and much thinking, and prospects of more society: so we shall wait in a kind of rest, 96-100; returns to Craigenputtock, Jane glad like me to be back; grieved to find a plantation burnt; Jane very feeble, has no nurse but myself: poor lassie, she is in bed, 101-103. Dr. Carlyle returns from abroad, 110, 111 *note:* a letter to him after his visit; leaves Scotsbrig and walks across the moors from Catlinns to meet his wife at Templand; hears an unedifying sermon at Closeburn; returns to Craigenputtock—feels so *harried* and so bereaved; piano has been re-tuned, new arrangement of furniture in the rooms. Visit from Emerson, "the most amiable creature in the world"; your earnest counsels for Tolerance will not fail of their effect on me; shooting let for £5 given to the Dame for pin-money, the *first* help this place ever brought us, 109-115. To Dr. Carlyle: augurs well of his company at Milan; visits Templand with Graham of Burnswark; Jane at Moffat ten days with her mother; alone in the most perfect seclusion any European was suffering or enjoying, "was glad enough to seek my little companion home again from Templand"; sympathy in the troubles of the Glens. Looking back over seven years, wonder at myself; looking forward, but for a fund of tragical indifference, I could lose head; going to write on the *Diamond Necklace* and the *St. Simonians;* books enough; have already read what Mill sent me, and have access to Barjarg Library. Tell us the biographic doings of your party dramatically, especially lyrically, these touches will bring us nearer than general views; above all be autobiographical, as you see I am. Jane says nothing can be added to this so minute letter but her sisterly love, 115-124; drove to Dumfries to fetch up our mother: Jamie's marriage fixed upon: she to continue at Scotsbrig, a *bad best* arrangement: proposes to build a house here for her; Glen now a near neighbour: going to smoke a pipe with him: his mental condition; deep tragedy of Badams's death, enquiries about those that were dear to him; Jane sends a message, 124-129. To his sister Jane: lends books; going to set off for London; Craigenputtock advertised to be let; buried alive here and must try to rise of ourselves; must go and tell our mother, you shall see me on the road, 129-132. To Dr. Carlyle:

each day here the express image of the last; went to Scotsbrig, glad, almost surprised to find there was still a living world; visits Alick at Catlinns; hears of poor old Aunt Fanny's death: the strange manner of it; kind words about his mother; no tenant for Craigenputtock; a servant found for London; to go thither palpably necessary, yet seems almost like a rising from the grave; trimming the flower borders though I shall not see them blow. Farewell, and love me and come back safe to me! 132-140. Pray for me only, that I do not become a scoundrel, in the highest garret I have no other prayer, 143. Sets out alone to seek a house in London, journey thither described; in wide quest of houses: Leigh Hunt accompanies; chance meeting with Irving, pathos of his Annandale laugh, 146-151. His mother's visit to Craigenputtock and farewell: hums the tune she has sung to him, on the coach roof; minute Annandale news; Mrs. Welsh's farewell visit. Dreary outlook as to employment; finds kind friends; doubtless there *is* a way of bringing a professed teacher and innumerable Ignorants together, 154-164. To his wife: it is long since I have been so happy as when I found your letter: fancy you, with one sure hope in your heart, all too overclouded otherwise, God bless you for it, and bring you safe: take my thanks for your cleverness, adroitness, and despatch. Is Chico actually with you? Thou little fool! yet dear even thy follies. Thousand thanks for your kind sentiment of *staying at home:* that *is* it, my little brave one, 164-167. Description of Chelsea and Cheyne Row: taking possession, furnishing, all things painted here in the colours of Hope, no doubt we shall have them painted in the dingier colours of Reality, 167-182; economics and commissariat department; will begin a book on the French Revolution, Periodical Authorship seems *done;* "Fanny Wright" goes lecturing, and I will engage to lecture twice as well; funds here already to keep us going above a year, 183-185; cost of living, 197; the Streets one of the strangest *newspaper columns* the eye ever opened upon, 191, 192, 304; London "amusements," 193. Preliminary perplexities as to writing *The French Revolution*, 211, 237: finds it a tough struggle; going to be a very queer book, 265-281: MS. of first volume destroyed, 287-301: is re-writing, 289-304, 346: completes it, 355. Delighted by a letter from his mother, 217, 221. *Sartor* has met with no recognition in these parts, but Emerson sends me the most cheering letter of thanks, 199; Hunt spends evenings with; Chelsea College; London street tumult a kind of marching music to me; company not deficient; Allan Cunningham, Hunt, Mill; London-born men seem fractions of a man; I sometimes long greatly for the old Irving of fifteen years ago, nay, the poor actual gift-of-tongues Irving has seemed desirable to me, 201-206; dines with Mr. and Mrs. Taylor; no hope in the Socinians; reads in Mill's face that he has given the editorship of the *London Review* to Fox; Mill offers to print the *Diamond Necklace;* disappointment on disappointment simplifies one's course; Heraud, too, has a periodical; heartily obliged to Emerson and to Father O'Shea; *tout va bien ici, le pain manque;* utter poverty should it even come has no terrors for me; admitted to see poor Irving, too likely he will die; Jane takes well with Chelsea, 207-216; Hunt a very boy for clear innocence, 224; sees the burning of the Houses of Parliament; nothing can exceed the obligingness of Mill, 227-231. "Friends of the species" and their singular creed; sees Allan Cunningham and his wife, George Rennie, Eastlake, Cockerell, the Austins, and Hayward; "the happiness of commonplace," 239, 240; I shall swim in the water, did I once know the currents, 251. To his mother: Jane introduced to Mrs. Somerville; description of Buller's "Radical meeting"; my *French Revolution* will keep me all winter, but if the people read it, or it be worth reading, we won't complain: I see you at Scotsbrig, with kind thoughts to your children, and assurance that they send you the like, 248-251; a new hat and a "*rifle-green*" coat; my poor Dame has a burnt foot and sits prisoner, but is getting better, 253; so motionless over the task-sheet the world is almost foreign to me, 271; homœopathy a delusion, 272, 294; in a *new* sort of health; in my mind, feel quite young yet and *growing* as when I was eighteen; daily life, 274-276; in America the sky's bounty is not whisked away as by art magic into hands that have not toiled for it; meets Southey; Henry Taylor's laugh reminds me of poor Irving; meeting with Wordsworth, 284-305; the *Globe,* all that has any fun in it is by Buller, 309; the "Literary World" defied—in the name of God; forwards "this good Emerson's letter"; "the Poor, I think, will get up and tell you how improved their condition is"; doubts of his own book, and books in general; will try to get something to do in the "National Education" which the Parliament is busy upon; invitation to lecture in America; illness of Charles Austin, 322-328; John Sterling, a new young figure risen on us: a whole retinue of curious persons belong to him; the elder Sterling; "Mr. Dunn, who refused a bishopric"; meets O'Connell; the Americans order "50 or 100 copies" of *Sartor,* only three to be had; commissions to Dr. Carlyle in Paris: maps, Vernet's *Caricatures, Ça-ira* for the piano, etc., 232-352; his mother visits Mrs. Welsh, 339, 359; sees the King in Hyde Park, 343; a letter from George Ripley; Jane getting Italian lessons; ill-off about servants, 352-364. No trip to Munich, having promised to see my mother yearly, must to Scotland, 357; Mrs. Welsh here, happy enough to be beside her child again; hot weather has withered us all up; Jane broke down into the most violent series of headaches; different forms of distraction amongst servants; better to have a small apartment and sweep and arrange it for myself; miserable arrangement as to master and servant, 359-361. To his wife (from Annan, 1835): present bad equipment for writing, and reasons for delay; describes journey and visit to her uncle at Liverpool: my mother well and cheerful; have heard much about Templand; a rocking of cradles and a quackling and lullabying in all these houses; the presents and playthings joyfully welcomed; approves of Alick's resolve to emigrate; all so sad, *spectral* here, yet like healing oil to be *let alone*, and see greenness round me. I do hope you are a little quieter, stronger; know at any rate for some comfort that I have all but hired you a servant. Is Harry (her pony) to be sold? Kiss your mother, and say that means my love. Love me, my dear lassie, and fear God, and I swear by Him there shall nothing go ill with us, 365-377. Asks Harry Inglis's help for a young orphan cousin, 381. Sterling proves by far the loveablest man I have met for many a year; article on, in the *North American Review*, 389-390; death of Alick's child Margaret, 392. That village of Ecclefechan gave me the strangest unearthly feeling, Hades itself were slight change to me from this fearful and wonderful mystery of a world; admires old Mirabeau's saying, "*Il a* HUMÉ *toutes les formules*"; am calm but energetic, 396-399

Carson, Dr., ii. 367
Catholic question, i. 199, 200
Cervantes. See *Don Quixote*
Chalmers, Dr., professor at St. Andrews, i. 114, 119; his resignation, 130
Characteristics, i. 335 *note;* accepted by Napier, 387; Carlyle's own opinion of, i. 387
Chelsea, description of, ii. 179-185; literary associations of, 182; Carlyle's removal to: his house, 169-171, 177-181
Chico, the canary-bird, ii. 165, 168, 169, 177
Cholera, i. 360; Carlyle does not fear, 369, 385, ii. 70; at Haddington, i. 386; ii. 23, 45; at Dumfries, 69
Clare, Countess of, Dr. Carlyle travelling physician to, i. 304, 310; mentioned, ii. 33, 80, 272, 354
Clerk, Robert, his strange death, i. 211
Clow, Robert, i. 266 *note;* his liking for *Sartor Resartus*, 282
Cobbett, William, i. 116 *note;* returned for Oldham, ii. 79
Cochrane, ii. 76, 120, 163
Cockerell, Mr., ii. 242
Coleridge, S. T., i. 319; death and character, ii. 201
Cook, Dr., candidate for the St. Andrews Professorship, i. 121, 131, 149
Coke, Mr., a disciple of Carlyle, i. 321, 322

Corn Law Rhymes, article by Carlyle, ii. 39, 49
Cornelius, artist, i. 123
Coronation of William IV., Carlyle sees the procession, i. 328, 329
Cousin, Victor, the London Professorship and, i. 103; mentioned also, 123, 191
Craigcrook, i. 64 *note;* dinner at, 77
Craigenputtock, Carlyle proposes to live at: his wife fond of the project, i. 34-41; Mrs. Welsh helps about negotiations, 45-56; Alexander Carlyle removes to, 58: will be a stronghold, 78; furnishing, 95; visitation of smoke, 117, 213; Carlyle removes to, 150; daily life at, 154, 175; new farm-house at, 162; Jeffrey visits, 169, 228, 232; hills gleaming with burning heath, 191; Alexander Carlyle's ill fortune at, 219, 286: decides to leave, 264-265; engraved at Weimar, 229, 239; stillness and beauty of, 175, 289; almost ghastly solitude of, 236, 339, 367, ii. 2, 47; winter at, i. 241, 252; " castle of many chagrins," 339; the Carlyles return for the summer of 1832, ii. 31; Mrs. Carlyle's better health at, 39; shooting let, 115, 214; preparations for final removal from, 138
Craik, G. L., ii. 361, 362
Cromwell, allusion to, i. 270
Cruthers and Johnson, Carlyle's article, i. 227 *note*
Culture, the only blessing to strive for, i. 71
Cunningham, Allan, a public dinner to, at Dumfries, i. 324 *note;* residence, ii. 181; calls

from, 206, 242; characterised, 259
Cunningham, Dr. Peter, mentioned, ii. 349; his book on New South Wales, 315

DANTE, a class of damned souls, the "respectable people" of this generation, ii. 362
Death, thoughts on, i. 138, 142, 144; the cup goes round, and who so cunning as to pass it by, 179; frightful even in a brute, 284; grown transparent, ii. 15
Demonology, Dr. Carlyle's article on, i. 248
De Quincey, i. 132, 182, 200
Detrosier, ii. 5
Diamond Necklace, ii. 120, 184: Mill offers to print at his expense, 208, 210
Diderot, i. 388; ii. 52, 76, 99
Diet, hints to Dr. Carlyle for an article on, i. 246
Dilke, C. W., his philosophy, i. 319; mentioned, 391
Dilletantism, i. 196
Disorder, man's duty is to remedy, i. 377
Dixon, Frank, i. 125
Dobie, "the preacher," i. 170 *note*
Don Quixote, i. 176; "few languages equal to Spanish, and few lips so melodious as those of Cervantes," 183
"Don Saltero's Coffee-house," ii. 179
Dow, minister of Irongray, ii. 295
Duncan, Rev. Henry, i. 77
Dunn, Rev. Mr., "refused a bishoprick," ii. 331; visits from, 348, 362, 390; his conversation, 397
Dynamism, i. 270

EASTLAKE, Sir Charles, ii. 242
Edinburgh, Carlyle settles at, i. 2;

literary society in, 133; fatal epidemic at, 386; compared with London, ii. 78, 88; power of thought has forsaken, 94
Edinburgh Review, Carlyle's articles in, 82, 83, 108, 112; *State of German Literature*, 104, 107; maltreatment of article on *Burns*, 163, 168; Napier editor of, 203; salary fair, vehicle respectable, 245; *Characteristics*, 356, 370, 373, 378, 387; ii. 75
Editors *v.* authors, i. 169 *note*
Education, German, study of, recommended, i. 134
Eichthal, Baron d', invites Dr. Carlyle to Munich, i. 73 *note*, 92; his hospitality, 115; mentioned, 124, 151
Eichthal, Gustave d', calls on Carlyle, ii. 5; Emerson and: message to, 113; mentioned, 333
Elections, ii. 79, 258
Emerson, visits Carlyle, ii. 113; cheering letters from, 199, 321; on *Sartor*, 211; wishes Carlyle to lecture in America, 326
Emigration, prevalence of, ii. 93; becoming inevitable, 335
Empson, Mr., mentioned, i. 319, 321; breakfast with, 326
Examiner, newspaper, preferred by Carlyle, i. 208; Fonblanque, editor, 318, 354, 393; irregularity in publication, ii. 232, 277, 293

FACTORY children, Overworked, ii. 92
"Fairest Phillis," ii. 152 *note*
Farming, done or nearly so, i. 264; a bad trade, 355; ii. 278; in America it were something, 279
Faust, i. 258, 262

Fenwick, Miss, ii. 284, 305
Fichte, reading, i. 72; "Fichte's mongrel," 91
Fonblanque, A., i. 318 *note*, 354; described, 359, 393; ii. 284
Forbes, David James, ii. 78 *note*
Foreign Quarterly Review, article on *Werner* for, i. 90; articles on *Goethe* in, 152, 163; ii. 39; *Reinecke Fuchs* in, i. 317; *Diderot* in, 76; alluded to, 120
Foreign Review, mentioned, i. 151, 238; *Life of Heyne* in, 163; *German Playwrights* for, 178; *Voltaire* and *Novalis* written for, 190; *Jean Paul* in, 227
Fox, editor of the *London Review*, ii. 207; mentioned, 240; editor of the *Repository*, 283
Fraser, James (of *Fraser's Magazine*), letter of Carlyle to, 103-115; report on reception of *Sartor Resartus*, 128; pays for it, 210; declines to reprint it, 321; arrangement with, as to publishing *French Revolution*, 184; characterised, 217; ii. 25, 183; mentioned also, i. 227; ii. 238, 283, 299
Fraser, William (editor of *Foreign Review*), article on *Schiller* sent to, i. 228; his connection with *Fraser's Magazine*, 217 *note*, 228, 238 *note;* ii. 106; negotiates for the Goethe seal, i. 278, 299; Carlyle dines with, 307; mentioned also, 308, 317, 328
Fraser's Magazine, its origin, i. 238 *note ;* Irving wishes Carlyle to become editor of, 309; *Sartor Resartus* to be printed in, ii. 99, 103: its reception in, 128; portrait of Carlyle in, 108, 109, 163
French Revolution, History of the. See under Carlyle, Thomas

Froude, Mr. J. A., his *Life of Carlyle*, its inaccuracies noted, i. 5, 29, 34, 269, 293, 295, 345; ii. 11, 31, 77, 202; "gey ill to deal wi'," as cited by, i. 44

GALLOWAY, MR., i. 109
German Literature, State of, in the *Edinburgh Review*, i. 104, 107
German Literature, A History of, Carlyle writing, i. 213-224; difficulties as to publishing, 225, 233, 261; Dr. Lardner and, 379 *note*, 389
German Playwrights, Carlyle's article, i. 178; an "unmystical paper," 182
German Romance, Specimens of, publication of, i. 9-20; reviews of, 31
Germany, education in, 134; Carlyle an honorary member of the Gesellschaft für ausländische Literatur, i. 239
"Gey ill to deal wi'," Mr. Froude's inaccurate rendering of the phrase, i. 44 *note*
Gleig, Mr., writes to Carlyle about a *Life of Goethe*, i. 216, 220
Glen, Archibald, ii. 117, 118, 126
Glen, W., mentioned, i. 313; characterised, 336 *note*, 364; boards near Craigenputtock, ii. 118-126; reads Homer with Carlyle, 118, 140, 220, 294
Goethe, letter to Carlyle from, i. 64: reply to, 72; request for a testimonial from, 121-128, 149; sends medals for Sir Walter Scott, 129-146, 157; Carlyle's earlier articles on, 152, 163; biography by Carlyle proposed, 216, 220; letters and gifts to Carlyle from, 226-239, 326-328; ornamental seal for, 278, 285, 299: acknowledgment of it from, 317; portrait of, in *Fraser's Magazine*, ii. 26 *note*; death of, 29; *Funeral Oration* and *Essay* on, 39, 53; alluded to, i. 258, 262; ii. 46, 123, 242
Graham, William, of Burnswark, i. 55, 136, 170; visit from, ii. 116; message to, 344
Grahame, Mary, her rye-straw bonnet, i. 116 *note*
Gray, William, ii. 118
Greave, Alison, i. 93, 102, 138
Greaves, Mr., i. 220
Grierson, John, death of, i. 179 *note*
"Grüne Gans," original of the, in *Sartor Resartus*, ii. 364 *note*

HADDINGTON, cholera at, i. 386
Hamilton, Captain T., i. 132
Hamilton, Sir William, pleasant evening with, i. 131; a genuine man, ii. 82
Hayward, A., friendly offices to Carlyle, i. 389 *note*; ii. 243
Hazlitt, i. 233
Hegel, death of, i. 386
Heraud, Mr., i. 306 *note*; ii. 209
Heyne, C. G., Carlyle's article on, i. 152, 163, 182; translation of Homer by, ii. 140, 141
Hoddam Hill, i. 41
Hogg, James, in London society, ii. 10
Homer, ii. 118; translations of, compared, 140
Homœopathic medicine, a delusion, ii. 272; its fame in London, 294
Hope, Thomas, his book on *Man* furnishes a text for *Characteristics*, i. 335, 356
Hunt, Henry, ii. 88 *note*
Hunt, Leigh, his *Lord Byron and Some of his Contemporaries*, i. 158; goes house-hunting with Carlyle, ii. 150, 162; "kindest of

men," 173; relations with Carlyle, 201; "clear innocence" of, "one of the cleverest men I ever spoke with," 224-230, 349; income of, 239; "a friend of the species," 241; mentioned also, 267
Hunt, Messrs., publishers, i. 34, 37, 44
Hyde Park, description of, ii. 341

INGLIS, H., quoted, i. 156; visit from, 177; letters to, 180, 192, 203; ii. 141, 377; his interest requested for a relative of Carlyle's, 381
Irving, Dr. David, i. 120, 384; ii. 89
Irving, Edward, letter to Carlyle from, i. 64; testimonial to him from, 77, 120; extravagancies noted in procedures and creed of, 125, 156, 318, 343, 351, 352, 371; praises Dr. Carlyle, 305; characterised, 250, 351; ii. 27, 80; Carlyle's affection and longing for, 206 : his last interviews with, 149, 212, 213; is thought to be dying, 213, 228

JAMESON, Mrs., ii. 243
Jeffray, Rev. Mr., ii. 51, 53
Jeffrey, Francis, Carlyle introduced to: interview with, invited to the Law Courts by, asked to "Germanise the public" in the *Edinburgh Review* by, i. 30, 31, 62: his liking for, 63-72: as to professorships asks advice of, 77-98: his claims urged by, 103-120: a visit with his wife to, 157: "offers me in the coolest and lightest manner the use of his *purse*": "writes often and half loves, half hates me with the utmost sincerity"; proposed visit from, 163-166; displeases Carlyle by hacking his article on *Burns;* visits Craigenputtock; admonitions to his host from ; a meeting with, at Dumfries, 201; visits Craigenputtock again, is well liked there; his generosity to Hazlitt; tries to find a publisher for the *German Literary History*, 332-336; becomes Lord Advocate; elected to parliament; in London, "his letters exclusively addressed to Jane have a very tumultuous, frothy, whirlpoolish character"; possible disastrous effect of St. Stephen's on a pretty little gem ; kindness of, to Dr. Carlyle, 273-298 : lends money to him, 60, ii. 52, 64 : a letter from, i. 279-281; proposes to find a government clerkship for Carlyle, 298; Carlyle takes MS. of *Sartor* to; is too busy for private talk; friendship with Carlyle waning: let me remember also that the pressure of such a situation as mine can be known to him (Jeffrey) only theoretically, 309-314; calls on the Carlyles, 366, 393, ii. 10: they meet him in Edinburgh, ii. 82 ; Carlyle hints as to a professorship in the gift of, 89; an accidental meeting with, 166, 307; calls at Chelsea, 315
Johnson, Carlyle's article, i. 271, 379, 388; ii. 21, 25
Johnstone, James, i. 14; a letter from Carlyle to, 102 ; ii. 294
Jones, Paul, ii. 96

KEEVIL, Richard, i. 23, 28, 35
Kensington Garden, ii. 149
"Kirk and a mill," i. 128
Kleinstädterei, i. 202
Knight, Payne, ii. 141

INDEX

LAING, Dr., i. 81
Lamartine, i. 191
Landalls, quoted, i. 59
Lardner, Dr., proposes to publish the *History of German Literature*, i. 379 *note*, 389
Larry, death of the horse, i. 284
Leslie, Prof., i. 120; death of, ii. 78
Lessing, i. 183
Life, Carlyle's philosophy of, i. 22, 83, 92; the truth lies beyond, 138; life beyond death, 142; pity is for the living, 145; man is born unto toil, 151, 153; Carlyle's views on, 193-198, 222, 273-276, ii. 2, 8; *sic vos non vobis* universal in, 266; to be accounted for, i. 392; given for work, ii. 48
Lockhart, i. 157. *See* Burns
London, the *littérateurs* of, 309; a *twilight* intellectual city, 360; the tumult of, 367; fog, 381, 385; great charm there, ii. 8; Carlyle settles in Chelsea, 169-178; streets full of interest, 191, 192, 205, 263, 304
London Review started by Mill and Molesworth, ii. 184, 198; editorship given to Fox, 207, 283, 363; united with the *Westminster*, 399
Luther, Carlyle's article on, i. 203; life of, to be "my best book," 221; his hymn translated, 235

MACAULAY, T. B., i. 149
Macculloch, Prof., i. 91
M'Diarmid, Mr. i. 199; ii. 45
Maclise, portrait of Carlyle by, ii. 25, 108
Macqueen, Nanny, i. 49; ii. 183, 214
Magazines, writing for, the death of literature, i. 273; below street-sweeping, 283
Maginn, Dr., ii. 109
Man of Feeling, i. 110
Marriage opposed by "friends of the species," ii. 241
Melbourne ministry, ii. 322
Mercury, The, i. 131
Mill, J. S., Carlyle's first meeting with, i. 320-359; MS. of *Sartor Resartus* lent to, 365, 393; one of the purest and worthiest of men, ii. 122; *London Review*, 184, 198; a London-born man, 205, 206; offers to print *The Diamond Necklace* at his own expense, 208; lends Carlyle books, 231-238; Carlyle's fears for, 240; loss of the MS. first volume of *The French Revolution*, 287-301
Mint, visit to the, i. 342
Milton quoted, i. 378; ii. 226
Mirabeau, ii. 238, 397
Mitchell, Mr. Robert, i. 8, 91
Moir, Mr. George, i. 126, 131
Molesworth, Sir Wm., ii. 184, 283, 298
Montagu, Mr. Basil, i. 165, 353, 358, 365
Montagu, Mrs. Basil, i. 64, 336, 353
Morning Watch, ii. 27
Müllner, Notes on, by Carlyle, i. 356, 359
Murray, Mr. John, i. 326; accepts MS. of *Sartor Resartus*, 337; returns it, 357

NAPIER, Mr. Macvey, letter from Carlyle to, on an editor's privileges, i. 169 *note*; editor of the *Edinburgh Review*, 203; Carlyle's intercourse with, in regard to articles for the *Review*, i. 242-260, 290-316, 353-

390; ii. 21, 39; his one fault, 75. See also *Edinburgh Review*
Napier, "Peninsular," ii. 331
Naples, Dr. Carlyle's sketches of, ii. 32; what to do and see at, 36
Napoleon's snuff-box, i. 57
Nelson, Ben., i. 176 *note*; ii. 372
New Monthly Magazine, i. 388 *note*; ii. 39
Nibelungen Lied, article on, i. 224, 261, 265; payment for it given to Dr. Carlyle, 296
Nicol, Principal, i. 119
North American Review, on *Sartor Resartus*, ii. 390
Novalis, article, i. 178, 190

O'CONNELL, Carlyle meets, ii. 328, 331; the *dining* man of the recess, 364
Orderliness, characteristic of Carlyle, i. 93 *note*
"Ornament to society," i. 171 *note*
O'Shea, Father, ii. 211
Owen, Robert, ii. 5

PAINTING and music, *artes perditæ*, i. 122
Paris, the wonders of, i. 190; Palais Royal, 191; commissions for Dr. Carlyle in, ii. 333, 352
Parliament Houses, the burning of the, ii. 227, 230
Peel, Sir Robert, ii. 323
Pepoli, Count, ii. 362
Poor, the, is their condition improving? ii. 323
Procter, B. W., i. 30; mentioned also, 120
Prophecy, not poetry, the want of the age, ii. 123

QUIN, Dr., ii. 294

RADICAL meeting, a, ii. 249

Radical Review. See *London Review*
Rebellion, a barren matter, ii. 270
Reform Bill, general stagnation caused by, i. 346-379; anxiety about, 369; delayed, ii. 9
Reinecke Fuchs, article on, i. 317
Rennie, Mr. George, bust of Thorwaldsen by, ii. 215, 242
Rhetoric, Professorship of, at London, i. 76; at Edinburgh, ii. 139
Richardson, Mrs., i. 139, 202
Richter, J. P. F., i. 9; article for *Edinburgh Review* on, 63-72; *Schmelzle's Journey*, 127; *Campaner Thal*, 132; second article on, 203, 227; poverty of, 263; Richter and Wordsworth, ii. 297
Ripley, Mr. George, Carlyle receives a letter from, ii. 347
Ritchie, Dr., quoted, i. 59
Robinson, Mr. H. Crabb, i. 59

ST. ANDREWS UNIVERSITY, Carlyle applies for a Professorship in, i. 114-121; not to be counted on, 127, 130; Dr. Cook as good as appointed, 149
Saint-Simon, i. 243
St. Simonians, a parcel from, i. 229; Goethe warns Carlyle against, 240; Carlyle translates the *Nouveau Christianisme*, 243; an upholstery aggregation, 363; mentioned also, ii. 120
Sartor Resartus, first mentioned, i. 234, 235; to be two articles, 237, 238; to be enlarged, 250; it must out; to be taken to London; both dross and metal in it, 261-2; not *right* yet, 271; Carlyle's opinion of, 239-300; drawing to a close; refused by Longmans, 307; left with Jeffrey; the sentiment of it not

shared in London; another effort to publish, 307-325; accepted by Murray; publication hindered by the Reform Bill; returned by Murray, and locked away; renewed hopes for, 337-379; *Teufelsdreck* changed to *Teufelsdröckh*, ii. 104 *note;* Carlyle's letter to Fraser describing the work, 103-108; appears in *Fraser;* meets with unqualified disapproval, 128, 145; printing completed; the payment for, 198-210; Fraser will not print in book form, 321; Sterling's letter on, 327, 332; order from America for copies, 332

Schelling, i. 72, 92, 122; message to, ii. 363

Schiller, article on, i. 228

Schlegel, i. 92, 104

Scott, Sir Walter, Carlyle neglects an offer of introduction to, i. 31; medals for, from Goethe, 129; mentioned, 91, 157, 322

"Segretario ambulante," ii. 178 *note*

Sharpe, General, needs increase of wisdom, i. 35 *note;* "our ain Hoddam, sir!" ii. 307, 308 *note*

"Sherra' muir," ii. 247 *note*

Signs of the Times, printing of, i. 203; alluded to, 226, 229, 322

Skinner, Captain, i. 133

Smeal, Betty, ii. 22

Socinians, ii. 207

Somerville, Mrs., characterised, ii. 245

Sorbonne, a forsaken crow-nest of theology, i. 190

Southey, R., Carlyle's description of, ii. 284, 295

Specimens of German Romance. See *German Romance*

Sterling, John, Carlyle's first acquaintance with, ii. 327; criticism of *Sartor Resartus* by, 327, 332; a retinue of curious persons belonging to, 331, 337; settles in Bayswater, 349; the lovablest man, 389; mentioned also, 376

Stewart, Dugald, his admiration for Cousin, i. 103, 123; death of, 165

Strachey, Mrs., Carlyle's great regard for, i. 221; a "*schöne Seele*": death of her husband, 387

TAIT, publishes *German Romance:* pays for it, 5, 20, 58; his magazine, 390: gives it up, ii. 163

Tait, Wull, sudden death of, i. 161

Tasso, Carlyle's proposed article on, i. 83, 90, 157

Taylor, Henry, i. 365; introduces Carlyle to Southey and to Wordsworth, ii. 295, 305; characterised, 349

Taylor, Mrs. (afterwards Mrs. Mill), ii. 200, 207, 208

Taylor, William, his *Survey of German Poetry*, reviewed by Carlyle, i. 242-245, 316; grieved at some parts of the review, 322

Templand, residence of Mrs. Welsh, i. 70

Teufelsdreck. See *Sartor Resartus*

"There was a piper had a cow," verses, ii. 206

Thomson, Rev. Andrew, i. 112

"Thornton, Cyril," i. 132

Thorwaldsen, ii. 215

VAUXHALL Gardens, ii. 193

Vernet, Charles, ii. 352

Villiers, Hyde, and Charles, i. 365

Villemain, i. 191

Voltaire, Carlyle blamed for condemning, i. 31; article on, 178, 190; portrait wanted, 191

Voss, his translation of Homer the best, ii. 140, 142

WAUGH, Bailie, i. 181 *note*
Waugh, Dr., ii. 372
Weimar, projected visit to, i. 221
Wellington, Duke of, Carlyle's opinion of, ii. 246, 249, 264 : described : the Waterloo dinner, 342
Welsh, Miss Jeannie, i. 55 *note;* last illness and death of, 137-144
Welsh, Dr. (Mrs. Carlyle's father), i. 308
Welsh, John, son-in-law of Knox, ii. 53
Welsh, Mrs. (Mrs. Carlyle's mother), visit to the Carlyles at Edinburgh, i. 51, 61; ii. 91 ; a letter from Carlyle to, i. 51-54; gives a cloak to Carlyle's mother, 204, 209; both nurse and doctor, 212; her patience, 216; an impromptu visit to, 231, 232 ; her troubles, 384; farewell visit to Craigenputtock, ii. 156 ; Carlyle's mother visits, 359; visits Chelsea, 359
Werner, *Zacharias*, article, i. 90
Westminster Review, i. 261, 265; united with Mill's *London Review*, ii. 398
William IV., coronation of, i. 325, 329; his rumoured insanity, ii. 166; should walk over to Hanover, 316; appearance described, 343
Wilson, Professor, testimonial from, i. 120; characterised, 91, 126; on Carlyle's speech at a dinner, 324
Wollstonecraft, Mary, ii. 66
Wordsworth, Carlyle meets, ii. 296, 305
Wotton Reinfred, Carlyle's novel, i. 27-62 ; "an angel of a hero," 65, 121 ; goes wholly to the fire, 62 *note*

YORSTOUN, Mrs., i. 138

THE END

Printed by R. & R. CLARK, *Edinburgh*